Sammy Addy's OM System "Olympus" OM-3 Guide to Smart Photography & Videography

Sammy Addy

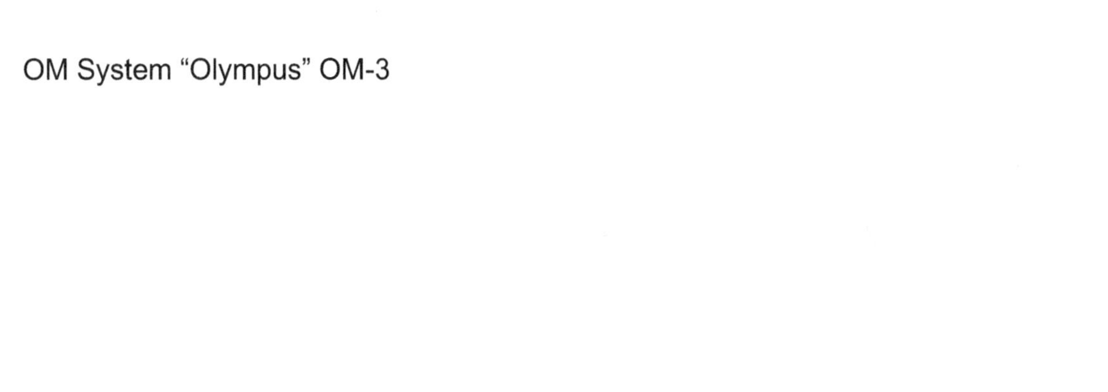

OM System "Olympus" OM-3

OM SYSTEM OM-3
Complete Camera User Guide

PART 1: Getting to Know Your OM-3

A plain-English, step-by-step guide for every photographer — beginner to advanced.

Welcome to the OM SYSTEM OM-3 — a beautifully designed, weather-sealed mirrorless camera built on the Micro Four Thirds system. Whether this is your very first camera or you are coming from a smartphone or an older model, this guide will walk you through every button, dial, menu, and setting in plain, simple language.

Before you take a single photo, take a few minutes to read Part 1. It will help you understand what every part of the camera does, how to handle it safely, and how to get it ready to shoot. Think of this section as your orientation tour of your new camera.

> **NOTE: How to Use This Guide**
> Every instruction in this guide tells you exactly where to look on the camera and what to do with your hands. When you see words in bold, they refer to a specific button or menu item you will find on the camera. When you see a numbered Step list, do each step in order.

1.1 What's in the Box

When you open the box for the first time, you should find the following items inside. Before you do anything else, lay everything out on a flat surface and check each item against this list.

Item	How to Identify It
OM-3 Camera Body	The main camera unit with the hand grip on the right side. It will have a red ring near the lens mount and the word "OM SYSTEM" on the front.
BLS-50 Rechargeable Battery	A small rectangular black battery roughly the size of a matchbox. The label reads "BLS-50" and shows the voltage.
BCH-1 Battery Charger	A small flat plastic charger with a fold-out plug. The battery slides in from the front. A green LED lights when charging is complete.

USB-C Cable	A short cable with a USB-C connector on one end. You can use this to charge the battery inside the camera or transfer photos to a computer.
Body Cap	A circular white or grey plastic cap that covers the lens mount hole on the front of the camera. It protects the sensor from dust.
Eyecup (Viewfinder Eyecup)	A small rubber cup around the viewfinder opening at the back of the camera. This is already attached to the camera.
Shoulder Strap	A fabric strap with metal clips on both ends. It attaches to the two strap lugs on the sides of the camera.
Quick Start Guide	A small folded booklet with basic setup instructions. This full guide you are reading now provides far more detail.

What Is NOT Included — and What You Should Buy

The OM-3 body does NOT come with a lens. You will need at least one Micro Four Thirds lens to take photos. The camera also does NOT include an SD card. You will need one of those too. Here is a shopping checklist for new users:

- SD Card — buy at least one SD card, UHS-I Speed Class 3 (U3) or faster. A 64GB card is a good starting size. For 4K video, use a V60 or V90 rated card.
- Micro Four Thirds Lens — the kit lens most commonly sold with the OM-3 is the M.Zuiko Digital ED 12-45mm f/4.0 PRO, which covers wide to short telephoto. If you bought only the body, any MFT lens will work.
- Extra Battery — the BLS-50 battery gives roughly 370 shots per charge. Buying a spare means you can always have one charging while shooting with the other.
- Camera Bag or Case — protects the camera and lens when travelling.
- Lens Cleaning Kit — a blower, soft brush, and cleaning cloth will keep your lens and sensor free of dust spots.

> **TIP: Check everything now**
> Count all the items in the table above before you put the box away. If anything is missing, contact your retailer immediately.

1.2 Physical Overview of the Camera Body

Before you touch any buttons, spend a moment simply looking at the camera from every angle. The diagrams in this section label every control you will use. When you read the word "left" or "right," it means left and right as you hold the camera up to your eye — as if you are about to take a photo.

Front of the Camera

The front is the side that faces your subject — the side with the big round lens mount hole in the middle.

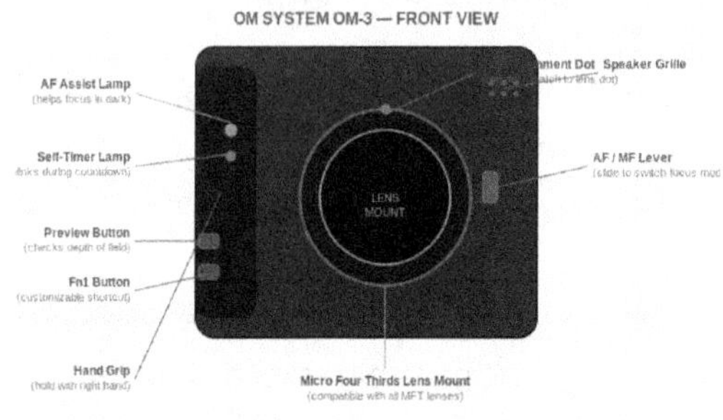

Figure 1.1 — OM-3 Front View with all controls labeled

Control	Location	What It Does
Hand Grip	Left side, front	The raised, rubberized bump on the left side of the front. Wrap your right hand around this for a secure, comfortable hold.
Lens Mount	Center, front	The large circular opening where you attach a lens. A red dot marks the alignment point used when fitting a new lens.
Lens Alignment Dot (Red)	Top of mount ring	A small red dot. When attaching a lens, align the red dot on the lens with this red dot on the body, then rotate the lens clockwise until it clicks.
AF Assist Lamp	Upper left of grip	A small orange-tinted LED. The camera fires this dim beam of light toward your subject to help the autofocus system work in dark environments.
Self-Timer Lamp	Below AF lamp	A small red LED. When you use the self-timer, this light blinks to count down before the shutter fires. Blinks slowly at first, then rapidly just before the photo is taken.
Preview Button	Left side of grip, front	A small rectangular button on the front of the grip area. Pressing and holding this button temporarily closes the lens aperture to the actual shooting aperture, so you can preview

		depth of field (how much of the scene will be in focus) before shooting.
Fn1 Button (front)	Left side of grip, front, below Preview	A customizable shortcut button. By default it is set to open a specific function, but you can reassign it to almost any camera setting you prefer (covered in Part 18).
AF / MF Lever	Right side of lens, front	A small sliding lever on the front of the camera near the lens. Slide it up to engage Autofocus (AF) — the camera focuses for you. Slide it down to switch to Manual Focus (MF) — you control focus by turning the lens ring.
Speaker Grille	Top right, front	A pattern of small holes. Sound from audio recorded in your videos plays through here during playback.

Back of the Camera

The back of the camera is what faces you when you hold the camera up to shoot. This side has the most buttons — everything you need to control and review your shots.

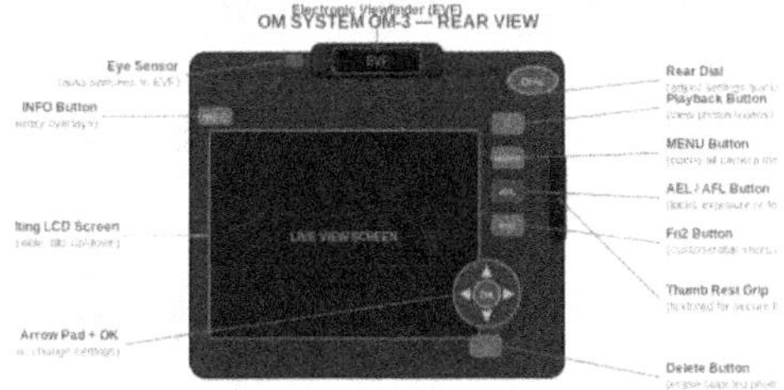

Figure 1.2 — OM-3 Rear View with all controls labeled

Control	Location on Back	What It Does
Electronic Viewfinder (EVF)	Top center hump	A small but high-resolution screen inside the eyepiece. Look through it with your eye to compose and shoot. It shows a live preview of your scene and all your settings.
Eye Sensor	Left of EVF eyepiece	A tiny infrared sensor just to the left of the viewfinder eyepiece. When your eye comes

		close to the viewfinder, this sensor detects it and automatically switches the display from the LCD screen to the EVF.
LCD Touch Screen	Center, back	A large 3-inch touchscreen that tilts up and down (not side to side). It shows a live view of your scene when you are composing shots. You can tap the screen to set your focus point or to take a photo. It also shows your photos and videos during playback.
INFO Button	Top-left of LCD	Pressing this button cycles through different information overlays on the screen. Each press shows a different combination of shooting data, histogram, level gauge, or a clean view with no overlays.
Rear Dial	Top right, back	A scroll wheel you roll with your thumb. In most shooting modes it adjusts your shutter speed or exposure compensation. You will use this constantly.
Playback Button	Upper right	Press this to enter Playback mode, where you can browse through your saved photos and videos. Press it again or half-press the shutter to return to shooting.
MENU Button	Right of LCD, upper	Opens the camera's menu system, which gives you access to every setting and customization option on the camera. Press it again to close the menu.
AEL / AFL Button	Right of LCD, middle	AEL stands for Auto Exposure Lock. AFL stands for Auto Focus Lock. Pressing this button locks either the exposure or focus (or both) so you can reframe your shot without the camera recalculating the exposure or focus.
Fn2 Button	Right of LCD, lower-mid	Another customizable shortcut button. Assign any frequently used function to it so you can access it with a single press (covered in Part 18).

4-Way Arrow Pad	Lower right	Four directional buttons arranged in a cross (Up, Down, Left, Right). Use these to navigate through menus, move the autofocus point around the frame, and change settings. Each direction button often also has a shortcut function printed on it (such as Drive, WB, ISO, Flash).
OK Button	Center of arrow pad	Press this to confirm a menu selection, or to open the Super Control Panel — a quick-access grid of the most important shooting settings.
Delete Button	Below arrow pad	In Playback mode, press this to delete the photo or video currently shown on screen. The camera will ask you to confirm before deleting.
Thumb Rest Grip	Far right edge	A rubberized raised area on the far right of the back. Place your right thumb here for a comfortable, secure grip while shooting.

Top of the Camera

The top plate of the OM-3 holds the most important shooting controls — the ones you will reach for every single time you pick up the camera.

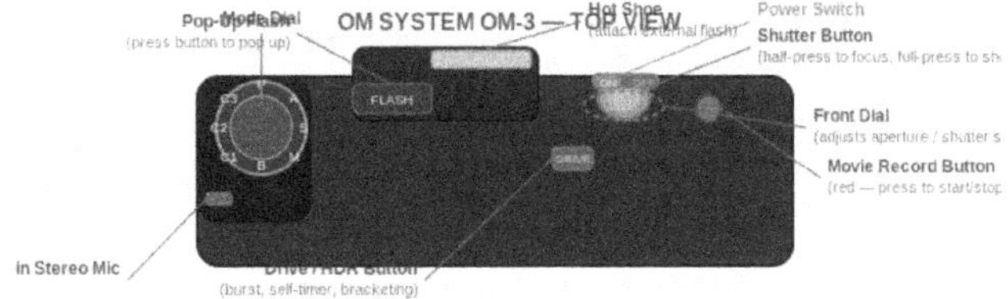

Figure 1.3 — OM-3 Top View with all controls labeled

Control	Location on Top	What It Does
Mode Dial	Top left	A large round dial that selects your shooting mode. Rotate it to choose from iAuto (fully automatic), P, A, S, M, B, or C1/C2/C3 (custom presets). The active mode is indicated by the marker line at the top of the dial.

Power Switch / ON-OFF	Around the shutter button	A lever that wraps around the shutter button. Slide it to ON to power up the camera; slide it to OFF to shut down. The camera will save your settings automatically when you switch it off.
Shutter Button	Top right, center	The most important button on the camera. Press it HALFWAY down to activate autofocus and exposure measurement — the camera focuses on your subject. Press it ALL THE WAY down to take the photo. Always press gently and smoothly to avoid camera shake.
Front Dial	Around / behind shutter	A textured wheel just behind and around the shutter button. Roll it with your index finger. In Aperture Priority (A) mode it adjusts aperture; in Shutter Priority (S) mode it adjusts shutter speed; in Manual (M) mode it adjusts aperture while the rear dial adjusts shutter speed.
Hot Shoe	Top center	A rectangular metal bracket on top of the camera body with electrical contacts inside. This is where you attach an external flash unit or other accessories (such as a wireless transmitter or microphone adapter).
Pop-Up Flash / Flash Button	Left of hot shoe, center-top	Press the small button to pop up the built-in flash. When the flash is raised, it fires automatically when needed. Push the flash head back down to close it when not in use.
Drive / HDR Button	Top, center-right	Opens the drive mode menu, where you can switch between single shot, burst (continuous), self-timer, and bracketing modes.
Movie Record Button	Top right, red button	A dedicated red button that starts and stops video recording. You can press it from any shooting mode — you do not need to switch the mode dial to video first.
Built-in Stereo Microphone	Top left area	Small openings in the top plate that record audio for your videos. They are stereo microphones, meaning they pick up sound from left and right. For better audio quality,

		you can connect an external microphone through the 3.5mm port on the left side.

Bottom of the Camera

The bottom of the OM-3 is simpler. It holds the battery, the SD card, and the tripod mount.

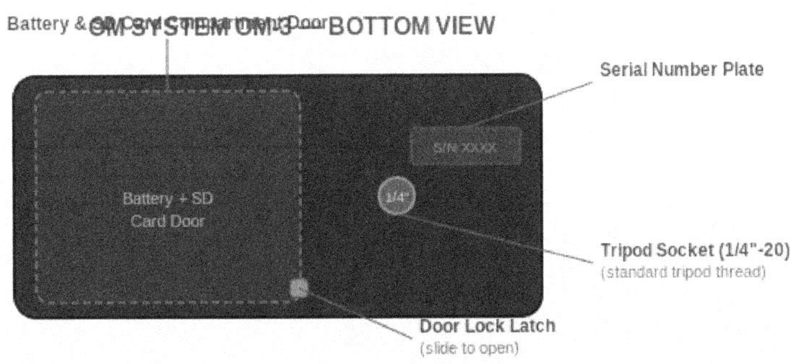

Figure 1.4 — OM-3 Bottom View

Control	Location on Bottom	What It Does
Battery / SD Card Compartment Door	Bottom left	A hinged door that covers the battery and SD card slots. Slide the door latch toward the open icon (usually a padlock or arrow symbol), then lift the door open.
Door Lock Latch	Edge of door	A small plastic slider on the edge of the compartment door. Slide it in the direction of the unlock symbol to open the door.
Tripod Socket (1/4"-20)	Bottom center-right	A threaded metal hole that accepts a standard 1/4" tripod screw. Screw your tripod head or quick-release plate into this hole to mount the camera on a tripod, monopod, or any compatible accessory.
Serial Number Plate	Bottom right area	A small label showing the camera's unique serial number. You may need this number for warranty registration or service.

Left Side of the Camera — Port Connections

The left side (as you hold the camera to shoot) has a rubber port cover that protects all the camera's input and output connections. Peel back the cover gently to access them.

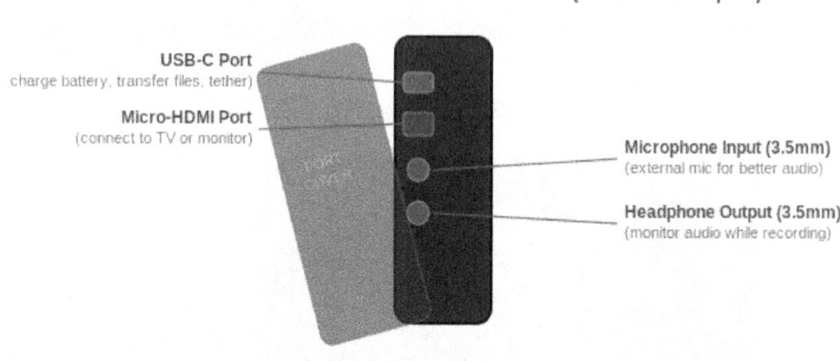

Figure 1.5 — OM-3 Left Side: Port cover open, ports labeled

Port	What It Is For
USB-C Port	The USB-C port serves three purposes. First, you can plug a USB-C cable from your computer into this port to transfer photos and videos. Second, you can plug the included USB-C cable into a USB charger or power bank to charge the BLS-50 battery while it is inside the camera. Third, you can use this port for tethered shooting — connecting the camera directly to a computer so photos appear on screen instantly.
Micro-HDMI Port	Connect a Micro-HDMI to full-size HDMI cable (not included) from this port to a television or external monitor. This lets you view your photos and videos on a large screen, or use an external monitor for critical focus while filming.
Microphone Input (3.5mm)	If you want better audio quality for your videos, plug an external microphone's 3.5mm mini-jack into this port. The camera will use the external microphone instead of the built-in one automatically.
Headphone Output (3.5mm)	Plug headphones or earphones into this port while recording video. You will hear the audio being recorded in real time, which lets you catch problems (wind noise, poor microphone placement) before it is too late.

NOTE: Keep the rubber cover closed

The rubber port cover keeps dust and moisture out. The OM-3 is weather-sealed — it can handle rain and dusty environments — but only when the rubber port cover is firmly closed. Always close it after use.

Right Side of the Camera

The right side of the camera (as you hold it to shoot) is much simpler. It has:

- Strap Lug (Right) — a small metal loop fixed to the right side of the camera body. This is one of the two points where you attach the shoulder strap.
- Right Edge of Hand Grip — the curved, rubberized right edge of the grip that your fingers wrap around when you hold the camera.

The left side of the camera (opposite the ports side) also has a strap lug — a second metal loop for attaching the other end of the shoulder strap.

1.3 Attaching and Removing a Lens

The Micro Four Thirds (MFT) Mount System

The OM-3 uses a lens system called Micro Four Thirds — often abbreviated as MFT or M43. This is a standard shared by Olympus, OM SYSTEM, and Panasonic cameras. What that means for you:

- Any lens labeled "Micro Four Thirds" or "MFT" will fit and work fully on your OM-3.
- The OM SYSTEM (formerly Olympus) lenses labeled "M.Zuiko Digital" are designed specifically for this camera and work best with it.
- Panasonic Lumix G-series lenses also fit and work well.
- Older "Four Thirds" lenses (a larger, older standard) can be used with an optional adapter.
- Full-frame lenses (Canon EF, Nikon F, Sony E, etc.) can be used with adapters, but they will not autofocus as effectively and you will lose some features.

How to Attach a Lens — Step by Step

WARNING: Never force a lens
The lens mount is precision-engineered. If you feel strong resistance when attaching a lens, stop. Check that you have aligned the red dot correctly. Never apply downward pressure to force it in — this can damage the mount.

Step 1: Power the camera OFF. Always attach or remove lenses with the camera turned off. This prevents the sensor from attracting dust and protects the autofocus motor.

Step 2: Hold the camera facing you with one hand supporting the bottom. With your other hand, hold the lens.

Step 3: Remove the body cap from the camera. The body cap is the white or grey round plastic disc covering the lens mount hole. Grip it and rotate it counter-clockwise (to the left) until it releases, then lift it away. Set it aside on a clean surface.

Step 4: Remove the rear lens cap from the lens. The rear lens cap is the cap covering the back end of the lens (the end that goes into the camera). Rotate it counter-clockwise to remove it.

Step 5: Look at the front of the camera and find the small RED DOT at the top of the lens mount ring.

Step 6: Look at the rear of the lens and find its own RED DOT or colored index mark.

Step 7: Align the two red dots. Hold the lens so its red dot lines up with the red dot on the camera body.

Step 8: Gently push the lens into the mount — do not rotate yet. It should slide in smoothly with the dots aligned.

Step 9: Rotate the lens clockwise (to the right) until you feel and hear a distinct CLICK. That click means the lens has locked securely in place.

Step 10: Gently try to wiggle the lens to confirm it is locked. There should be no movement.

TIP: Keep your body cap

Whenever you remove the lens, always put the body cap back on immediately. Even a few seconds with the sensor exposed allows dust to settle on it — and dust spots on the sensor show up as dark blobs in your photos.

How to Remove a Lens — Step by Step

Step 1: Power the camera OFF.

Step 2: Hold the camera body securely with one hand.

Step 3: Locate the LENS RELEASE BUTTON on the front of the camera body. It is a small round button positioned just to the left of the lens mount ring.

Step 4: Press and hold the Lens Release Button with your thumb.

Step 5: While holding the button, rotate the lens COUNTER-CLOCKWISE (to the left) with your other hand. It will rotate approximately 45 degrees before stopping.

Step 6: Lift the lens straight out away from the camera body.

Step 7: Immediately place the rear lens cap back onto the lens, and place the body cap back onto the camera body.

Body Cap and Front Lens Cap

The body cap (on the camera) and the front lens cap (on the front of the lens) both work the same way — push it onto the mount and rotate clockwise to lock; rotate counter-clockwise to remove. Always put these caps back on when not shooting.

1.4 Inserting the Battery and SD Card

Which Battery Does the OM-3 Use?

The OM-3 uses the Olympus / OM SYSTEM BLS-50 Lithium-Ion rechargeable battery. Key facts you need to know:

- Battery model: BLS-50 (also compatible with the older BLS-5 and BLS-1 batteries, though the BLS-50 is recommended)
- Voltage: 7.2V, Capacity: 1210mAh
- Expected shots per charge: approximately 370 shots (CIPA standard), but real-world performance will vary depending on how often you use the LCD screen, viewfinder, flash, and video.
- Charging time: approximately 2.5 hours with the included BCH-1 charger, or slower when charging via the USB-C port inside the camera.

NOTE: Charge before first use
The battery is shipped with only a partial charge. Before your first shoot, charge the battery fully — either in the included BCH-1 charger or by plugging a USB-C cable into the camera body. A full charge takes about 2.5 hours with the external charger.

How to Insert the Battery — Step by Step

Step 1: Make sure the camera is powered OFF.

Step 2: Turn the camera upside down so the bottom faces up.

Step 3: Find the battery/SD card compartment door on the bottom of the camera. It is a large hinged door on the left side of the bottom.

Step 4: Slide the door lock latch in the direction of the OPEN or UNLOCK symbol. The door will spring open slightly.

Step 5: Open the door fully — it will hinge away from the camera on a small plastic hinge.

Step 6: Look inside. You will see two slots. The battery slot is the larger one on the right side (when the camera is upside down with the door facing you).

Step 7: Hold the battery so that the gold or silver electrical contacts face INTO the camera. The BLS-50 is shaped so it only fits in one correct orientation — a small raised ridge prevents you from inserting it upside down.

Step 8: Slide the battery into the slot. Press it gently until you hear a soft click as the internal latch engages.

Step 9: Gently try to pull the battery back out. If it holds firmly in place, it is locked correctly.

Step 10: Close the compartment door and push it until it clicks shut. Slide the latch to the LOCKED position.

How to Remove the Battery

Step 1: Power the camera OFF.

Step 2: Open the battery/SD card compartment door (same as above).

Step 3: Inside the battery slot, you will see a small orange or grey plastic eject lever beside the battery.

Step 4: Push or slide that lever — this releases the battery latch.

Step 5: The battery will spring out slightly. Pull it out completely.

Step 6: Close and lock the compartment door.

WARNING: Never remove the battery while the camera is ON
Always power off the camera first. Removing the battery while the camera is powered on can corrupt your SD card or damage the camera's internal settings.

Which SD Cards Are Compatible?

The OM-3 has one SD card slot that accepts the following card types:

Card Type	Speed Class Needed	Best For
SDHC (up to 32GB)	U3 / Class 10 minimum	Standard JPEG shooting. Not ideal for RAW or video.
SDXC (64GB to 2TB)	U3 / V30 or faster	RAW files, burst shooting, Full HD video. Best all-round choice.
SDXC (64GB to 2TB)	V60 or V90	4K video recording. Required for high-bitrate 4K. Look for V60 or V90 on the card label.

UHS-II SDXC	V60 / V90	4K video and very fast burst shooting. The OM-3 supports UHS-II for faster write speeds.

TIP: Buy name-brand cards
Stick to reputable brands: SanDisk, Sony, Lexar, or Delkin. Cheap off-brand cards may work sometimes but can fail without warning — and a card failure means lost photos.

How to Insert the SD Card — Step by Step

Step 1: Power the camera OFF.

Step 2: Open the battery/SD card compartment door on the bottom of the camera.

Step 3: The SD card slot is the smaller slot on the left side (when the camera is upside down with the door facing you).

Step 4: Hold the SD card so the label faces toward the back of the camera and the gold contacts face toward the front of the camera (away from you).

Step 5: The notched corner of the SD card should be at the bottom-left. The card is shaped so it can only go in one way — do not force it if it does not slide in easily.

Step 6: Gently push the card in until you feel a slight resistance, then push a little more firmly until you hear a soft click. The card is now locked in.

Step 7: Close and lock the compartment door.

How to Remove the SD Card

Step 1: Power the camera OFF and make sure the access lamp (a small light near the card slot) is not blinking. Never remove the card while it is blinking — this means data is being written and removing the card will corrupt your files.

Step 2: Open the compartment door.

Step 3: Gently push the SD card inward (push it down into the slot). You will feel a click, and the card will spring up slightly.

Step 4: Pull the card out and store it safely.

How to Tell When the Battery Is Low

The OM-3 shows battery level in two places:

- On the LCD screen and in the EVF: a battery icon appears in the corner. When it is full, the icon is completely filled. As the battery drains, segments disappear. When only one segment remains or the icon blinks, the battery needs charging soon.

- When the battery is completely empty, the camera will display a warning message and then shut down automatically.
- Before an important shoot, always check the battery level and charge if needed.

> **TIP: Cold weather drains batteries faster**
> In temperatures below 10°C (50°F), battery performance drops significantly. Carry a spare battery in a warm pocket and swap them if the camera drains faster than usual.

1.5 Powering the Camera On and Off

Location of the Power Switch

The power switch is a lever that wraps around the base of the shutter button on the top right of the camera. It has two positions:

- ON — slide the lever so the green or white section with "ON" is visible. The camera will power up, and the LCD screen or EVF will light up within 1 to 2 seconds.
- OFF — slide the lever back to the OFF position. The camera saves your current settings, turns off the screens, and shuts down within about 1 second.

The lever requires a deliberate push in one direction — it will not accidentally switch on or off while in your bag.

How to Turn the Camera On

> **Step 1:** Make sure the battery is inserted and an SD card is loaded.
>
> **Step 2:** Slide the power lever to ON. The lever moves to the right when you push it away from you.
>
> **Step 3:** The rear LCD screen will light up and display a live view of whatever the lens is pointed at. You are ready to shoot.

> **TIP: First startup**
> The very first time you power on the camera, it will ask you to set the language, date, time, and time zone. Follow the on-screen prompts using the arrow pad and OK button. This is covered in detail in Part 2.

How to Turn the Camera Off

> **Step 1:** Slide the power lever back to OFF.

Step 2: The screen will go dark and the camera will shut down. Any settings you changed are automatically saved.

Auto Power-Off — What It Is and How to Change It

If you do not press any button or turn any dial for a set period of time, the OM-3 will automatically turn off the screens and enter a sleep state to save battery power. This is called Auto Power-Off (sometimes called Sleep Mode).

By default the camera goes to sleep after 1 minute of inactivity. To wake it up from sleep, just press the shutter button halfway — the camera will be ready to shoot within about 1 second.

To change the Auto Power-Off time, follow these exact steps:

Step 1: Press the MENU button (on the back of the camera, to the right of the LCD screen).

Step 2: The menu system opens. You will see a row of icon tabs along the top of the screen.

Step 3: Use the LEFT or RIGHT arrow buttons on the 4-way pad to navigate to the SETUP MENU tab. It looks like a wrench or gear icon (usually the last tab on the right).

Step 4: Press the DOWN arrow to move into the menu list below the tab.

Step 5: Scroll DOWN using the DOWN arrow until you find "Power Save" or "Auto Power Off."

Step 6: Press the RIGHT arrow or OK button to enter that submenu.

Step 7: You will see a list of time options: 1 min, 3 min, 5 min, 10 min, or Off (never auto-off).

Step 8: Use the UP or DOWN arrows to highlight your preferred time.

Step 9: Press OK to confirm.

Step 10: Press the MENU button to close the menu and return to shooting.

NOTE: When to disable Auto Power-Off
If you are shooting on a tripod with the camera set to wait for a remote trigger, consider setting Auto Power-Off to a longer time or turning it off temporarily. Otherwise the camera will sleep before you get the shot.

1.6 How to Hold the Camera Correctly

Holding the camera correctly is one of the most overlooked skills in photography. A bad grip causes camera shake — and camera shake causes blurry photos. A good grip is also more comfortable, giving you better control over every button and dial.

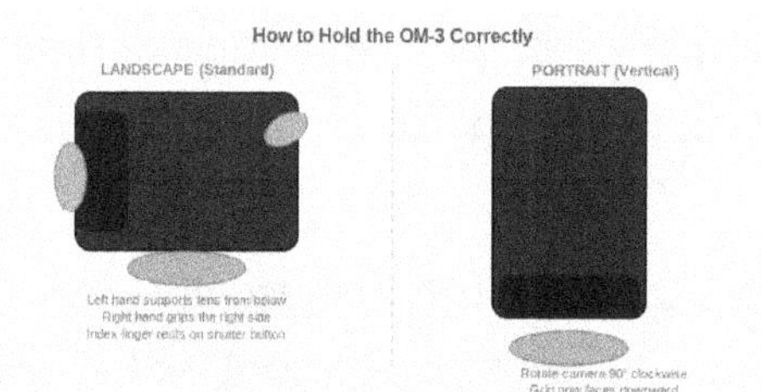

Figure 1.6 — Correct landscape and portrait camera grip

Correct Grip for Still Photos (Landscape / Horizontal)

This is the standard horizontal grip — used for most everyday photos.

- RIGHT HAND: Place your right hand around the grip bump on the right side of the camera. Wrap your middle, ring, and little fingers underneath the grip. Your thumb rests on the thumb rest on the back. Your index finger rests lightly on top of the shutter button — do not press yet, just rest it there.
- LEFT HAND: Slide your left hand under the camera and lens. Your palm should support the bottom of the lens. Your fingers can gently wrap around the lens barrel. This hand does the heavy lifting — it supports the weight of the lens, especially important if the lens is large.
- ELBOWS: Tuck both elbows in toward your body. This creates a stable triangle between your two hands and your chest, greatly reducing camera shake.
- BREATHING: Just before pressing the shutter, take a breath, let half of it out, then press the shutter gently and smoothly. This technique, borrowed from rifle shooting, dramatically reduces blur from breathing movement.
- VIEWFINDER: When possible, press the camera lightly against your face and look through the EVF. The contact between the camera and your face adds a third stabilization point.

Correct Grip for Vertical (Portrait) Shots

To take a photo that is taller than it is wide (called portrait orientation), rotate the camera 90 degrees.

- Rotate the camera clockwise when looking from the front — so the shutter button ends up at the bottom.
- Your right hand now grips the right side of the camera (which is now the top). Your right thumb will be at the bottom.
- Your left hand supports the lens from below as before.
- Tuck your elbows in. Your right elbow may need to point upward — keep it in toward your body as much as possible.

> **TIP: Use the tilting screen for low shots**
> For photos taken from very low to the ground, flip the LCD screen upward so you can see the image while the camera is near the floor. This saves you from lying face-down on the ground.

Correct Grip for Video Recording

Holding the camera steadily for video is even more important than for stills, because any shake is very visible in moving footage.

- Use the landscape grip described above, with both elbows tucked in.
- If you are walking while filming, bend your knees slightly and walk with a gentle, gliding step — almost as if walking on ice. This absorbs your footsteps and prevents the bouncy walk that ruins handheld video.
- Extend your left arm slightly further out from your body, creating a longer lever — this helps dampen small shakes.
- Consider using a tripod or a small handheld gimbal for any footage that lasts more than a few seconds. Even the OM-3's excellent 5-axis image stabilization has limits.
- Hold your breath while filming critical moments, just like with stills.

> **TIP: Use the neck strap as stabilization**
> Wrap the neck strap around your wrist (not your neck) and hold the camera forward at arm's length, with the strap taut and under tension. This creates resistance that steadies the camera — a common trick for low-angle shots.

End of Part 1 — Getting to Know Your OM-3

Next: Part 2 — Initial Setup (Language, Date, SD Card Formatting, App Connection)

Part 2 — Initial Setup

You have inspected every part of your OM-3, attached a lens, loaded the battery and SD card, and powered it on for the first time. Now you are going to complete the camera's one-time setup wizard, confirm your language and date settings, format your SD card correctly, and optionally connect the camera to your smartphone. None of these steps take more than a few minutes, and when you are finished you will have a camera that is perfectly configured and ready to shoot.

Work through sections 2.1 to 2.4 in order the first time you set up the camera. After that you can return to any individual section whenever you need to change a setting.

2.1 First-Time Setup Wizard

The very first time you power on the OM-3 — before a single photo has ever been taken — the camera detects that it has not yet been configured and automatically launches a short setup wizard. This wizard walks you through four quick screens: choosing a display language, setting the current date, setting the current time, and selecting your time zone.

> **NOTE: When does the wizard appear?**
>
> The wizard appears only on the very first power-on after purchase, or after you perform a full factory reset (covered in Part 19). If you bought a used camera, the wizard may not appear — go straight to Section 2.2 to check and correct the language, date, and time manually.

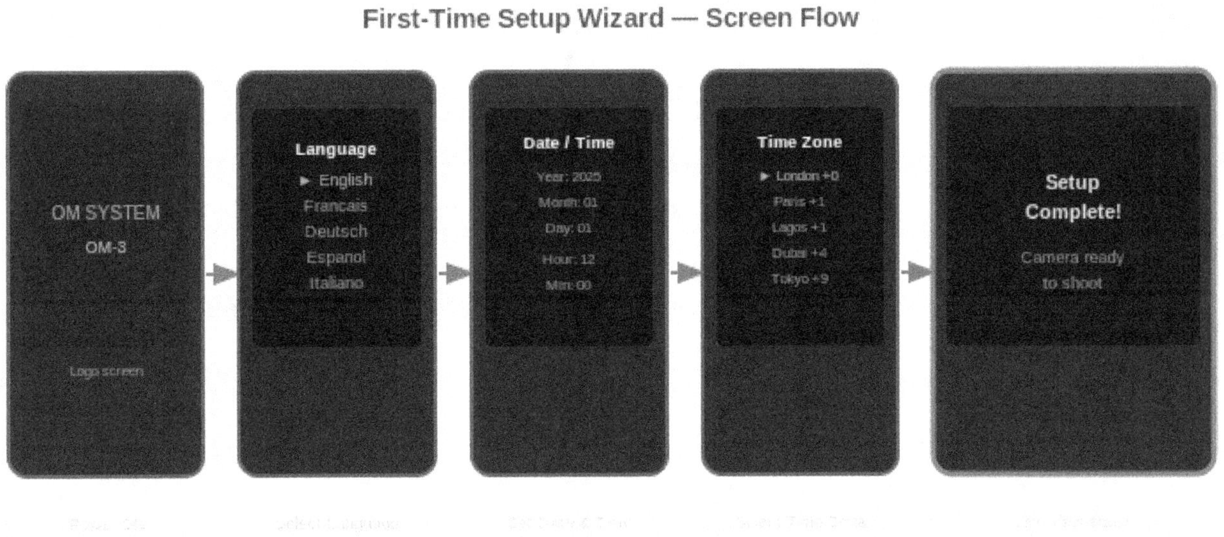

First-Time Setup Wizard — Screen Flow

Figure 2.1 — The four-screen first-time setup wizard, from power-on to ready

What Happens When You Power On for the First Time

Slide the power lever to ON. The camera shows the OM SYSTEM boot logo for about one second, then immediately jumps to the first wizard screen. You will not see the live viewfinder at this point — the wizard must be completed before the camera lets you shoot.

The wizard is completely controlled using the four arrow buttons and the OK button on the back of the camera. Here is a quick reminder of what those buttons do inside the wizard:

Button	What It Does Inside the Wizard
UP arrow	Moves the selection cursor up through a list, or increases a number value (such as the year or hour).
DOWN arrow	Moves the selection cursor down through a list, or decreases a number value.
LEFT arrow	Moves to the previous field (for example, from the "Month" field back to the "Year" field).
RIGHT arrow	Moves to the next field (for example, from the "Year" field forward to the "Month" field).
OK button	Confirms your current selection and advances to the next screen.

Wizard Screen 1 of 4 — Select Language

The first screen shows a scrollable list of languages. The list is in alphabetical order. English is near the top.

Step 1: Look at the screen. You will see a list of language names. One of them is highlighted in blue — that is the currently selected language.

Step 2: Press the UP or DOWN arrow to scroll through the list until "English" (or your preferred language) is highlighted.

Step 3: Press OK to confirm your language choice. The screen will immediately change to the date-setting screen.

TIP: Can't read the screen?

If the camera was pre-set to a language you do not understand, scroll down toward the bottom of the language list — most language names are written in their own script AND in English transliteration. Alternatively, count the position: English is the first or second option in most firmware versions.

Wizard Screen 2 of 4 — Set the Date

The second screen shows a date entry field with separate boxes for Year, Month, and Day. The camera's cursor starts on the Year field.

Step 1: The Year field is highlighted. Press UP or DOWN to increase or decrease the year until it shows the correct current year.

Step 2: Press the RIGHT arrow to move to the Month field.

Step 3: Press UP or DOWN to set the correct month (shown as a number — 01 = January, 12 = December).

Step 4: Press the RIGHT arrow to move to the Day field.

Step 5: Press UP or DOWN to set the correct day of the month.

Step 6: When all three fields (Year, Month, Day) show the correct date, press OK to confirm.

NOTE: Date format

The OM-3 displays dates in Year / Month / Day order by default (for example, 2025 / 04 / 18 for the 18th of April 2025). This format can be changed later in the Setup Menu if you prefer Month / Day / Year or Day / Month / Year.

Wizard Screen 3 of 4 — Set the Time

The third screen looks similar to the date screen, but now shows Hour and Minute fields. The camera uses a 24-hour clock format by default (where 1:00 PM = 13:00, midnight = 00:00).

Step 1: The Hour field is highlighted. Press UP or DOWN to set the correct hour in 24-hour format. For example: 2 PM = 14, 6 PM = 18, 11 PM = 23.

Step 2: Press the RIGHT arrow to move to the Minute field.

Step 3: Press UP or DOWN to set the correct minute.

Step 4: Press OK to confirm the time.

TIP: Switching to 12-hour clock

If you prefer a 12-hour clock with AM/PM, you can change this after setup: go to MENU → Setup Menu (wrench) → Date/Time → set the time format to 12h. This is covered fully in Section 2.2.

Wizard Screen 4 of 4 — Select Time Zone

The final wizard screen shows a list of world cities with their UTC offset. Choosing the correct city (or the city in your time zone) ensures the camera's clock stays accurate and that photos are time-stamped correctly.

> **Step 1:** A list of city names and UTC offsets appears. Scroll through the list using the UP or DOWN arrows.
>
> **Step 2:** Find the city that is in your time zone. You do not need to find your exact city — just find any city in the same time zone. For example, if you are in West Africa (UTC+1), you can select "Lagos," "Casablanca," or "Paris" — all are UTC+1.
>
> **Step 3:** Press OK to confirm your time zone.
>
> **Step 4:** The camera will briefly show a confirmation screen or go directly to live view — this means setup is complete.

After the Wizard — Camera is Ready

Once you press OK on the time zone screen, the wizard closes and the camera's live view appears on the LCD screen. You will see whatever the lens is pointed at on the screen. The camera is now configured and ready to take photos.

> **TIP: Write down your settings**
>
> If you ever need to reset the camera to factory defaults for troubleshooting, you will need to go through the wizard again. It only takes two minutes if you already know your preferred language, date, time, and time zone.

2.2 Setting Language, Date, Time, and Time Zone

Even if the setup wizard already captured these settings, it is worth knowing how to find and change them later. You may want to adjust the time after travelling to a different country, or switch the clock to 12-hour format, or change the date format. All of these settings live inside the Setup Menu.

Understanding the Menu System — A Quick Orientation

Before diving into specific settings, here is a simple map of how the OM-3's menu system is organized. Every setting in this guide will refer back to this structure.

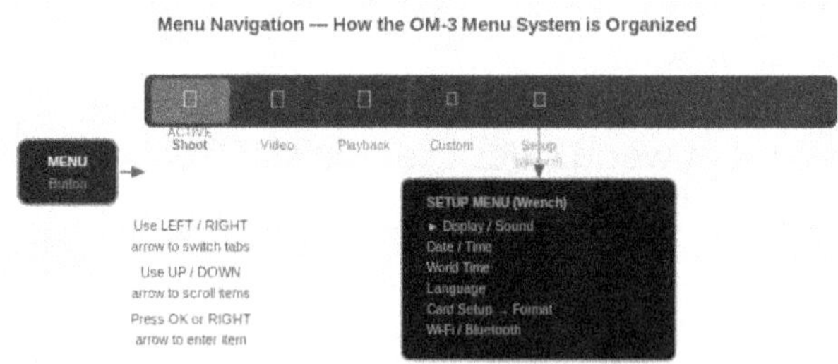

Figure 2.2 — How the OM-3 menu is organized: tabs along the top, items listed below

The menu is divided into five main tabs, represented by icons along the top of the screen. Think of each tab as a folder:

Tab Icon	Tab Name	What It Contains
Camera icon	Shooting Menu	All settings that affect how a photo is taken — image quality, focus, drive mode, white balance, ISO, metering, and more.
Video camera icon	Video Menu	All settings specific to video recording — resolution, frame rate, audio, and video stabilization.
Triangle / Play icon	Playback Menu	Settings for reviewing photos — slideshow, print settings, RAW development, and photo editing.
Gear icon	Custom Menu	Advanced customization — reassigning buttons, adjusting dials, fine-tuning autofocus behavior, and much more.
Wrench icon	Setup Menu	Camera-level settings — language, date/time, Wi-Fi, SD card, display brightness, power saving, and firmware. This is where you are working in Part 2.

How to Open the Setup Menu — Exact Steps

Step 1: Press the MENU button. It is on the back of the camera, to the right of the LCD screen. The word MENU is printed on or above it. The menu system opens immediately.

Step 2: Look at the top of the screen. You will see a row of five small icons in a dark bar — these are the menu tabs. The currently active tab is highlighted or underlined.

Step 3: Press the RIGHT arrow button repeatedly until you reach the rightmost tab — the one that looks like a wrench. This is the Setup Menu. You may need to press RIGHT four or five times depending on which tab was last active.

Step 4: Once the wrench tab is selected, press the DOWN arrow to move your cursor into the list of menu items below the tab row.

Step 5: You are now inside the Setup Menu and can scroll through its items using the UP and DOWN arrows.

NOTE: Quick tip — getting back

At any point while inside the menus, press the MENU button once to go back one level. Press it again to close the menu entirely. You can also press the shutter button halfway to exit the menu and return to live view.

Finding and Changing the Language — Step by Step

Step 1: Open the Setup Menu (follow the steps above).

Step 2: Scroll DOWN through the menu items using the DOWN arrow until you see the item labeled "Language" with a small flag or globe icon next to it.

Step 3: Press the RIGHT arrow or press OK to enter the Language selection screen.

Step 4: A list of languages appears. Scroll UP or DOWN to highlight your preferred language.

Step 5: Press OK to confirm. The entire menu system immediately switches to the selected language.

Step 6: Press the MENU button to close the menu.

TIP: If the menus change to a language you can't read

Scroll to the bottom of the language list — the word for each language is usually written in that language, but you can count positions. If you know English was the 2nd item, simply press DOWN once from the top. Alternatively, count the languages alphabetically — Arabic, Chinese, Czech, Danish, Dutch, English.

Setting the Date and Time — Step by Step

Step 1: Open the Setup Menu.

Step 2: Scroll DOWN to the item labeled "Date/Time" and press OK or RIGHT to enter it.

Step 3: A date and time entry screen appears, similar to the wizard. Fields are: Year, Month, Day, Hour, Minute.

Step 4: Press LEFT or RIGHT to move between fields.

Step 5: Press UP or DOWN to change the value of the highlighted field.

Step 6: When all fields show the correct date and time, press OK to save.

Changing the Date Format

By default the OM-3 shows dates as Year/Month/Day. If you prefer a different order, change it here:

Step 1: Inside the Date/Time screen, look for a field or separate option labeled "Date Format" or an icon showing the date order.

Step 2: Press RIGHT to enter the Date Format setting.

Step 3: Three options appear: Y/M/D (Year first), M/D/Y (Month first — common in the USA), D/M/Y (Day first — common in Europe and many other regions).

Step 4: Highlight your preferred format and press OK.

Changing the Clock to 12-Hour (AM/PM) Format

The camera defaults to a 24-hour clock. To switch to 12-hour with AM/PM:

Step 1: Inside the Date/Time screen, find the field labeled "Clock Display" or a small icon showing "24h" or "12h."

Step 2: Press RIGHT to enter the clock format option.

Step 3: Select "12h" and press OK.

Step 4: The time display will now show AM or PM.

Setting the Time Zone — Step by Step

Step 1: Open the Setup Menu.

Step 2: Scroll DOWN to "World Time" (it may also appear as "Time Zone" in some firmware versions). Press OK or RIGHT to enter it.

Step 3: Two options appear: "Home" and "Alternative" (or "Travel"). Home is your primary time zone. Alternative/Travel is a second time zone you can set for when you are travelling.

Step 4: Select "Home" and press RIGHT or OK.

Step 5: A list of world cities and UTC offsets appears. Scroll UP or DOWN to find your time zone. Cities are sorted by UTC offset (from UTC-12 at the top to UTC+14 at the bottom).

Step 6: Highlight your city or any city in the same time zone and press OK.

Step 7: The clock will immediately update to the correct time for that zone.

Step 8: Press MENU to close.

NOTE: Daylight Saving Time (DST)

The OM-3 does not automatically adjust for daylight saving time. When your country switches to or from summer time, go to the Date/Time menu and manually add or subtract one hour. Alternatively, use the World Time menu and switch to a city that does not observe DST as your primary zone.

2.3 Formatting the SD Card

Formatting an SD card means erasing everything on it and preparing the card's internal file structure specifically for your OM-3 camera. This is one of the most important steps you can take before you start shooting seriously — and it is something you should do every time you insert a new or used card into the camera.

Why You Should Always Format the Card In-Camera

Many photographers skip this step and assume a card is ready to use straight from the shop, or after deleting photos on a computer. This is a mistake. Here is why formatting in-camera matters:

- A fresh card from the shop is usually formatted for use with Windows computers (FAT32 or exFAT). The OM-3 can read these cards, but formatting in-camera creates a folder structure tailored to the camera's own file management system, which prevents file-numbering errors and folder conflicts.
- A card previously used in a different camera (even another OM SYSTEM camera) may have a different internal folder structure. Formatting in the OM-3 removes all traces of the previous camera's structure.
- Deleting individual photos — whether on the camera or on a computer — does not fully clean the card. Over time, partial files, hidden system files, and fragmented data accumulate and can cause the camera to slow down when writing files or even cause card errors mid-shoot. Formatting cleans all of this away instantly.
- Formatting takes approximately 3 seconds. It is fast, it is safe (assuming you have copied any important files off the card first), and it dramatically reduces the risk of a corrupt card ruining a shoot.

WARNING: Copy your photos BEFORE formatting

Formatting permanently deletes every file on the SD card. Before you format, make sure you have copied all the photos and videos you want to keep to a computer or external drive. There is no undo button and no way to recover files after formatting.

How to Format the SD Card — Exact Menu Path

The exact path is: MENU → Setup Menu (wrench icon) → Card Setup → Format

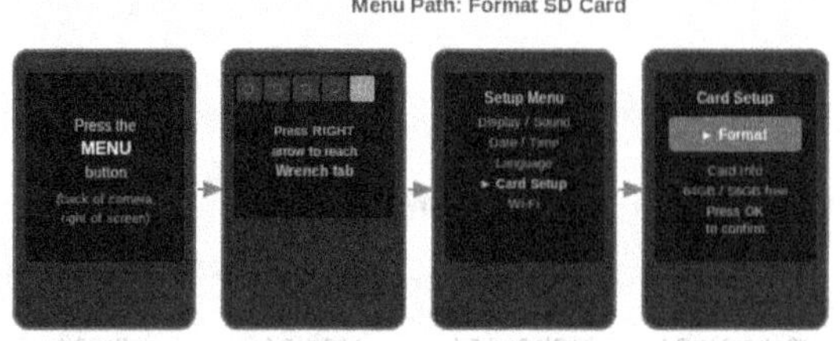

Figure 2.3 — Step-by-step screen flow for formatting the SD card

Step 1: Press the MENU button on the back of the camera.

Step 2: Navigate to the Setup Menu by pressing the RIGHT arrow until you reach the wrench icon tab at the far right.

Step 3: Press the DOWN arrow to move into the menu list.

Step 4: Scroll DOWN with the DOWN arrow until you see "Card Setup." Press OK or RIGHT to enter it.

Step 5: A submenu opens. You will see "Format" at the top and "Card Info" below it (Card Info just shows the card's capacity and remaining space — pressing it does nothing harmful).

Step 6: Highlight "Format" using the UP or DOWN arrow if it is not already highlighted.

Step 7: Press OK. The camera shows a confirmation dialog: "All data on card will be deleted. Format card? YES / NO." The cursor is on NO by default — this safety measure prevents accidental formatting.

Step 8: Press the LEFT arrow to move the cursor to YES.

Step 9: Press OK to confirm. The camera formats the card. A progress bar or spinning icon appears for about 2 to 5 seconds.

Step 10: When formatting is complete, the camera returns to the Card Setup menu. The card is now ready to use.

TIP: Format after every major shoot

Many professional photographers format their SD card at the start of every new shoot (after copying the previous session's files). This keeps the card clean and fast, and eliminates the possibility of leftover files from a previous session appearing in a new shoot's file sequence.

What Formatting Deletes — and What It Does Not

Formatting DOES delete:	Formatting does NOT delete:
Every photo and video file on the card	The camera's internal settings (these are stored in the camera body, not the card)
Every hidden system file and folder	The firmware (the camera's operating software — also stored internally)
Every custom folder created by other cameras	The images stored on a different card (only the inserted card is affected)

Corrupted or fragmented file index data	Files on your computer or hard drive that you previously copied from the card

NOTE: Quick format vs full format

The OM-3 performs a quick format — it erases the card's file index (the table of contents) rather than overwriting every byte of data. This is why formatting is so fast. However, it also means that with specialized data recovery software, a forensics expert could theoretically recover recently formatted files. If you need to completely destroy the data for privacy reasons, repeat the format 3 times or use a dedicated data-shredding tool on a computer.

2.4 Connecting to the OM SYSTEM App

What the OM SYSTEM App Does

The OM SYSTEM app (previously called the OI.Share app) is a free application made by OM SYSTEM for both iOS and Android smartphones. Once connected to your camera via Bluetooth or Wi-Fi, the app lets you:

- Control the camera remotely from your phone — set shutter speed, aperture, ISO, and other settings without touching the camera. Useful for self-portraits, wildlife shots from a hide, or tripod work where touching the camera would cause shake.
- See a live view from the camera on your phone's screen — useful when the camera is mounted on a tripod at an angle you cannot easily look through the viewfinder.
- Transfer photos and videos wirelessly to your smartphone, ready to share on social media or send to family — without needing a cable or computer.
- Use your smartphone as a remote shutter release — tap the screen to take a photo.
- Geotag your photos — if your phone has GPS, the app can embed location data into each photo's metadata. The OM-3 does not have built-in GPS, so the app provides this via your phone.
- Remotely change focus point — tap anywhere on your phone's live view screen to move the autofocus point on the camera.

TIP: Geotagging without extra hardware

The GPS geotag feature is one of the most useful reasons to connect the app. Enable it in the app settings and your photos will automatically be tagged with the exact location where they were taken — which makes organizing travel photos much easier later.

How to Download the OM SYSTEM App

Your Phone	Where to Find It	Search For

iPhone / iPad (iOS 14.0 or later)	Apple App Store	"OM SYSTEM" — look for the official app by OM Digital Solutions
Android phone / tablet (Android 8.0 or later)	Google Play Store	"OM SYSTEM" — look for the official app by OM Digital Solutions

The app is free. Install it, open it, and create a free account if prompted. You do not need an account to use the basic wireless control and transfer features, but an account lets you back up preferences.

Enabling Bluetooth and Wi-Fi on the OM-3

The camera's wireless connection system uses Bluetooth to establish the initial pairing with your phone, then automatically switches to Wi-Fi for transferring photos (since Wi-Fi is faster). You need to enable both in the camera's menu.

Step 1 — Enable Bluetooth

Step 1: Press the MENU button on the back of the camera.

Step 2: Navigate to the Setup Menu (wrench icon tab) by pressing RIGHT.

Step 3: Press DOWN to enter the menu list.

Step 4: Scroll DOWN to find "Wi-Fi / Bluetooth" or "Wireless Connection" and press OK or RIGHT to enter it.

Step 5: Inside the wireless settings, look for "Bluetooth" and press OK or RIGHT to enter it.

Step 6: You will see an ON / OFF toggle. Use the arrow keys to select "ON" and press OK to confirm.

Step 7: The camera's Bluetooth radio is now active. A small Bluetooth icon may appear in the corner of the LCD screen.

Step 2 — Enable Private Connection (Recommended)

The "Private Connection" setting is a dedicated one-to-one pairing mode between the camera and your specific phone. This is the recommended connection method because it is more stable and reconnects automatically each time.

Step 1: Still inside the "Wi-Fi / Bluetooth" menu, look for "Private Connection" and press OK or RIGHT.

Step 2: A QR code or device name appears on the camera's screen — for example, "OM-3-A1B2C3." This is the name the camera broadcasts so your phone can find it.

Step 3: Leave this screen open on the camera — do not press any button. Now pick up your phone.

Pairing the Camera to Your Smartphone — Step by Step

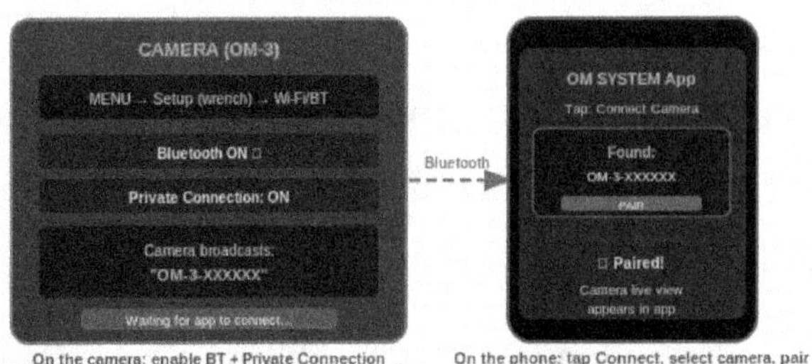

Figure 2.4 — Camera broadcasts its name; the app on the phone finds and pairs with it

On Your Smartphone — First-Time Pairing

Step 1: Open the OM SYSTEM app on your phone.

Step 2: Tap the connection icon or tap "Connect Camera" on the app's home screen. The app will scan for nearby cameras.

Step 3: Your camera's name (for example, "OM-3-A1B2C3") will appear in the list. Tap it.

Step 4: A pairing confirmation may appear on both the camera screen and your phone. On the camera, press OK to accept. On the phone, tap "Pair" if prompted.

Step 5: Wait 5 to 10 seconds. The app will connect to the camera, switch to Wi-Fi automatically, and then show you a live view of what the camera lens sees.

Step 6: Pairing is complete. You are now connected.

TIP: After the first pairing

Once you have paired the camera and phone once, they remember each other. On future sessions: turn on the camera, enable Bluetooth if needed (or leave it always on), open the app, and tap "Connect" — the camera and phone reconnect automatically, usually within 5 seconds.

If the Connection Fails — Troubleshooting

Problem	Most Likely Cause	Solution
Phone cannot find the camera	Bluetooth is off on the camera or the phone	On the camera: check MENU → Setup → Wi-Fi/Bluetooth → Bluetooth is ON.

		On the phone: check phone Settings → Bluetooth is ON.
Camera appears in list but pairing fails	Interference from other Bluetooth devices nearby	Move away from crowded areas, try again. Also ensure the camera is not already connected to a different phone.
App connects but live view does not appear	Wi-Fi on phone switched off	Check phone Settings → Wi-Fi is ON. The app uses Bluetooth to pair but switches to Wi-Fi for live view — both must be on.
Connected but transfer is very slow	Phone is far from camera or physical obstruction	Move the phone within 5 metres (15 feet) of the camera with no walls in between for best speed.
Forget pairing and start fresh	Incorrect pairing saved	On camera: MENU → Setup → Wi-Fi/Bluetooth → Reset Wi-Fi Settings. Then repeat the pairing steps above.

Connecting via QR Code (Alternative Method)

If you have difficulty with the Bluetooth pairing method, the OM-3 provides an alternative: a QR code that the app can scan directly to connect.

Step 1: Press MENU → Setup Menu → Wi-Fi/Bluetooth → QR Code Connection (the exact label varies by firmware version — look for any option mentioning QR Code).

Step 2: A large QR code appears on the camera's LCD screen.

Step 3: Open the OM SYSTEM app on your phone.

Step 4: Look for a QR code scan option in the app's connect screen.

Step 5: Point your phone's camera at the OM-3's screen and scan the QR code.

Step 6: The connection establishes automatically.

NOTE: Keep the port cover closed during wireless use

You do not need any cables for wireless connection — the camera transmits via its internal Bluetooth and Wi-Fi antennas. Always keep the rubber port cover on the left side of the camera fully closed when no cables are plugged in.

NOTE: Battery consumption

Bluetooth and Wi-Fi use battery power. If you are shooting all day and do not need the wireless features, go to MENU → Setup → Wi-Fi/Bluetooth → Bluetooth → OFF. You can turn it back on whenever you need it. Keeping Bluetooth on in low-power mode uses very little battery; Wi-Fi uses more.

Part 3 — Understanding the Displays

The OM-3 gives you two ways to see your scene before you shoot — the Electronic Viewfinder (EVF) that you look through with your eye, and the rear LCD touchscreen that you hold out and look at. Both show a live image of what the camera sees through the lens in real time, and both are covered with useful information overlays that tell you everything about your current camera settings at a glance.

This part of the guide explains every single icon and indicator you will see on both displays, how to switch between them, how to use the Super Control Panel to change settings instantly without diving into menus, and how to cycle through different information display modes using the INFO button.

By the end of this section you will be able to look at either screen, understand every piece of information displayed, and change any setting you need within a few seconds — all without opening the main menu.

3.1 The Electronic Viewfinder (EVF)

What the EVF Is and How to Look Through It

The Electronic Viewfinder — abbreviated EVF — is the small eyepiece at the top of the back of the camera. It looks like the viewfinder on traditional cameras, but instead of optical glass it contains a tiny, high-resolution electronic screen (2.36 million dots on the OM-3) that shows you a live digital image from the camera's sensor.

To use the EVF, simply bring the camera up to your eye and position your eye roughly 2 to 3 centimetres away from the rubber eyecup. The image will fill your vision. If the image looks blurry, find the small diopter adjustment dial just to the right of the eyepiece (it looks like a tiny ridged wheel). Turn it slowly left or right until the image becomes sharp for your eye. You should only need to do this once.

Feature	Detail
Resolution	2.36 million dots — high enough to judge fine focus and detail
Refresh rate	Up to 120 fps — motion appears very smooth with no perceivable lag
Magnification	0.74x equivalent — slightly smaller than life-size but larger than many competitors
Eye relief	21mm — comfortable even if you wear glasses
Diopter range	-4 to +2 diopters — adjustable without glasses for most prescription strengths
Brightness	Adjustable — auto-adjusts to ambient light or set manually in Custom Menu J

TIP: Use the EVF in bright sunlight

On a bright sunny day, the rear LCD screen can be hard to see due to glare. Bring the camera to your eye and use the EVF instead — it is completely unaffected by sunlight and gives you a more stable shooting platform because the camera is pressed against your face.

Every Icon and Indicator in the EVF — Each One Explained

The diagram below shows the full EVF display with every overlay visible. In normal shooting, not all of these will be visible at once — the INFO button (covered in Section 3.5) lets you choose how much information you want to see. But every icon listed here will appear at some point, so you need to know what each one means.

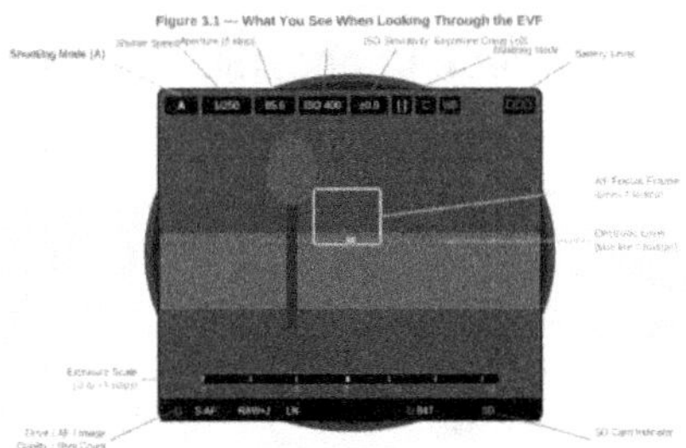

Figure 3.1 — The EVF display with all information overlays active and labeled

Top Row — Shooting Settings

Across the top of the EVF you will see a row of your most important shooting settings. These are the numbers that directly control how your photo will look.

Icon / Display	Location in Top Row	What It Shows	What Changes It
Shooting Mode letter (e.g. A, P, S, M)	Far left	The current shooting mode selected on the Mode Dial. A = Aperture Priority, P = Program, S = Shutter Priority, M = Manual, B = Bulb, iA = Auto.	Turn the Mode Dial on top of the camera.
Shutter Speed (e.g. 1/250)	Left of center	How long the shutter stays open. 1/250 means one two-hundred-and-fiftieth of a second. A larger bottom number = faster shutter = less motion blur. In Bulb mode it shows BULB.	Rear dial (in S and M modes).
Aperture (e.g. f/5.6)	Center	The size of the lens opening. A lower f-number (like f/1.8) means a wider opening —	Front dial (in A and M modes).

		more light, blurrier background. A higher f-number (like f/16) means a smaller opening — less light, sharper background.	
ISO (e.g. ISO 400)	Right of center	The sensor's light sensitivity. ISO 200 = low sensitivity, clean image. ISO 6400 = high sensitivity, bright image in dark conditions but with more grain (noise).	Front dial or SCP or rear dial in some modes.
Exposure Compensation (e.g. ±0.0)	Right	How much you have deliberately made the photo brighter (+) or darker (-) beyond what the camera's meter recommends. At ±0.0 you are following the meter exactly.	Press and hold the AEL button and turn the rear dial, or press the arrow pad up/down shortcut.
Metering Mode icon (circle with dot)	Right side	Which metering pattern the camera uses to measure light. A small dot in a circle = Spot. A dot in center of larger circle = Centre-weighted. Filled segments = ESP (multi-zone). Small square = Highlight.	SCP or Custom Menu.
Flash mode icon (lightning bolt)	Right side	Whether the flash will fire and in what mode. Lightning bolt = Auto or Fill. Bolt with A = Auto. Bolt crossed out = Flash off.	Press the Flash button on top or use SCP.
WB (White Balance abbreviation)	Right side	The current white balance setting. AWB = Auto White Balance. Numbers (e.g. 5500K) = manual Kelvin setting. Sun icon = Daylight. Cloud = Cloudy.	SCP or Menu.

Battery icon (rectangle with segments)	Far right	The remaining battery charge. Three segments = full. Two = medium. One = low. A blinking empty icon = critically low — charge or swap immediately.	Automatic — no action needed except to charge.

Center of the Frame — Focus and Composition Aids

Overlay	What It Looks Like	What It Means
AF Focus Frame	A green rectangle or set of brackets around your subject	This shows where the camera is focusing. Green = camera has found and locked focus on this area. Red or orange = camera is struggling to focus (reframe or switch to manual focus). White = the area the camera is targeting but has not yet locked.
Electronic Level (Horizon Line)	A thin horizontal dashed blue line across the middle of the frame	Shows whether the camera is held level left to right. When the camera tilts, a second orange or yellow line appears at an angle. Align the two lines to shoot a perfectly level horizon. The centre dot turns green when level.
Grid Lines (if enabled)	A faint 3x3 grid of lines across the entire frame	Helps with composition — for example, placing your subject at the intersection of two grid lines (the rule of thirds). Turn on/off in Custom Menu D → Grid Display.
Face/Eye Detection Frame	A small white rectangle around a detected face, with brackets on the eyes	The camera has detected a human face and locked onto it. The eye brackets show which eye is being tracked. This appears automatically when Face Detection is turned on.

Exposure Scale — The Most Important Indicator

The exposure scale is a horizontal bar that runs near the bottom of the frame. It has a zero mark in the middle and tick marks extending left (minus, = underexposed / darker) and right (plus, = overexposed / brighter), usually from -3 to +3 stops.

A small pointer (a white triangle or line) moves left or right depending on whether the camera thinks your current settings will produce a correctly exposed photo. When the pointer is exactly at zero, the camera calculates the exposure is correct. If the pointer is to the left, the image will be too dark at the current settings. To the right, it will be too bright.

- In Auto, P, A, or S mode — the camera automatically moves settings to keep the pointer near zero. You can push it deliberately left or right using Exposure Compensation.
- In Manual (M) mode — the pointer shows you whether your chosen combination of aperture, shutter speed, and ISO will produce the correct exposure. You adjust manually until the pointer reaches zero (or wherever you deliberately want it).

TIP: Trust your eyes, not just the meter

The exposure meter tries to make every scene average middle grey. If you are photographing a snow scene or a dark room, the meter will try to make them both look the same shade of grey. Use Exposure Compensation (+) for bright snowy scenes and (-) for intentionally dark and moody shots.

Bottom Row — Drive, Format, and Storage Information

Display	What It Shows
Drive mode icon (square or stack of squares)	The current drive mode: single shot (one square), burst/continuous (overlapping squares), or self-timer (clock icon).
AF mode text (e.g. S-AF, C-AF, MF)	The active autofocus mode — Single AF, Continuous AF, or Manual Focus.
Image quality (e.g. RAW+J, JPEG, RAW)	Whether photos are saved as RAW files, JPEG files, or both simultaneously. RAW+J means both are saved with every shot.
Image size code (e.g. LN, MN, SN)	The JPEG image size and compression level. L = Large, M = Medium, S = Small. N = Normal compression, F = Fine compression.
Shot counter (number with camera icon)	How many more photos can be stored on the SD card at your current image quality setting. This number counts down as you shoot.
SD card indicator	Shows that an SD card is inserted and functioning. If it blinks red, the card is being written to — do not remove it.

The Eye Sensor — How It Automatically Switches to the EVF

Just to the left of the EVF eyepiece on the back of the camera is a tiny infrared proximity sensor. This sensor emits an invisible infrared beam. When your eye (or any object) comes within about 3 to 4 centimetres of the eyepiece, the beam is interrupted and the sensor detects the presence of your eye.

In the camera's default automatic mode, here is exactly what happens when you lift the camera to your eye:

Step 1: Your eye approaches the EVF eyepiece.

Step 2: The eye sensor detects your eye within a fraction of a second.

Step 3: The rear LCD screen switches off instantly.

Step 4: The EVF screen switches on and shows the live image.

Step 5: You look through the viewfinder and shoot as normal.

Step 6: When you lower the camera away from your eye, the sensor detects the absence of your eye.

Step 7: The EVF switches off and the rear LCD switches back on automatically.

NOTE: Sensitivity and false triggers

The eye sensor can sometimes be triggered by objects other than your eye — for example, the camera bumping against your clothing while it hangs around your neck. If this drains your battery, go to Custom Menu J and change the EVF/Monitor setting to "Monitor Only" while you are not actively shooting through the viewfinder.

The sensitivity of the eye sensor cannot be adjusted directly, but the speed at which it responds can be influenced by the EVF display settings in Custom Menu J.

3.2 The Rear LCD Screen

Tilting and Adjusting the LCD Screen

The OM-3's rear LCD screen is a 3-inch, 1.037 million dot touchscreen that tilts up and down on a hinge. It does not rotate sideways (it is not a fully articulating screen). Here is what the tilt allows you to do:

Tilt Direction	Angle Available	When to Use It
Straight back (flat)	Default position	Normal shooting — looking straight at the back of the camera.
Tilt up	Approximately 80 degrees upward	Low-angle shooting — hold the camera near the ground and angle the screen up so you can see it while looking down. Great for street photography and flower shots.
Tilt down	Approximately 45 degrees downward	High-angle / overhead shooting — hold the camera above your head and angle the screen downward so you can see it while looking up. Useful for shooting over crowds.
Face the screen forward (selfie position)	180 degrees — screen fully forward	Self-portraits and vlogging — the screen faces the same direction as the lens so the subject in front of the camera can see themselves while shooting.

To tilt the screen, grip the top edge of the LCD panel with your left hand and gently pull it away from the camera body. Then angle it up or down to your preferred position. It will hold any position you set it in. To return it flat, push it gently back until it clicks flush with the camera body.

> **WARNING: Handle the hinge gently**
> Do not force the screen past its mechanical limits. Pushing it further than it naturally goes can crack the hinge mechanism. The tilt range is clearly felt — stop when you feel resistance.

Every Icon and Indicator on the LCD — Each One Explained

The LCD screen shows exactly the same information as the EVF. Every icon described in Section 3.1 (shooting mode, shutter speed, aperture, ISO, exposure compensation, metering, flash, white balance, battery, AF frame, exposure scale, drive mode, image quality, shot count) appears in the same positions on the LCD. Refer to the EVF table above for the meaning of each one.

The diagram below shows the full LCD live view, oriented as you see it when holding the camera to shoot. The labeling is identical to the EVF diagram.

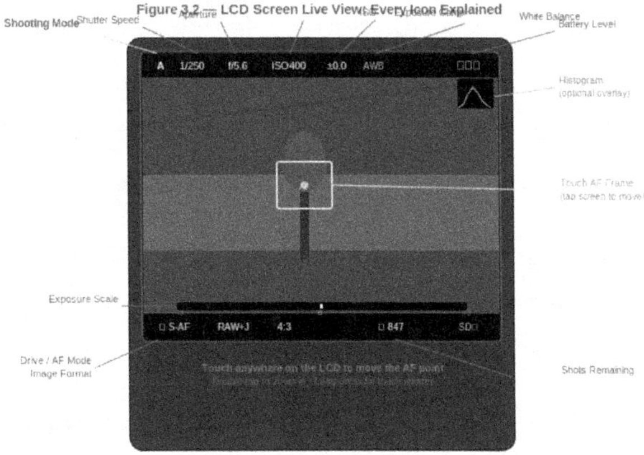

Figure 3.2 — The LCD screen in live view mode, with all overlays and icons labeled

One additional element appears on the LCD that is not in the EVF: the touch-target feedback. When you tap the LCD screen to set a focus point, the camera draws a green square or circle at the point you tapped, confirming where it will focus. This does not appear in the EVF.

> **TIP: Histogram in the corner**
>
> You can choose to display a small live histogram in the corner of the LCD or EVF — a real-time graph of the photo's brightness distribution. A histogram bunched to the left means the photo is dark; bunched to the right means it is bright; spread across means well-balanced exposure. Enable it by pressing INFO until the histogram mode appears (Section 3.5).

Touchscreen Functions — Tap to Focus, Tap to Shoot

The OM-3's LCD is a fully touch-sensitive screen. You can interact with it using your finger in the following ways:

Touch Gesture	What It Does	How to Use It
Single tap	Moves the autofocus point to where you tapped	During live view, tap anywhere on the screen. A green square appears at that point, and the camera focuses there. This is called Touch AF.
Double tap	Zooms in to the tapped area at 5x or 10x magnification for focus checking	Double-tap on any area. The camera zooms the live view in so you can check sharpness. Double-tap again or press the

		shutter button halfway to zoom back out.
Long press (touch and hold)	Activates Touch Shutter — the camera focuses and fires the shutter at the tapped point	Touch and hold the area you want in focus. The camera automatically focuses and takes the photo. Useful for one-handed selfies.
Swipe left/right	Moves between photos during Playback mode	In Playback mode, swipe left to go to the next photo, swipe right to go to the previous one.
Pinch to zoom	Zooms into a photo during Playback	In Playback mode, use two fingers and spread them apart to zoom in. Pinch them together to zoom back out.

Enabling and Disabling Touch Controls

If you want to prevent accidental touches while shooting (for example, if you are shooting through the viewfinder and your nose might touch the screen), you can disable the touchscreen:

Step 1: Press the MENU button.

Step 2: Navigate to the Custom Menu (gear icon tab) using the LEFT/RIGHT arrows.

Step 3: Scroll down to Custom Menu D (Display / Sound settings).

Step 4: Enter Custom Menu D and scroll to find "Touch Screen Settings" or "Touch Control."

Step 5: Press OK to enter it. A submenu appears with options for Live View touch control and Playback touch control.

Step 6: Select "Off" for the controls you want to disable and press OK to confirm.

Step 7: Press MENU to exit.

TIP: Partial touch disable

You can disable the touch shutter (to prevent accidental shots) while keeping touch AF active (to quickly move the focus point). This is a useful combination for handheld EVF shooting — you can use your nose without firing the shutter accidentally, but still reposition your focus point with a quick tap when you lower the camera.

3.3 Switching Between EVF and LCD

The Four Display Modes Available

The OM-3 offers four different ways to control which display is active. You choose the one that suits your shooting style and assign it in the camera's Custom Menu J (the EVF settings menu).

Figure 3.3 — EVF / LCD Display Switching

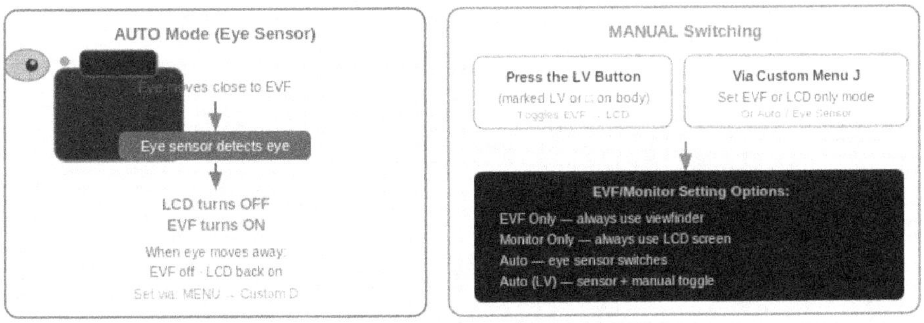

Figure 3.3 — Auto (eye sensor) switching on the left; manual options on the right

Mode Name	What It Does	Best For
EVF Only	The EVF is always on. The LCD screen stays off.	Sports, wildlife, and action shooting where you always have the camera to your eye. Saves LCD battery drain.
Monitor Only (LCD Only)	The LCD screen is always on. The EVF stays off.	Landscape, architecture, studio, and video work where the camera is frequently on a tripod or held at arm's length.
Auto (Eye Sensor)	Eye sensor controls the switch. Eye near EVF = EVF on, LCD off. Eye away = LCD on, EVF off.	General everyday shooting — the camera intelligently switches for you. This is the factory default.
Auto (LV + Eye Sensor)	Eye sensor works as above, but you can also manually override using the LV button at any time.	Advanced users who want the best of both — automatic switching plus the ability to lock to one display when needed.

How to Switch Between EVF and LCD Manually

The quickest manual method is the LV button. On the OM-3, there is a dedicated button for toggling the display — look for a button labeled LV (for Live View) on the back of the camera. It is typically located near the top right area of the back panel, or it may be assigned to one of the function buttons.

Step 1: While looking at the LCD screen in live view, locate the LV button on the back of the camera.

Step 2: Press the LV button once. The LCD screen will turn off and the EVF will turn on.

Step 3: Press the LV button again. The EVF turns off and the LCD turns back on.

NOTE: LV button behavior depends on display mode

The LV button only acts as a manual toggle when the display mode is set to "Auto (LV + Eye Sensor)." In "EVF Only" or "Monitor Only" modes, pressing LV does nothing. In standard "Auto" mode, it may not be assignable to this function. Check your Custom Menu J setting first if the LV button does not seem to toggle the display.

How to Set Up Automatic Switching — Exact Steps

Step 1: Press the MENU button on the back of the camera.

Step 2: Press the RIGHT arrow to navigate to the Custom Menu (gear/cog icon tab). Continue pressing RIGHT until you reach the last Custom Menu section which is labeled J (or find the EVF section).

Step 3: Inside Custom Menu J, scroll to find "EVF / Monitor" or "EVF-Autoswitch" setting.

Step 4: Press OK or RIGHT to enter it.

Step 5: You will see the four options: EVF Auto, Monitor, EVF, Auto (LV). Use the UP/DOWN arrows to highlight your preferred mode.

Step 6: Press OK to confirm.

Step 7: Press MENU to close.

Adjusting the Eye Sensor Sensitivity (If Needed)

If the eye sensor switches displays unexpectedly — for example, getting triggered while the camera hangs at your side — you can adjust the delay or disable the sensor:

Step 1: Go to MENU → Custom Menu J.

Step 2: Look for "EVF Auto Switch" or "Eye Sensor."

Step 3: You may find options for the sensor's detection area or a switch delay. Setting a slightly longer delay prevents quick accidental triggers.

Step 4: Press OK to save, then MENU to close.

3.4 The Super Control Panel (SCP)

What the SCP Is and Why It Is Useful

The Super Control Panel — shortened to SCP — is one of the most powerful and time-saving features on the OM-3. It is a single screen that displays up to 16 of your most important shooting settings all at once, arranged in a grid. From this single screen you can view and change all of them without ever opening the main menu.

Think of the SCP as a quick-access dashboard. Instead of pressing MENU and navigating through five different menus to change your White Balance, AF mode, Drive mode, and ISO, you open the SCP and change all four in under 15 seconds. For fast-changing shooting situations — a bird about to fly, a child about to laugh — the SCP can be the difference between getting the shot and missing it.

How to Open the SCP — Press the OK Button

To open the Super Control Panel from live view (while the camera is in shooting mode and showing you the scene through the lens):

Step 1: Make sure you are in live view — the camera is powered on, not in playback or menu mode.

Step 2: Press the OK button once. It is the button in the center of the four-way arrow pad on the back of the camera.

Step 3: The Super Control Panel appears on the LCD screen (or in the EVF if you are looking through the viewfinder).

Step 4: The panel shows a grid of setting tiles. One tile will be highlighted in blue — this is the currently selected tile.

Step 5: To close the SCP and return to live view, press the shutter button halfway or press the MENU button.

NOTE: SCP in different shooting modes

Some tiles in the SCP will appear greyed out in certain shooting modes. For example, in Aperture Priority (A) mode, the Shutter Speed tile will be greyed out because the camera controls shutter speed automatically. In iAuto mode, most tiles are greyed out because the camera controls everything. In Manual (M) mode, all tiles are available.

How to Navigate the SCP with the Arrow Pad

Step 1: Press OK to open the SCP.

Step 2: Use the UP, DOWN, LEFT, and RIGHT arrow buttons to move the blue highlight from tile to tile across the grid.

Step 3: The currently selected tile is highlighted in blue. The name and current value of that setting are also shown in larger text below or beside the grid.

Step 4: To change the highlighted setting: either press OK again to enter a full selection screen for that setting, or simply turn the front dial or rear dial to cycle through the options directly.

Step 5: After changing a setting, the tile updates immediately to show the new value.

Step 6: Move to the next setting you want to change and repeat.

Step 7: When finished, press the shutter button halfway to exit the SCP and return to live view, ready to shoot.

Every Setting in the SCP — Each One Explained

The diagram below shows the full SCP layout with all 16 tiles. Every tile is described in the table that follows.

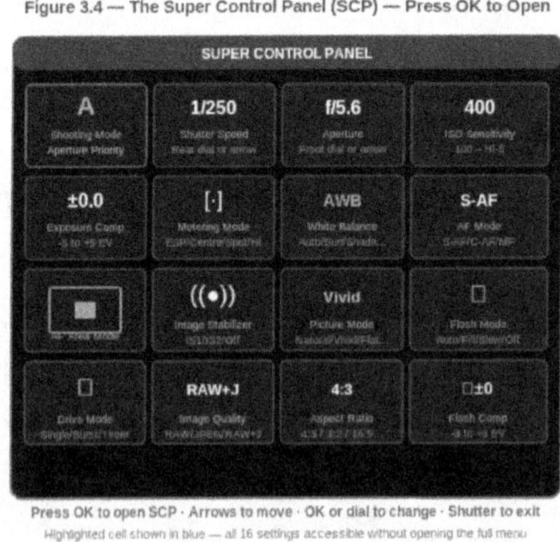

Figure 3.4 — The Super Control Panel: all 16 settings visible at once, changeable in seconds

SCP Tile	What It Controls	Options Available	How to Change It
Shooting Mode	The mode dial position —	iAuto, P, A, S, M, B, Custom modes	Highlight and press OK, then select a mode.

	which shooting mode is active		(Easier: just turn the Mode Dial directly.)
Shutter Speed	How long the shutter stays open — controls motion blur and exposure time	30 seconds to 1/8000 second, plus BULB	Highlight, then turn the rear dial. Or press OK and enter a value.
Aperture	The size of the lens opening — controls depth of field and exposure	Depends on your lens (e.g. f/1.8 to f/22)	Highlight, then turn the front dial. Or press OK and enter a value.
ISO Sensitivity	How sensitive the sensor is to light — controls brightness and noise	Low, 200, 400, 800, 1600, 3200, 6400, 12800, 25600, Hi-1 to Hi-5, or Auto	Highlight and turn the front or rear dial, or press OK for a list.
Exposure Compensation	Deliberately makes the photo brighter (+) or darker (-) than the meter suggests	-5 EV to +5 EV in 1/3 or 1/2 stop increments	Highlight and turn the rear dial, or press OK for a scale.
Metering Mode	Which pattern the camera uses to measure the brightness of the scene	ESP (multi-zone), Centre-weighted, Spot, Highlight-weighted	Highlight, press OK, select from the list.
White Balance	The color temperature correction applied to the image to make whites look white	AWB, AWB Warm, Daylight (5500K), Shade (7500K), Overcast (6000K), Incandescent (3000K), Fluorescent (various), Flash, Underwater,	Highlight, press OK, scroll through icons and select.

		Custom (CWB), Kelvin (K)	
AF Mode	Whether the camera focuses once (and holds) or continuously tracks moving subjects	S-AF (Single), C-AF (Continuous), MF (Manual), S-AF+MF, C-AF+TR (Tracking)	Highlight, press OK, select from list.
AF Area Mode	Which part of the frame the camera uses to find and lock focus	Single target (small), Single target (large), 9-point zone, 25-point zone, All targets (camera chooses), Custom zone	Highlight, press OK, select the pattern from the visual diagram.
Image Stabilization	The in-body 5-axis optical image stabilization system	IS1 (all-direction stabilization), IS2 (horizontal only — for panning), IS3 (vertical only), Off	Highlight, press OK, select mode.
Picture Mode / Profile	The overall color and tone profile applied to JPEG images	Natural, Vivid, Muted, Portrait, Monotone, Custom 1-4, ePortrait, Art Filters	Highlight, press OK, scroll through and select.
Flash Mode	How the built-in or external flash behaves	Auto, Fill-in, Red-eye reduction, Slow Sync, Slow Sync + Red-eye, Off	Highlight, press OK, select.
Drive Mode	Whether the camera takes one photo or multiple, and the timing	Single shot, Sequential L (low speed burst), Sequential H (high speed burst), Anti-shock, Silent, Self-timer 2s, Self-timer 12s, Custom self-	Highlight, press OK, select.

		timer, HDR, Bracketing	
Image Quality (Format)	Whether photos are saved as RAW, JPEG, or both	RAW, JPEG Large Fine (LF), JPEG Large Normal (LN), JPEG Medium Fine, JPEG Small Fine, RAW+JPEG (various combinations)	Highlight, press OK, select.
Aspect Ratio	The proportional shape of the image frame	4:3 (native MFT), 3:2 (matches 35mm film), 16:9 (widescreen video look), 1:1 (square), 3:4 (tall portrait)	Highlight, press OK, select.
Flash Exposure Compensation	Makes the flash fire more or less brightly than its automatic setting	-3 EV to +3 EV in 1/3 stop increments	Highlight and turn a dial, or press OK for a scale.

TIP: Learn the SCP grid by heart

After a week of shooting with the OM-3, you will know instinctively that White Balance is in the second row, third column, and AF Mode is second row, fourth column. The SCP grid becomes muscle memory very quickly and dramatically speeds up your workflow.

How to Change a Setting Inside the SCP — Detailed Walkthrough

Let us walk through a complete example: changing the White Balance from Auto (AWB) to Daylight because you are shooting outside in sunshine.

Step 1: Press OK to open the SCP. The grid of tiles appears on screen.

Step 2: Look for the tile labeled AWB or showing the White Balance icon. It is in the second row, third column of the SCP.

Step 3: Press the RIGHT arrow three times from the leftmost position to move to the WB tile, or navigate directly to it using the arrow pad.

Step 4: The WB tile is now highlighted in blue. You will see the label "White Balance" and the current setting "AWB" appear at the bottom of the panel.

Step 5: Press OK to enter the White Balance selection screen. A row of white balance icons appears.

Step 6: Press RIGHT to move to the sun icon (Daylight / 5500K).

Step 7: Press OK to confirm. The panel returns and the WB tile now shows the sun icon instead of AWB.

Step 8: Press the shutter button halfway to exit the SCP and return to live view. Your white balance is now set to Daylight.

You can also use the dials to change many settings without entering the sub-screen. For example, to change ISO: highlight the ISO tile, then simply turn the front dial. The ISO value changes live on the tile as you turn the dial. Press the shutter halfway when you reach your desired value.

3.5 Information Display Modes

The INFO Button — Location and Function

The INFO button is located on the back of the camera, above and to the left of the LCD screen. It is a small rectangular button with the word INFO printed on or near it. Pressing it once cycles to the next display mode; pressing it again cycles to the next; and so on, looping back to the beginning after the fifth mode.

The INFO button works both in live view (while composing a shot) and in playback mode (while reviewing images). The display modes it cycles through are different in each context — this section covers live view modes.

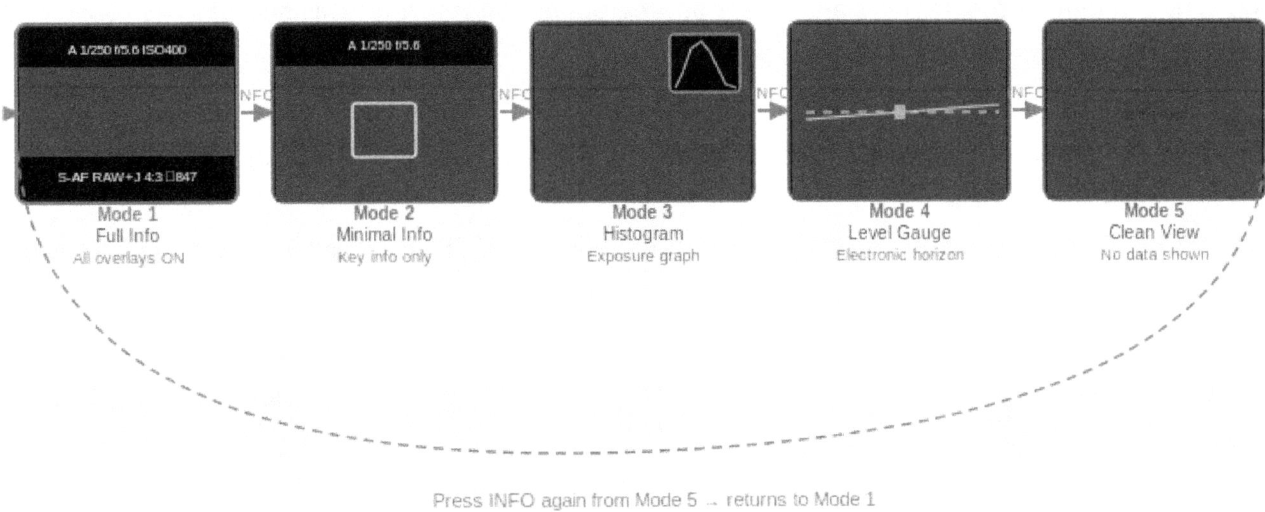

Figure 3.5 — The five INFO display modes, cycled with each press of the INFO button

The Five Display Modes — Each One Explained

Mode 1 — Full Information Display

This is the default mode when you first power on the camera. Every available information overlay is visible simultaneously:

- Top bar with shooting mode, shutter speed, aperture, ISO, exposure compensation, metering, flash, and white balance
- Bottom bar with drive mode, AF mode, image quality, aspect ratio, shot counter, and SD card status
- Exposure scale bar near the bottom of the frame
- Battery icon in the top right
- Electronic level horizon line across the center
- AF frame (focus point indicator)

This mode gives you complete situational awareness — you can see everything at a glance without pressing a single button. It is ideal when you are learning the camera or in any situation where you want to confirm all your settings at once. The downside is that the overlays can make it harder to judge composition when the frame is very busy.

Mode 2 — Minimal Information Display

This mode shows only the most essential settings — typically the shooting mode, shutter speed, aperture, and perhaps ISO — in a small strip at the top of the frame. The bottom bar and most other overlays are hidden.

Use this mode when you know your settings are correct and you want a cleaner view of your scene for composing. Wildlife photographers and street photographers often prefer this because the subject fills more of the visual frame without distraction.

- The AF frame is still visible even in minimal mode.
- The electronic level is hidden, but can be re-enabled independently in settings.

Mode 3 — Histogram Display

This mode adds a live histogram in one corner of the screen (usually the top right). Everything from Mode 1 remains visible, but the histogram overlay is now active.

The histogram is a bar graph showing the distribution of brightness across the photo, from pure black on the left to pure white on the right. The height of the bars at any point shows how many pixels in the scene have that brightness.

Histogram Shape	What It Means	What to Do
Bars pushed mostly to the left	Photo will be underexposed (too dark)	Increase exposure compensation (+) or adjust settings to let in more light.
Bars pushed mostly to the right	Photo will be overexposed (too bright) — highlights may be blown out with no detail	Decrease exposure compensation (-) or reduce exposure.
Bars cut off abruptly at the far right edge	Highlight clipping — the brightest areas of the scene will have no detail, just pure white	Reduce exposure to recover highlights. Even -1/3 stop often restores detail.
Bars cut off at the far left edge	Shadow clipping — the darkest areas will be pure black with no detail	Increase exposure slightly, or accept it as a creative choice for dramatic shadows.
Bars spread smoothly across the full width	Well-balanced exposure with detail in both shadows and highlights	Good exposure. Continue shooting.

TIP: Use the histogram for critical exposure

The histogram is far more reliable than your eyes for judging exposure correctly. Your eyes adapt to the brightness of the screen and the ambient light around you. The histogram always tells you the mathematical truth about the photo. Experienced photographers check it constantly.

Mode 4 — Level Gauge Display

This mode adds a large, easy-to-read electronic level gauge to the display. It works in two axes: left-right tilt (rolling) and front-back tilt (pitching).

- The main horizontal line shows left-right tilt. When this line is perfectly horizontal and coloured blue (or green on some firmware versions), the camera is level from side to side.
- A small indicator on the line shows the degree of tilt — the further from center, the more the camera is tilted.
- When you tilt the camera forward or back (like pointing up at the sky or down at the ground), a second axis indicator shows this pitch angle.
- When both axes read zero (level and straight), the indicator changes colour to green or turns solid, confirming the camera is perfectly level.

This mode is particularly valuable for landscape photography (where a tilted horizon is a common and distracting mistake), architectural photography (where vertical lines must be truly vertical), and any tripod work where precise leveling matters.

> **TIP: Electronic level vs a hot shoe bubble level**
>
> The OM-3's 5-axis stabilization system provides very accurate electronic leveling. For most photography it is more than precise enough. However, for critical architectural or panoramic work where multiple images will be stitched together, a physical spirit level in the hot shoe provides even greater confidence.

Mode 5 — Clean View (No Overlays)

The fifth mode removes all information overlays from the screen completely. You see only the pure live image from the lens with no text, no icons, no bars, and no lines — just the scene.

This is useful for:

- Critically judging the artistic composition of a scene without any distractions.
- Showing the live image to a client or subject — they see exactly what the camera sees without being confused by technical readouts.
- Video recording preview — see how the final video frame will look without clutter.

Your settings are still active and still controlling the camera — you simply cannot see them on screen. Press INFO once more to cycle back to Mode 1 and see all your settings again.

> **NOTE: Settings still work in Clean View**
>
> Removing the overlays in Mode 5 does not change any setting. Your aperture, ISO, shutter speed, and everything else stays exactly as you set it. Clean View only affects what you see on the display, not how the camera operates.

Summary — When to Use Each Display Mode

Display Mode	Best Shooting Situation
Mode 1 — Full Info	Learning the camera · Checking all settings before an important shot · Any time you want complete awareness of your settings
Mode 2 — Minimal Info	Street photography · Wildlife · Any fast-paced shooting where clean composition view matters more than seeing all data
Mode 3 — Histogram	Landscape · Studio · Any situation where precise, reliable exposure is critical
Mode 4 — Level Gauge	Landscape horizons · Architecture · Tripod work · Panoramas · Any scene where straight lines matter
Mode 5 — Clean View	Artistic composition study · Showing the live view to a subject or client · Video framing

TIP: Customise what appears in each mode

The OM-3 lets you choose which elements appear in each INFO mode via Custom Menu D (Display / Sound). For example, you can set Mode 2 to show the histogram AND minimal info text, combining what you find most useful. Experiment and set it up to suit your shooting style.

Part 4 — Shooting Modes (Mode Dial)

The Mode Dial is one of the most important controls on your OM-3. It sits on the top-left of the camera body and determines who is in charge of your camera's exposure settings — you, the camera, or a mix of both. Every mode on the dial produces a fundamentally different shooting experience, and choosing the right mode for the right situation is a skill that separates great photographers from casual ones.

This part of the guide explains every mode position on the dial in plain English, with real-world examples of when to use each one, exactly how to operate the controls in that mode, and what you will see on the screen when it is selected. We start with the fully automatic mode and move progressively toward full manual control.

> **NOTE: You do not need to master every mode immediately**
>
> Most photographers use two or three modes the majority of the time. Read through all sections so you understand what each mode is for, then focus on the modes that match the type of photography you want to do. Return to the others as your skills grow.

4.1 How to Use the Mode Dial

Location of the Mode Dial

The Mode Dial is the large, round, ridged dial on the top-left of the camera — the left side when you are holding the camera ready to shoot. It has nine positions arranged in a circle, each labeled with a letter or abbreviation. A small red line or marker at the top of the dial shows which mode is currently selected.

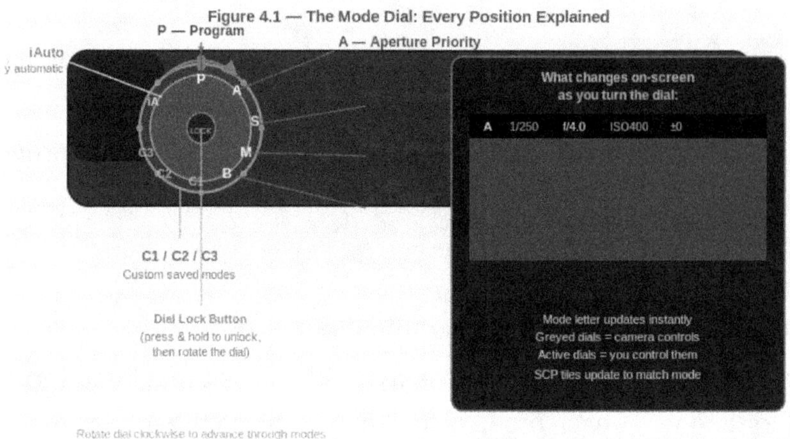

Figure 4.1 — The Mode Dial with every position labeled and the on-screen changes explained

How to Turn the Mode Dial

The Mode Dial on the OM-3 has a built-in lock mechanism to prevent you from accidentally changing modes while shooting. To turn the dial, you must press and hold the unlock button in the center of the dial while rotating it at the same time.

Step 1: Look at the top of the camera. Find the Mode Dial on the left side and locate the small button in the very center of the dial.

Step 2: Press the center button down with your left thumb and hold it.

Step 3: While holding the center button down, use your left thumb and index finger to rotate the dial clockwise or counter-clockwise to the mode you want.

Step 4: Release the center button once you have the correct mode aligned with the red marker line at the top of the dial.

Step 5: Look at the LCD screen or EVF — the shooting mode letter will have updated to confirm the change.

TIP: One smooth motion

> With a little practice you can press and rotate simultaneously with one thumb in a single smooth motion. It becomes natural very quickly. If you find the lock button stiff at first, this is normal — it loosens slightly with regular use.

What Changes on Screen When You Turn the Dial

The moment you move the Mode Dial, several things change simultaneously on the LCD and EVF:

- The shooting mode letter in the top-left corner of the display updates instantly to show your new mode (for example, the letter changes from A to S).
- The shutter speed and aperture readouts may change — some values become bold and white (meaning you control them), while others become grey (meaning the camera controls them automatically).
- The front dial and rear dial functions change — in A mode the front dial adjusts aperture; in S mode it adjusts shutter speed. These changes happen automatically.
- The Super Control Panel (if open) updates — any greyed-out tiles reflect settings the camera now controls in the new mode.
- If you switch from a semi-automatic mode to iAuto, most tiles in the SCP will grey out as the camera takes control.

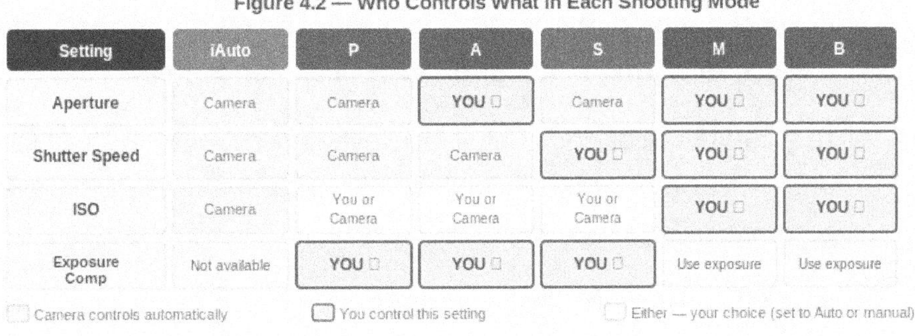

Figure 4.2 — Who Controls What in Each Shooting Mode

Setting	iAuto	P	A	S	M	B
Aperture	Camera	Camera	YOU □	Camera	YOU □	YOU □
Shutter Speed	Camera	Camera	Camera	YOU □	YOU □	YOU □
ISO	Camera	You or Camera	You or Camera	You or Camera	YOU □	YOU □
Exposure Comp	Not available	YOU □	YOU □	YOU □	Use exposure	Use exposure

□ Camera controls automatically   □ You control this setting   □ Either — your choice (set to Auto or manual)

Figure 4.2 — Who controls what in each mode: green = camera, blue = you, yellow = your choice

4.2 iAuto Mode — Fully Automatic

iAuto (Intelligent Auto) is the green-label mode on the Mode Dial, usually marked as iA. In this mode, the OM-3 takes control of virtually every photographic setting and makes all the decisions for you. Your only job is to point the camera at your subject and press the shutter button. The camera figures out everything else.

What the Camera Controls in iAuto

Setting	What the Camera Does Automatically
Shutter Speed	Chooses a shutter speed fast enough to prevent motion blur for the type of subject detected.
Aperture	Selects an aperture appropriate for the scene — wider for dim environments, narrower for bright scenes with multiple subjects at different distances.
ISO	Automatically raises ISO in low light and keeps it low in bright conditions to balance noise vs. brightness.
White Balance	Reads the color of the ambient light and applies the correct white balance — warm for indoor tungsten, cool for overcast skies.
Focus	Uses all AF target points plus face/eye detection to find and lock onto the most likely subject. Prioritizes faces and eyes automatically.
Flash	Pops up and fires the flash automatically when the camera detects the scene is too dark for a sharp handheld shot without it.
Drive Mode	Stays in single-shot mode unless the camera detects rapid subject motion, in which case it may enable continuous shooting.
Image Stabilization	Activates IS1 (full 5-axis stabilization) automatically.
Scene Recognition	Identifies the type of scene (portrait, landscape, close-up, night scene, backlit subject, etc.) and optimizes all settings for that scene type.

What You Can Still Control in iAuto

Even in iAuto, a small number of things remain under your control:

- Zoom — you still control the lens zoom (or zoom ring if using a manual zoom lens).

- Focus point — you can tap the touchscreen to tell the camera which subject to focus on, though the camera still manages the actual focus distance.
- Framing and composition — you decide what goes in the frame and where.
- Whether to fire the shutter — you still press the button. Half-press to focus and meter; full press to shoot.

How to Shoot in iAuto — Step by Step

Step 1: Turn the Mode Dial to iA (the green position, usually at approximately the 10 o'clock position on the dial).

Step 2: The camera screen shows the live view. You will see the mode letter iA in the top-left corner.

Step 3: Point the camera at your subject. The camera will begin scanning the scene, looking for faces and identifying the scene type.

Step 4: If the camera detects a face, you will see a white or yellow rectangle appear around it — this is the face detection frame.

Step 5: Press the shutter button HALFWAY down. You will hear or feel a small click as the autofocus confirms a lock — the AF frame turns green and the shutter speed/aperture values in the display settle on their chosen values.

Step 6: Without lifting your finger, press the shutter button ALL THE WAY down to take the photo.

Step 7: The camera saves the image to the SD card. The access lamp on the side blinks briefly.

TIP: Review your shot

After taking a photo, press the Playback button on the back of the camera to immediately review the image on the LCD screen. Zoom in by pinching the screen or using the rear dial to check sharpness. Press the shutter button halfway to return to shooting.

When to Use iAuto — and When Not To

Good situations for iAuto	Situations where iAuto may struggle
Handing the camera to someone unfamiliar with photography	Scenes where the camera misidentifies the subject — e.g., photographing a tree instead of a person

Documenting everyday moments quickly without thinking about settings	Very dark scenes where the flash firing is unwanted (concerts, candlelit dinners)
Learning what the camera is capable of before exploring manual modes	Creative shots that require deliberate blur, silhouettes, or non-standard exposure
Fast-moving social situations where stopping to adjust settings means missing the moment	Scenes with strong backlighting where the camera meters incorrectly

REAL-WORLD SCENARIO: Family birthday party indoors

You are at a birthday party. The room has mixed lighting — some overhead bulbs, some candles, and a window. Children are moving around. You just want to capture the moments without fussing with settings.

Turn the dial to iA. Point at your subject, half-press to focus, full press to shoot. The camera handles the flash, white balance, ISO boost for indoors, and fast enough shutter to freeze the kids. Result: well-exposed, sharp, correctly colored photos with no effort.

4.3 Program Mode (P)

Program mode (P) is like iAuto with a crucial difference: you can override the camera's automatic choices when you want to. In P mode, the camera still automatically selects both the shutter speed and aperture to produce what it calculates as a correct exposure. However, all other settings — ISO, white balance, drive mode, AF mode, flash mode, and exposure compensation — are under your full control.

Program mode also has a special feature called Program Shift (sometimes called Flexible Program), which lets you change the shutter/aperture combination the camera has chosen without changing the overall exposure.

What the Camera Controls in P Mode

- Shutter Speed — the camera selects this automatically.
- Aperture — the camera selects this automatically.
- Both are chosen together to give the same total exposure — there are many valid combinations of shutter and aperture that result in the same amount of light reaching the sensor.

What You Control in P Mode

- ISO — set manually or leave on Auto.
- White Balance — full manual control or Auto.
- Exposure Compensation — push the overall exposure brighter (+) or darker (-) without changing the shutter/aperture relationship.
- Flash Mode — choose Auto, Fill, Off, etc.

- AF Mode — choose S-AF, C-AF, or MF.
- Drive Mode — single, burst, self-timer, etc.

Program Shift — change the shutter/aperture pair without changing total exposure (see below).

How to Use Program Shift

Program Shift is one of the most useful features of P mode. It works like this: the camera picks a specific combination — say, 1/125 at f/5.6. If you would prefer a faster shutter speed (perhaps because your subject is moving), you can shift the program to 1/500 at f/2.8. The total exposure stays the same, but the creative effect changes.

Step 1: Turn the Mode Dial to P.

Step 2: The camera automatically picks a shutter/aperture combination and shows it on screen.

Step 3: Turn the FRONT DIAL (the wheel around the shutter button) to the left or right.

Step 4: As you turn, the shutter speed increases and the aperture opens wider (or vice versa), while the exposure scale stays at zero.

Step 5: An asterisk (*) or the letter P with a star (P*) may appear on screen to indicate that Program Shift is active.

Step 6: Shoot as normal. The shifted values remain active until you rotate the front dial back to center, change mode, or turn the camera off.

TIP: P mode is great for beginners who want control

Many photographers use P mode as their everyday mode. It lets you concentrate on composition and moment-catching while the camera handles the technical exposure math. Reach for exposure compensation when the camera's guess is wrong, and use Program Shift when you need a specific motion or depth effect.

REAL-WORLD SCENARIO: Street photography on a sunny day

You are walking through a market. Scenes change every few seconds. You want clean, correctly exposed shots without stopping to set aperture or shutter each time.

Set the dial to P. Set ISO to 400 (or Auto ISO with a max of 1600). Leave white balance on AWB. Set exposure compensation to -1/3 if the market is very bright. Now shoot freely —

> *the camera makes the exposure decisions while you focus entirely on finding great moments.*

4.4 Aperture Priority Mode (A)

Aperture Priority mode (A) is the mode where you set the lens aperture (the f-stop number) and the camera automatically chooses the shutter speed needed to produce a correctly exposed photo. This is the most popular semi-automatic mode among photographers and is extremely versatile.

Why would you want to control aperture? Because aperture directly controls depth of field — how much of the scene appears sharp, and how blurry the background is. This is often the single most important creative decision in a photograph.

Figure 4.4 — How Aperture (f-stop) Affects Depth of Field

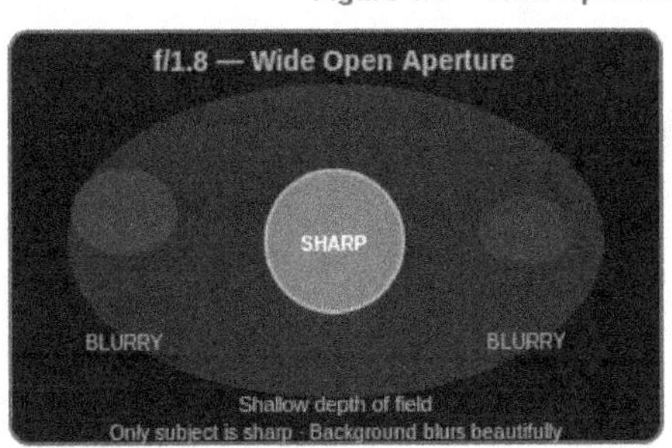

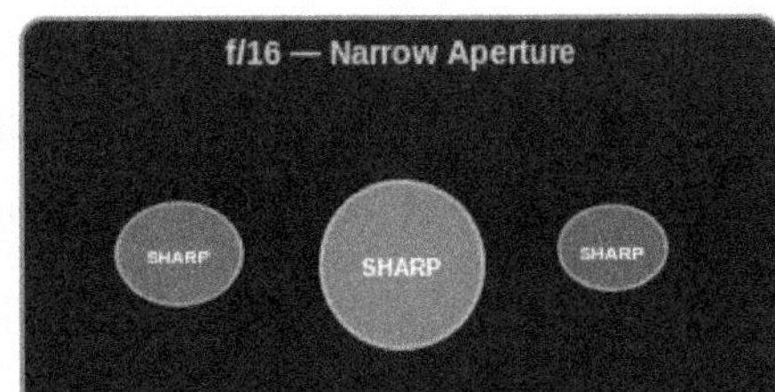

Figure 4.4 — Aperture controls depth of field: f/1.8 blurs the background; f/16 makes everything sharp

Understanding Aperture Numbers

Aperture is expressed as an f-number (also called f-stop). The f-number scale seems backwards at first — a smaller number means a WIDER aperture (bigger opening), and a larger number means a NARROWER aperture (smaller opening). Here is a quick reference:

f-number	Aperture Size	Depth of Field	Best Used For
f/1.4 – f/2.8	Very wide (lots of light)	Very shallow — only a thin slice is sharp	Portraits, low light, subject isolation with blurry background
f/2.8 – f/5.6	Wide (good light)	Shallow to moderate	Portraits, documentary, indoor photography
f/5.6 – f/8	Medium	Moderate — subject and some background sharp	General photography, groups, events
f/8 – f/11	Medium-narrow	Deep — most of the scene is sharp	Landscapes, architecture, sharpest point of most lenses

f/11 – f/22	Very narrow (less light)	Very deep — near and far all sharp, some diffraction	Landscape, still life, macro

How to Use Aperture Priority Mode — Step by Step

Step 1: Turn the Mode Dial to A.

Step 2: The display shows the current aperture value (e.g., f/5.6) in bold white, and the shutter speed in grey (meaning the camera will set it automatically).

Step 3: Turn the FRONT DIAL (the ridged wheel around or behind the shutter button) to change the aperture. Turn left toward smaller f-numbers (wider aperture) or right toward larger f-numbers (narrower aperture).

Step 4: Watch the aperture number update on screen as you turn the dial. Also watch the shutter speed — as you open the aperture, the shutter speed gets faster; as you narrow the aperture, the shutter slows down. The camera is always compensating to maintain the same exposure.

Step 5: Set your ISO manually or use Auto ISO.

Step 6: Check the exposure scale. If the shutter speed the camera has chosen is shown in red or blinking, it means the camera cannot achieve the correct exposure at your chosen aperture — either the scene is too dark (and the shutter would need to be impossibly slow) or too bright. Adjust your aperture or ISO.

Step 7: Half-press the shutter to confirm focus. Full-press to shoot.

TIP: Watch the shutter speed in A mode

In A mode, you set the aperture and the camera picks the shutter speed. If you choose a very narrow aperture (like f/16) indoors, the camera might select a shutter speed of 1/10 second or slower, which will cause blur from hand shake. Either widen the aperture, raise the ISO, or use a tripod.

Using Exposure Compensation in A Mode

Exposure compensation is particularly powerful in A mode. It lets you intentionally make the photo brighter or darker without changing your carefully chosen aperture:

Step 1: While in A mode, press and hold the AEL button (on the back of the camera) with your thumb.

Step 2: While holding AEL, turn the REAR DIAL to the right to increase exposure compensation (+) or to the left to decrease it (-).

Step 3: Alternatively, on the arrow pad, the UP button may be a direct shortcut to exposure compensation adjustment — press it and the compensation scale appears.

Step 4: Watch the exposure scale move left (darker) or right (brighter) as you adjust.

Step 5: Release and shoot. The compensation value stays active until you reset it to ±0.

REAL-WORLD SCENARIO: Portrait photography outdoors

You are photographing a friend in a park. You want a sharp face with a beautifully blurred green background behind them.

Set the dial to A. Turn the front dial to f/2.8 (or the widest aperture your lens offers). Set ISO to Auto. Focus on your friend's eyes using face/eye detection. The camera picks a fast shutter speed automatically. The background blurs into a soft wash of colour. Shoot.

REAL-WORLD SCENARIO: Landscape at sunrise

You want a landscape photo where the mountains in the distance and the wildflowers in the foreground are both sharp.

Set the dial to A. Turn the front dial to f/11. Put the camera on a tripod (the shutter speed will be slow). Focus one-third into the scene. Press the shutter. Both foreground and background are sharp.

4.5 Shutter Priority Mode (S)

Shutter Priority mode (S) is the opposite of Aperture Priority. You set the shutter speed — how long the camera's sensor is exposed to light — and the camera automatically selects the aperture needed for a correct exposure. This mode is all about controlling motion.

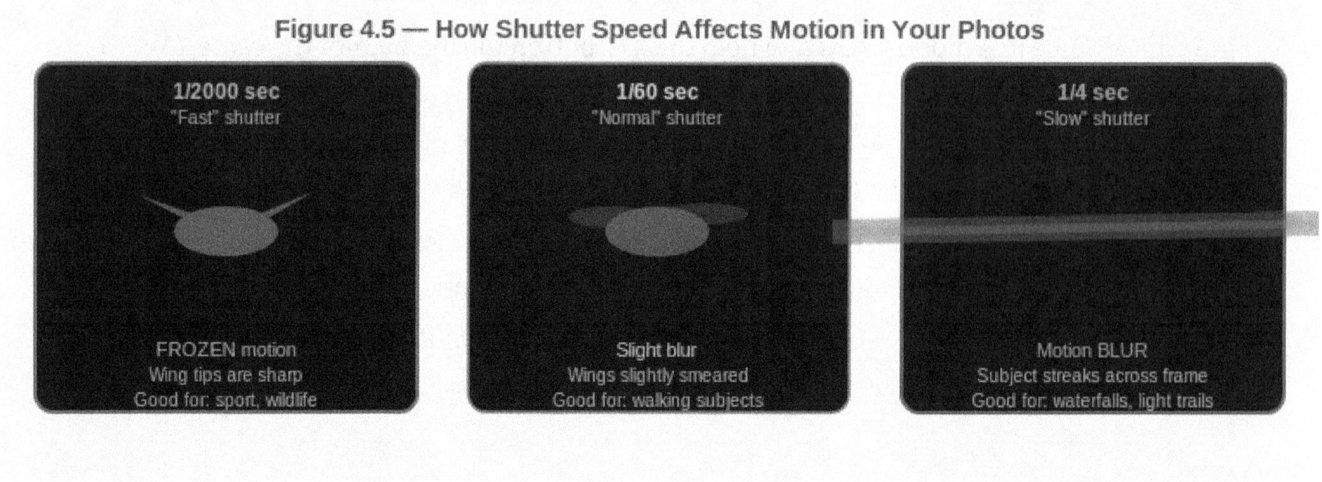

Figure 4.5 — How Shutter Speed Affects Motion in Your Photos

1/2000 sec
"Fast" shutter
FROZEN motion
Wing tips are sharp
Good for: sport, wildlife

1/60 sec
"Normal" shutter
Slight blur
Wings slightly smeared
Good for: walking subjects

1/4 sec
"Slow" shutter
Motion BLUR
Subject streaks across frame
Good for: waterfalls, light trails

Figure 4.5 — Shutter speed controls motion: fast freezes action, slow creates blur

Understanding Shutter Speeds

Shutter Speed	Motion Effect	Typical Use
1/4000 – 1/2000 sec	Freezes very fast motion completely	Birds in flight, motorsport, athletes at peak speed
1/1000 – 1/500 sec	Freezes most fast motion	Football, basketball, children running, fast animals
1/250 – 1/125 sec	Freezes moderate motion; safe for handheld	Everyday people, slower sports, street photography
1/60 – 1/30 sec	Some motion blur on fast subjects; risk of hand shake	Walking subjects, controlled scenes, use IS
1/15 – 1/4 sec	Clear motion blur on anything moving; tripod needed	Panning shots, moving crowds, waterfall silky effect
1 sec and slower	Strong, dramatic blur or light trails	Waterfalls, light trails, star movement, Milky Way
30 sec and longer	Extreme long exposure (use Bulb mode)	Star trails, very dark scenes, creative light painting

How to Use Shutter Priority Mode — Step by Step

Step 1: Turn the Mode Dial to S.

Step 2: The display shows the shutter speed in bold white (you control this) and the aperture in grey (the camera sets this).

Step 3: Turn the REAR DIAL to change the shutter speed. Turn right for faster speeds (larger numbers like 1/1000); turn left for slower speeds (smaller fractions like 1/30 or whole seconds like 1").

Step 4: Watch how the aperture value the camera selects changes as you adjust. If you choose a very fast shutter speed in dim light, the camera may open the aperture as wide as it will go and still not achieve correct exposure — the aperture value will blink red, warning you.

Step 5: If the aperture is blinking, either slow the shutter speed slightly or raise the ISO to give the camera more room to work with.

Step 6: Set ISO manually or use Auto ISO for flexibility.

Step 7: Half-press to focus, full-press to shoot.

TIP: The panning technique in S mode

Panning is when you follow a moving subject with the camera while shooting at a slow shutter speed (around 1/30 to 1/60 sec). The subject stays relatively sharp while the background blurs into horizontal streaks, creating a dramatic sense of speed. Set S mode to 1/30 or 1/60, set drive mode to high-speed burst, track the subject with the camera, and shoot a burst while you pan.

REAL-WORLD SCENARIO: Child's football match

Your child is playing football. They run fast. You want sharp, frozen action shots with no blur.

Set the dial to S. Turn the rear dial to 1/1000 second. Set ISO to Auto (the camera will raise it as the light changes). Set drive mode to Sequential H (high-speed burst). Track the subject and hold the shutter. The camera fires multiple shots per second, all with motion frozen.

4.6 Manual Mode (M)

In Manual mode (M), you set every exposure parameter yourself — aperture, shutter speed, AND ISO. The camera makes no automatic exposure decisions. Every element of the exposure is entirely under your control. This is the mode used by photographers who want complete, predictable, repeatable control over their images.

NOTE: Manual mode is not harder — it is more intentional

Many beginners avoid Manual mode because it sounds intimidating. But Manual mode does not require you to guess settings from scratch. The camera still shows you the exposure scale — a live meter that tells you whether your chosen settings will produce a bright, dark, or correctly exposed photo. Manual mode simply means the camera will not change anything without you asking it to.

What You Control in Manual Mode

- Aperture — set with the FRONT DIAL.
- Shutter Speed — set with the REAR DIAL.
- ISO — set manually via the SCP or ISO shortcut, or set to Auto ISO if you prefer the camera to manage just this one element.
- Exposure Compensation — not applicable as a separate control in M mode; instead you adjust one of the three values directly.

How to Use Manual Mode — Step by Step

Step 1: Turn the Mode Dial to M.

Step 2: The display shows both shutter speed and aperture in bold white — both are now under your control.

Step 3: Look at the EXPOSURE SCALE at the bottom of the frame. The marker starts wherever your current settings put it — it may be at zero already, or it may be to the left (underexposed) or right (overexposed).

Step 4: Turn the FRONT DIAL to set your desired aperture. Choose based on how much depth of field you want.

Step 5: Turn the REAR DIAL to set your desired shutter speed. Choose based on how you want motion to look.

Step 6: Watch the exposure scale. The marker moves as you change values. Bring the marker to zero for the camera's idea of correct exposure. Deliberately move it left for a darker (moody) image, or right for a brighter one.

Step 7: Set ISO by pressing the ISO shortcut button (or using the SCP) to the value you want.

Step 8: Once satisfied with all three values, half-press the shutter to confirm focus, then full-press to shoot.

Manual Mode with Auto ISO — A Powerful Combination

Many experienced photographers use Manual mode with one exception: they leave ISO on Auto. This gives them complete creative control over aperture (depth of field) and shutter speed (motion), while the camera handles ISO automatically to keep the exposure correct regardless of changing light. This is the best of both worlds for dynamic shooting environments.

Step 1: Set the Mode Dial to M.

Step 2: Set your aperture with the front dial (e.g., f/8 for a landscape).

Step 3: Set your shutter speed with the rear dial (e.g., 1/250 for handheld).

Step 4: Go to the SCP (press OK) and set ISO to Auto ISO.

Step 5: Shoot. The camera raises or lowers ISO automatically as the light changes, keeping exposure correct, while your aperture and shutter stay exactly as you set them.

TIP: Use Manual mode for consistent results across a series

If you are photographing a wedding reception or a product series where the lighting does not change, setting Manual mode and locking all three values means every photo in the series will have identical exposure. No shot-to-shot variation from the camera's metering changing its mind.

REAL-WORLD SCENARIO: Studio photography with a flash

You are photographing a product on a white background with a studio strobe light. The flash always fires at the same power. You need every shot to be perfectly identical.

Set mode to M. Set shutter to 1/200 (sync speed for flash). Set aperture to f/8. Set ISO to 200. Every photo will have identical exposure because Manual mode ignores the ambient light and uses only the settings you fixed. The flash provides consistent illumination. Every shot is identical.

4.7 Bulb Mode (B)

Bulb mode is a special long-exposure mode. The shutter opens the moment you press the shutter button fully down and stays open for as long as you keep the button held. The shutter closes the moment you release the button. This gives you a time exposure that can last from a fraction of a second to many minutes or even hours.

The name "Bulb" comes from the early days of photography, when photographers used a rubber pneumatic bulb (like a small squeeze ball) connected to the camera by a tube to hold the shutter open without touching the camera directly — which would cause vibration and blur.

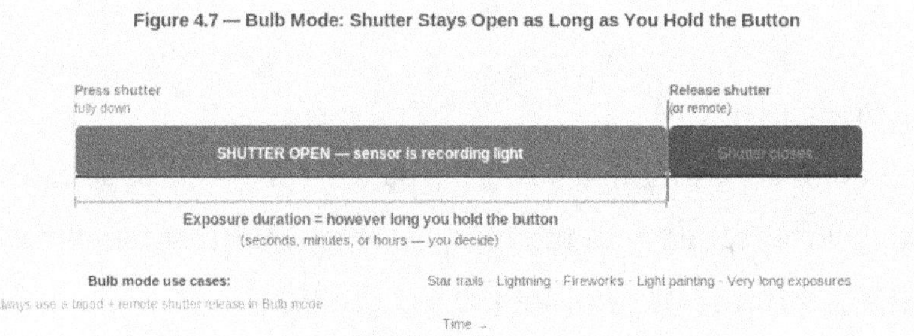

Figure 4.7 — In Bulb mode the shutter stays open for exactly as long as you hold the shutter button

What You Control in Bulb Mode

- Aperture — set with the front dial before starting the exposure.
- ISO — set manually.
- Exposure Duration — determined entirely by how long you hold the shutter button. A timer may appear on screen counting the elapsed seconds.

How to Use Bulb Mode — Step by Step

Step 1: Mount the camera on a stable tripod. Any movement during a Bulb exposure will cause blur across the entire image, not just the subject.

Step 2: Turn the Mode Dial to B.

Step 3: Set your aperture with the front dial. For star trails or fireworks, f/5.6 to f/8 is a good starting point. For light painting, f/8 to f/11.

Step 4: Set ISO. For star trails (very dark sky), ISO 800 to 3200 works well. For fireworks, ISO 100 to 200 is sufficient because fireworks are bright.

Step 5: Use a remote shutter release if you have one — plug it into the USB-C port or use the OM SYSTEM app on your smartphone as a remote. Pressing the shutter directly causes camera shake when you press and again when you release.

Step 6: If using the physical shutter button without a remote, use the 2-second self-timer (available in drive mode) to delay the start of the exposure so your pressing motion has settled before the shutter opens.

Step 7: Frame your shot. In a dark scene you may need to use a torch to focus first, then switch to manual focus (MF) to lock the focus distance.

Step 8: Press and hold the shutter button (or lock your remote release). The shutter opens. A timer on screen counts the elapsed seconds.

Step 9: When you have waited long enough, release the shutter button. The shutter closes and the image is processed.

Step 10: Review the image on the LCD. Adjust ISO or aperture and try again if needed.

TIP: Use LIVE BULB or LIVE TIME mode for monitoring

The OM-3 supports Live Bulb and Live Time modes (accessible via the drive or shooting menu). In these modes, the LCD updates every few seconds during the exposure, showing you a preview of how the image is building up in real time. This is invaluable for getting the exposure right without guesswork. Find it in the Shooting Menu under Bulb/Time settings.

WARNING: Very long exposures generate heat

Exposures longer than 30 seconds can cause the camera's sensor to generate heat, which may introduce colored noise (hot pixels) in very dark areas of the image. The OM-3 has a noise reduction processing feature for long exposures that takes a second, identical-length exposure with the shutter closed immediately after your shot, and uses the result to subtract the noise pattern. Enable this in the Shooting Menu under Noise Reduction. Note that it doubles your wait time between shots.

Subject	Suggested Settings	Typical Duration
Star trails (full arc)	f/5.6, ISO 800, wide lens	20 to 60 minutes
Milky Way (single frame)	f/2.8 or wider, ISO 3200-6400, 20-25mm lens	15 to 25 seconds (use 500 rule)
Fireworks	f/8, ISO 100-200	2 to 8 seconds (one burst)
Light painting	f/8, ISO 200	10 to 30 seconds (while you paint)
Lightning (storm)	f/8, ISO 200-400	5 to 30 seconds (wait for strike)
Waterfall silky effect	f/11-16, ISO 100, ND filter	2 to 30 seconds

4.8 Custom Modes (C1, C2, C3)

The OM-3 has three Custom Mode positions on the Mode Dial, labeled C1, C2, and C3. These are programmable modes — you configure all your preferred camera settings exactly as you want them for a specific type of photography, save that complete configuration to a Custom Mode slot, and then recall the entire setup instantly any time by turning the dial to that position.

Custom Modes are one of the most practical features on the OM-3. Once configured, they let you switch from your landscape setup to your portrait setup to your bird photography setup in under one second — a single twist of the dial — without having to touch a single menu or change a single setting manually.

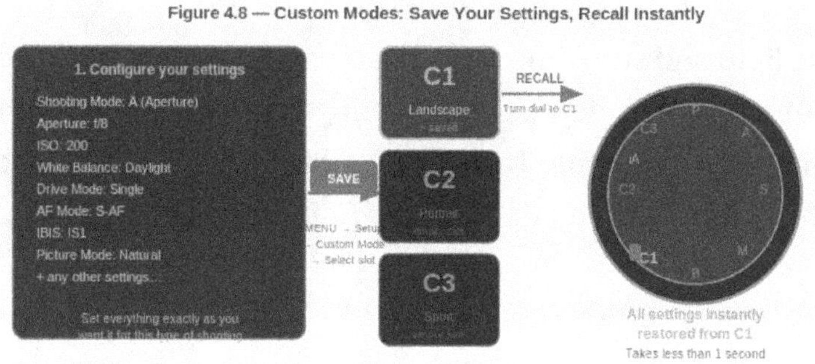

Figure 4.8 — Save your complete settings to C1/C2/C3, then recall them instantly by turning the dial

What Custom Modes Save

A Custom Mode saves an enormous number of settings simultaneously. Here is a partial list of what gets stored:

- Shooting mode (A, S, M, P, B)
- Aperture value
- Shutter speed
- ISO value (or Auto ISO with its min/max limits)
- Exposure compensation value
- White balance setting
- AF mode (S-AF, C-AF, MF)
- AF area mode (single target, zone, all-target, etc.)
- Face/Eye detection on or off
- Drive mode (single, burst, self-timer, etc.)
- Image quality (RAW, JPEG, RAW+JPEG)
- Aspect ratio
- Image stabilization mode
- Picture Mode / color profile
- Flash mode
- Metering mode
- Most Custom Menu settings active at the time of saving

NOTE: Not everything is saved in a Custom Mode

A few things are not saved: the current battery level (obviously), the number of photos on the card, GPS data, and some Wi-Fi/Bluetooth settings. Also note that if you change a setting after selecting C1/C2/C3 on the dial, those changes are temporary and the slot returns to its saved values next time you select it. If you want to update the saved values permanently, you must re-save to the slot.

How to Configure and Save Your Settings to C1, C2, or C3

Saving to a Custom Mode is a two-part process: first, set up everything on the camera exactly the way you want it; second, save those settings to the Custom Mode slot.

Part A — Set Up Your Camera Exactly as You Want

Step 1: Turn the Mode Dial to any standard mode (A, S, M, P) that you want to be the base for this Custom Mode. For a landscape preset, you might choose A (Aperture Priority).

Step 2: Set your preferred aperture using the front dial. For landscape, f/8 or f/11.

Step 3: Set ISO to 200 or enable Auto ISO with a maximum of 800.

Step 4: Open the SCP (press OK) and set White Balance to Daylight (sun icon).

Step 5: Set AF Mode to S-AF.

Step 6: Set Drive Mode to Single shot.

Step 7: Set Image Stabilization to IS1.

Step 8: Set Picture Mode to Natural.

Step 9: Set Image Quality to RAW+JPEG.

Step 10: Set Aspect Ratio to 4:3 (native MFT ratio).

Step 11: Adjust any other settings through the menus — AF area mode, metering, noise reduction, etc. — until everything is configured exactly as you want it for this type of shooting.

Part B — Save to the Custom Mode Slot

Step 1: Press the MENU button.

Step 2: Navigate to the SETUP MENU (wrench icon tab) using the RIGHT arrow.

Step 3: Scroll DOWN through the Setup Menu items until you find "Custom Mode" or "Reset/Custom Mode" and press OK or RIGHT to enter it.

Step 4: A list of three slots appears: C1, C2, and C3.

Step 5: Use the UP/DOWN arrows to highlight the slot you want to save to (for example, C1).

Step 6: Press OK or RIGHT to enter that slot's options.

Step 7: You will see an option labeled "Set" or "Register" or "Save Settings." Highlight it and press OK.

Step 8: The camera asks you to confirm. Select YES and press OK.

Step 9: The camera saves all your current settings to that slot. A brief confirmation message appears.

Step 10: Press MENU to close.

TIP: Name your Custom Modes mentally

The camera does not let you rename C1/C2/C3, but you can put a small sticky label on the camera body near the mode dial as a reminder — for example, 'C1 = Landscape, C2 = Portrait, C3 = Birds.' After a few weeks you will remember without the label.

How to Use Custom Modes — Recalling Your Saved Settings

Step 1: Hold the center lock button of the Mode Dial down.

Step 2: Rotate the dial to C1, C2, or C3 — whichever slot contains the preset you want.

Step 3: Release the button. All saved settings are instantly loaded. The mode letter C1, C2, or C3 appears on screen.

Step 4: Look at your aperture, shutter speed, ISO, and other values on the display — they will show the saved values from when you last saved to that slot.

Step 5: Shoot as normal. You are now using your custom preset.

Temporarily Changing Settings While in a Custom Mode

While your dial is set to C1, C2, or C3, you can still change any setting temporarily — just as you would in any other mode. For example, if C1 is your landscape preset but you want to quickly switch to f/16 for a specific shot, turn the front dial. The aperture changes for that shot.

The key point: these temporary changes are NOT permanently saved back to the slot. If you turn the dial away from C1 and then return to C1, all the original saved settings are loaded again.

If you want to permanently update the preset with your new settings, go through the save process again (Menu → Setup → Custom Mode → C1 → Save Settings → Yes).

Suggested Custom Mode Configurations

Slot	Suggested Name	Mode	Key Settings
C1	Landscape	A	f/8–f/11, ISO 200, Daylight WB, S-AF, Single drive, IS1, Natural picture mode, RAW+JPEG
C2	Portrait	A	f/2.8–f/4, ISO Auto (max 1600), AWB, S-AF with Face/Eye detection ON, Single drive, IS1, Portrait picture mode, RAW+JPEG
C3	Action / Birds	S	1/2000 sec, ISO Auto (max 6400), AWB, C-AF+Tracking, Sequential High burst, IS2, Natural/Vivid, JPEG Large Fine

TIP: Re-save after firmware updates

After updating the camera's firmware, it is good practice to re-check your Custom Mode settings and re-save them, as firmware updates occasionally reset certain Custom Menu entries that Custom Modes depend on.

Part 5 — Physical Controls: Every Button and Dial Explained

The OM-3 puts a remarkable number of controls at your fingertips — dials, levers, buttons, and a touchscreen — all positioned so that the most frequently used controls are reachable without ever lowering the camera from your eye. This part of the guide covers every single physical control on the camera body: where it is, what it does by default, how to operate it, and in some cases how to customize it.

The three diagrams below give you a complete map of every control on the front, back, and top of the camera. Refer to these diagrams as you read through each section.

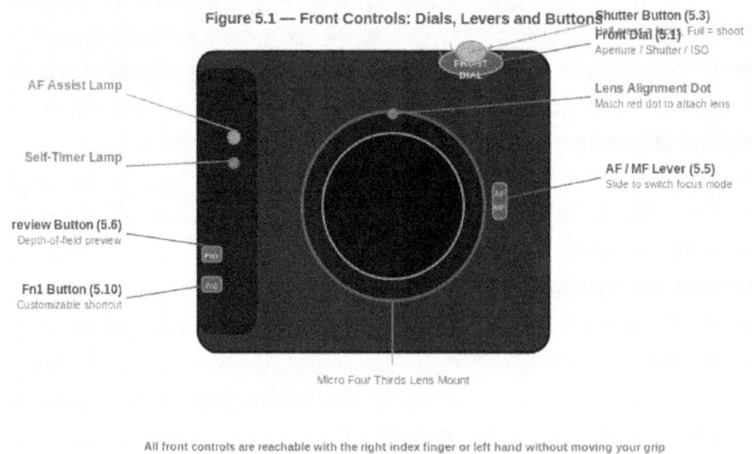

Figure 5.1 — Front of the OM-3: all controls labeled

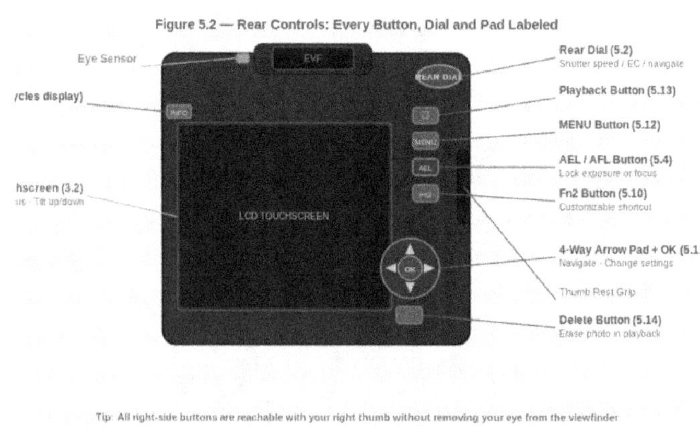

Figure 5.2 — Back of the OM-3: all controls labeled

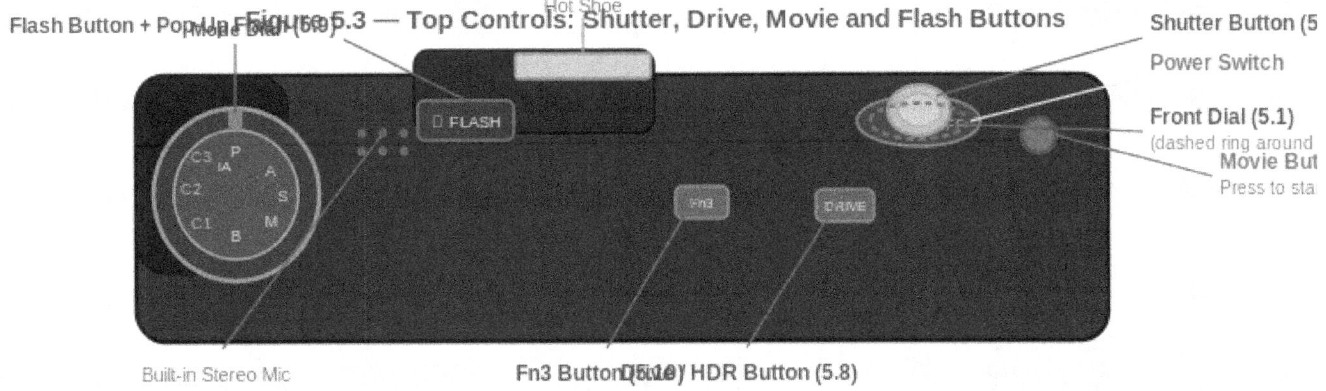

Figure 5.3 — Top of the OM-3: all controls labeled

5.1 The Front Dial

Location

The Front Dial is a ridged, rotating wheel located on the top-right of the camera's front face, surrounding or positioned just behind the shutter button. You operate it with the first joint of your right index finger, rolling it forward (away from you) or backward (toward you) without moving your grip.

What the Front Dial Does in Each Shooting Mode

Front Dial function by shooting mode:

iAuto: Not active — camera controls all exposure settings

P: Program Shift — changes shutter/aperture combination while keeping total exposure constant

A: Sets the Aperture (f-stop) — roll forward for narrower aperture (higher f-number), backward for wider (lower f-number)

S: Not primary dial — in S mode the Rear Dial controls shutter speed. Front Dial may adjust ISO if configured

M: Sets the Aperture — same as A mode. Use front dial for aperture, rear dial for shutter speed

B: Sets the Aperture for the long exposure

C1/C2/C3: Inherits the function saved in the custom mode configuration

How to Use the Front Dial

Step 1: With the camera powered on and in live view, rest your right index finger gently against the ridged surface of the front dial.

Step 2: Roll the dial forward (away from the camera toward the lens) to increase the value (e.g., increase aperture to f/11 in A mode).

Step 3: Roll it backward (toward the shutter button side) to decrease the value (e.g., open aperture to f/2.8).

Step 4: Watch the relevant number update in real time on the LCD screen or EVF as you turn.

Step 5: No button press is needed to activate the front dial — it is always active when the camera is in shooting mode.

TIP: Front dial with ISO

In many modes you can press the ISO button shortcut (usually the OK button or a dedicated Fn button) and then turn the front or rear dial to adjust ISO without opening the full menu. Configure this in Custom Menu B (Button/Dial settings).

Customizing the Front Dial Direction

If you prefer rolling the dial the other way to increase values, you can reverse the dial rotation direction: go to MENU → Custom Menu B → Dial Direction → Reverse. This is a personal preference and does not affect any other function.

5.2 The Rear Dial

Location

The Rear Dial is an oval or round scroll wheel on the upper-right area of the back of the camera, reachable by your right thumb without shifting your grip. It is the most frequently used dial for exposure control while shooting.

What the Rear Dial Does in Each Shooting Mode

Rear Dial function by shooting mode:

iAuto: Not active for exposure — used to navigate menus when in menu mode

P: Adjusts Exposure Compensation (+/- brightness) — roll right to brighten, left to darken

A: Adjusts Exposure Compensation — same as P mode

S: Sets the Shutter Speed — roll right for faster speeds, left for slower

M: Sets the Shutter Speed — left/right. Front dial handles aperture simultaneously

B: Not used for exposure duration (that is controlled by how long you hold the shutter)

Menu navigation: In any menu, the rear dial scrolls through items — same as the UP/DOWN arrow buttons

How to Use the Rear Dial

Step 1: With the camera in live view and shooting mode selected, place your right thumb on the ridged surface of the rear dial.

Step 2: Roll the rear dial to the right (clockwise when viewed from above) to increase the value — faster shutter speed, or more positive exposure compensation.

Step 3: Roll it to the left (counter-clockwise) to decrease the value.

Step 4: In M mode: the rear dial controls shutter speed while the front dial controls aperture — use both simultaneously for full manual control.

TIP: Quick EC adjustment in A mode

In Aperture Priority, turn the rear dial right to brighten the image, left to darken. This is the fastest way to apply exposure compensation — faster than going through the SCP or holding the AEL button.

5.3 The Shutter Button — Half-Press vs. Full-Press

Location

The Shutter Button is the large, slightly concave silver or grey button on the top-right of the camera, surrounded by the power switch lever. Your right index finger rests naturally on it when you hold the camera correctly.

Figure 5.3b — The Two-Stage Shutter Button: Half-Press and Full-Press

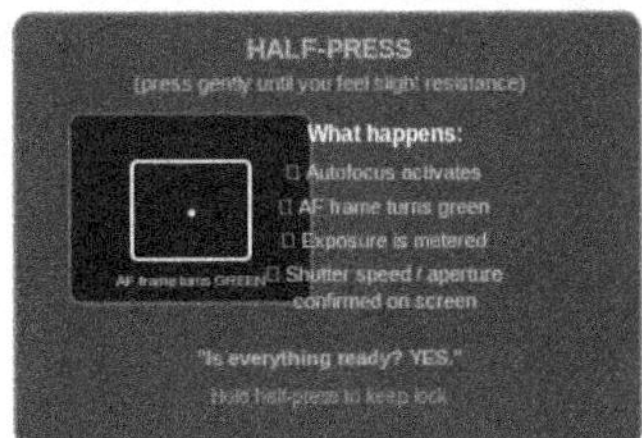

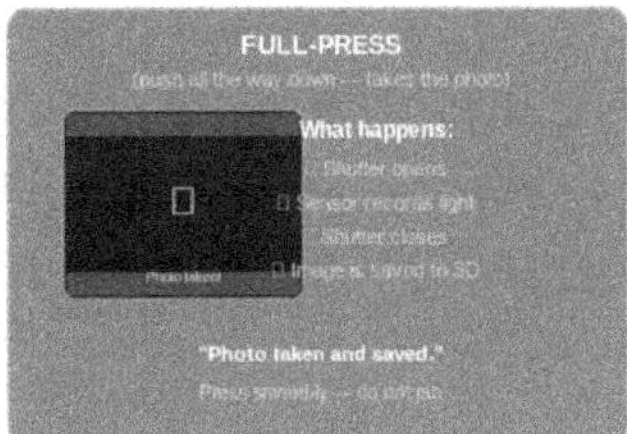

Figure 5.3b — The two-stage shutter button: half-press activates AF and metering; full-press fires the shutter

The Two-Stage Press — Understanding the Difference

The shutter button has two distinct pressure levels. These are not just light vs. heavy — they are two separate electronic triggers. Understanding this distinction is fundamental to good photography with any camera.

Press Stage	How Much Pressure	What Happens	When to Use It
Half-Press	Gentle — press until you feel light resistance, then stop	Autofocus activates and locks. Exposure is measured. The AF frame turns green when focus is confirmed. Shutter speed and aperture values settle on screen.	Before every photo. Hold here while you check focus and framing. Reframe if needed while keeping the half-press held.
Full-Press	Press all the way through the resistance point to the bottom	The shutter opens, the sensor records the image, the shutter closes. The photo is processed and saved to the SD card.	Once you are satisfied with the focus and composition. Press smoothly without jabbing.

The Correct Technique for Pressing the Shutter

How you press the shutter button has a direct effect on image sharpness. A jabbing or stabbing motion — especially at slow shutter speeds — causes the camera to move at the moment of exposure, resulting in blur. Here is the correct technique:

- Rest, do not press. Keep your finger resting lightly on the shutter button at all times while shooting. The button should feel like an extension of your finger, not a separate thing you reach for.
- Breathe first. Take a breath, let half of it out, then hold gently while you shoot.
- Squeeze, do not stab. Apply increasing pressure smoothly and deliberately, as if squeezing water from a sponge. The shutter fires when the pressure reaches the full-press point.
- Follow through. Keep the pressure applied for a fraction of a second after the shutter fires before releasing. This prevents the release motion from causing camera movement.

TIP: Half-press to wake the camera from sleep

If the camera has gone into sleep mode (screen off after auto power-off), a half-press of the shutter button wakes it up instantly — typically in under one second — and you are ready to shoot without turning it off and on again.

Shutter Button Shortcut — Exit Menus Instantly

A half-press of the shutter button closes any open menu, SCP panel, or playback screen and returns the camera immediately to shooting mode. This is the fastest way to get back to live view from anywhere in the camera interface.

5.4 The AEL / AFL Button

Location

The AEL/AFL button is on the back of the camera, on the right side, above the center of the 4-way arrow pad. It is labeled AEL or marked with a star symbol (*). It sits exactly where your right thumb lands naturally when holding the camera in landscape orientation.

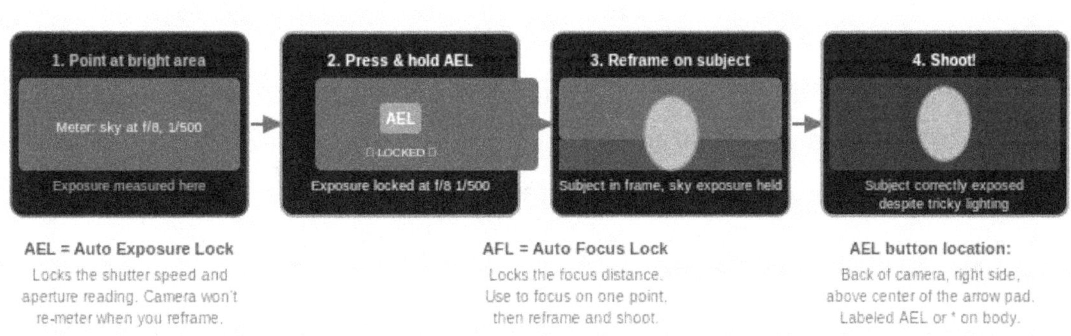

Figure 5.4 — AEL workflow: meter a bright area, lock the exposure, reframe, shoot the subject correctly

What AEL Means — Auto Exposure Lock

AEL stands for Auto Exposure Lock. Pressing and holding the AEL button freezes the camera's exposure reading at the value currently on screen. The camera will not re-meter the scene when you reframe — the shutter speed and aperture stay exactly where they were when you pressed AEL. This is powerful when your subject is in a lighting situation that would fool the camera's meter.

What AFL Means — Auto Focus Lock

AFL stands for Auto Focus Lock. In some configurations, pressing AEL also locks focus at the current distance. This lets you focus on one point, then reframe so your subject is off-center, without the camera refocusing on the background.

Default AEL Button Behavior on the OM-3

By default, pressing and holding the AEL button locks both exposure (AEL) and focus (AFL) simultaneously. Releasing the button releases the lock. You can configure the button to lock only exposure, only focus, or toggle the lock on/off with a single press — this is covered in the customization steps below.

How to Use the AEL Button — Step by Step

Step 1: Point the camera at the area of the scene where you want to meter the light. For example, if your subject is backlit by a bright window, point at your subject's face — not the window.

Step 2: Half-press the shutter button to let the camera take an exposure reading.

Step 3: Without lifting your shutter finger, press and hold the AEL button with your right thumb. You will see a small AEL indicator or asterisk (*) appear on the screen, confirming the lock.

Step 4: Still holding AEL, reframe the shot to your preferred composition.

Step 5: Full-press the shutter to take the photo. The exposure stays at the locked values regardless of what is in the new frame.

Step 6: Release the AEL button. The lock is released and normal metering resumes.

Customizing the AEL Button Behavior

You can change what the AEL button does by going to: MENU → Custom Menu A (AF/MF settings) → AEL/AFL Mode. The options available are:

Mode	What It Does
AEL Hold	Locks exposure only while the button is held. Releasing the button releases the lock. (Default)
AEL Toggle	One press locks exposure; a second press releases it. Useful when you want to lock for a longer period without holding the button.
AFL Hold	Locks focus only while held. Good for focus-recompose technique without using half-press.
AFL Toggle	Toggle focus lock on/off with each press.
AEL+AFL Hold	Locks both exposure and focus while held.
AEL+AFL Toggle	Toggles both exposure and focus lock.

> **TIP: Back-button focus technique**
>
> Many advanced photographers reassign the AEL button to act as the sole autofocus trigger — a technique called back-button focus. In this setup: the shutter button ONLY fires the shutter (no focusing). Pressing AEL focuses. This gives you separate, independent control over focus and exposure with two thumbs. Configure it in Custom Menu A → AFL Mode → AFL Hold, and in Custom Menu A → Shutter AF → OFF.

5.5 The AF / MF Lever

Location

The AF/MF lever is a small sliding switch on the front of the camera, positioned to the right of the lens mount ring. Slide it with your left thumb or left index finger. It has two positions: AF (top position) and MF (bottom position).

What the Lever Does

Lever Position	Mode Activated	What Changes	When to Use
AF (top position)	Autofocus — the camera focuses automatically	The camera's autofocus motor is active. Half-pressing the shutter or pressing AEL triggers focusing. The AF mode set in the menu (S-AF, C-AF) is now in effect.	Most everyday shooting — portraits, events, travel, street photography, wildlife. Any time you want the camera to handle focus.
MF (bottom position)	Manual Focus — you control focus by rotating the focus ring on the lens	The autofocus motor is disengaged. The focus ring on the lens barrel becomes active. Focus peaking and magnification aids activate automatically to help you judge sharpness.	Macro photography, astrophotography, studio work, situations where the camera struggles to focus (low contrast, glass, dark scenes), or when you want precise creative control of focus.

How to Switch Between AF and MF

Step 1: Locate the AF/MF lever on the front of the camera, to the right of the lens mount.

Step 2: Slide the lever upward to engage Autofocus (AF). The AF mode indicator (S-AF, C-AF) appears on screen.

Step 3: Slide the lever downward to engage Manual Focus (MF). The letters MF appear on screen. The lens's focus ring is now active.

Step 4: When in MF, rotate the focus ring on the lens barrel (the ring closest to the camera body on most lenses) to adjust focus. The image on screen sharpens or blurs as you turn.

Step 5: Use the magnified view (double-tap the LCD or use the Fn button assigned to Magnify) to check critical sharpness.

Manual Focus Assist Features (Active in MF Mode)

- Focus Peaking — highlights the edges of in-focus areas with a coloured outline (typically red, white, or yellow). Enable it in Custom Menu A → Peaking. When the coloured edges appear on your subject, that area is in focus.
- Magnified View — press a Fn button assigned to Magnify (or double-tap the LCD) to zoom in to the center of the frame at 5x or 10x to check fine focus. Press the shutter halfway to zoom back out.
- Focus Distance Scale — some lenses display a focus distance readout on screen showing the approximate distance in meters or feet.

TIP: S-AF+MF mode

There is also a combined mode called S-AF+MF. In this mode, the camera autofocuses when you half-press the shutter, then allows you to fine-tune focus manually by rotating the focus ring afterward — all without touching the AF/MF lever. Enable it in Custom Menu A → AF Mode → S-AF+MF.

5.6 The Preview Button

Location

The Preview button is a small rectangular button on the FRONT of the camera, located on the left side of the grip area, above the Fn1 button. It is sometimes labeled Preview or with a small depth-of-field icon. Reach it with your left thumb when your left hand is supporting the lens from below.

What the Preview Button Does

The Preview button temporarily closes the lens aperture to the actual aperture value that will be used when you take the shot. Normally when you look through the viewfinder, the lens aperture is wide open (at its maximum) regardless of what aperture you have set, because a wider aperture lets in more light and gives you a brighter viewfinder image. This is helpful for composing and focusing, but it means you cannot see the true depth of field effect.

When you press and hold the Preview button, the lens aperture closes to your set f-stop value. The viewfinder image will darken (because less light enters), but you will now see exactly how much of the scene will be sharp in the final photo. Areas that appear sharp on screen will be sharp in the photo. Areas that appear blurry will be blurry in the photo.

How to Use the Preview Button

Step 1: Set up your shot in Aperture Priority (A) or Manual (M) mode with your chosen aperture.

Step 2: Compose the shot and half-press the shutter to focus.

Step 3: While keeping the camera still, press and hold the Preview button on the front of the camera with your left thumb.

Step 4: The aperture closes to your set value. The screen darkens — this is normal. Look at the background behind your subject: if it is blurry, your aperture gives a shallow depth of field; if it is sharp, you have deep depth of field.

Step 5: Release the Preview button. The aperture opens wide again and the viewfinder brightens.

Step 6: Adjust your aperture if needed and preview again before shooting.

NOTE: Preview button can be reassigned

By default the Preview button shows depth-of-field preview. You can reassign it to any other function via MENU → Custom Menu B → Button Function → Preview. This is useful if you rarely use DoF preview and would prefer a different shortcut at this location.

5.7 The Movie Record Button

Location

The Movie Record button is the RED circular button on the top-right of the camera's top plate, to the right and slightly above the shutter button. It is red so you can identify it instantly by feel and by sight. It is the only red button on the camera body.

What the Movie Record Button Does

Pressing the Movie Record button starts video recording immediately — regardless of which position the Mode Dial is set to. You do not need to switch to a special video mode first. When recording, pressing the button again stops recording and saves the video file.

How to Record Video

Step 1: Power on the camera and compose your shot in any shooting mode.

Step 2: Press the red Movie Record button ONCE firmly. Video recording begins immediately. A red recording indicator (REC) and a time counter appear on the LCD screen.

Step 3: Shoot your scene. The camera records video using your current video settings (resolution, frame rate) as set in the Video Menu.

Step 4: Press the Movie Record button ONCE again to stop recording. The camera processes and saves the video file to the SD card. This may take a few seconds for longer recordings.

Video Indicator	What It Means
REC (flashing red dot)	Camera is actively recording video — do not remove the SD card
Time counter (e.g. 00:02:34)	How long the current recording has been running
Remaining time (e.g. 01:22:00 remaining)	Estimated remaining recording time on your SD card at the current quality setting
Temperature warning icon	The camera is getting warm — if it becomes too hot, recording stops automatically
SD card indicator blinking	Video data is being written — card is busy

TIP: Movie button in any mode

You can record video in P, A, S, or M mode, not just with the dial on the video position. When you record in A mode, the camera uses your set aperture for the video. In M mode it uses your exact aperture and shutter speed. This is useful for vloggers and filmmakers who want consistent exposure across photos and video in the same shoot.

NOTE: Maximum clip length

Individual video clips are limited to approximately 29 minutes 59 seconds per clip due to file system constraints. If you need to record longer than this, the camera will stop and automatically start a new clip. This is a limitation of most mirrorless cameras, not a fault.

5.8 The Drive / HDR Button

Location

The Drive button is on the top plate of the camera, to the left of the shutter button area. It is labeled DRIVE, or sometimes shown with a burst/stack icon. Press it with your right index finger after moving slightly left from the shutter button.

What the Drive Button Opens

Pressing the Drive button opens the Drive Mode selection screen. Drive mode determines how many photos the camera takes each time you fully press the shutter, and controls timing behavior like self-timers. The full list of available drive modes on the OM-3 is:

Drive Mode	Symbol	What It Does
Single (default)	□ (single square)	Takes one photo per full shutter press. The shutter will not fire again until you release and press again. Best for most still photography.
Sequential Low (SL)	□□ stacked (slower)	Burst shooting at a lower frame rate — approximately 5 fps. Good for moderately fast subjects where you do not need the fastest rate. Uses the mechanical shutter.
Sequential High (SH)	□□□ stacked (faster)	Burst shooting at a higher frame rate — up to 30 fps in electronic shutter mode (Pro Capture), or around 15 fps with mechanical shutter. Best for fast action.

Anti-Shock (ACS)	Camera with waves symbol	Adds a small delay (adjustable from 0 to 30 seconds) between mirror-less shutter release and actual capture to eliminate any vibration from the shutter mechanism.
Silent (S)	Camera with mute symbol	Uses the electronic shutter only — fully silent operation with no mechanical click. Useful in quiet environments. May have rolling shutter distortion with very fast subjects.
Self-Timer 2s	Clock with 2	Delays the shutter by 2 seconds after you press the button. Useful for camera-shake elimination on a tripod without a remote.
Self-Timer 12s	Clock with 12	Delays the shutter by 12 seconds after you press the button. Gives you time to walk into the frame for a self-portrait.
Custom Self-Timer	Clock with C	Set a custom delay (1-30 seconds) and number of shots (1-10). Useful for group photos where you need time to compose yourself.
HDR	HDR label	Shoots a bracketed sequence of exposures and automatically blends them into a single high-dynamic-range image in-camera.
Bracketing (BKT)	BKT label	Shoots a series of exposures at different values (AE bracket, WB bracket, Focus bracket, Art Filter bracket). Each type is configured separately in the Shooting Menu.
Pro Capture L / H	Pro capture icon	Pre-captures frames before you fully press the shutter, storing up to 35 frames. Releases them backward in time when you press. L = lower frame rate, H = higher.

How to Change the Drive Mode

Step 1: Press the DRIVE button on the top of the camera.

Step 2: A drive mode selection screen appears on the LCD. The current mode is highlighted.

Step 3: Use the LEFT or RIGHT arrow buttons (or turn the rear dial) to move through the available drive modes.

Step 4: When the mode you want is highlighted, press OK to confirm and return to live view.

Step 5: The drive mode icon in the bottom-left of the live view display updates to show your selection.

TIP: Drive mode via SCP

You can also change drive mode from the Super Control Panel without pressing the Drive button. Press OK to open the SCP, navigate to the Drive tile (bottom-left area of the panel), press OK, and select from the full list.

5.9 The Flash Button and Pop-Up Flash

Location

The Flash button is on the top-left area of the camera's top plate, just to the left of the EVF hump. The built-in pop-up flash unit is housed in the hump above the lens on the front of the camera. Pressing the Flash button causes the flash head to spring upward automatically.

How to Open and Use the Pop-Up Flash

Step 1: Press the FLASH button on the top plate once. The flash head springs upward automatically with a soft click.

Step 2: The flash is now active and ready to fire. A flash icon (lightning bolt) appears on the display.

Step 3: Compose your shot and shoot as normal. The flash fires automatically when the shutter opens.

Step 4: To close the flash, push the flash head gently back down until it clicks flat against the camera body. Do NOT force it — it should close smoothly with light pressure.

Flash Modes — Changing How the Flash Fires

Once the flash is raised, you can change the flash mode via the Super Control Panel or the Shooting Menu. The available flash modes on the OM-3 are:

Flash Mode	Icon	What It Does	Best For
Auto Flash	A⚡	Flash fires automatically when the camera detects the scene is too dark	General indoor shooting, events

Fill-In Flash	⚡ (solid)	Flash fires on every shot regardless of ambient light level	Outdoor portraits to fill shadows on faces, backlit subjects
Red-Eye Reduction	⚡👁	Flash fires a short pre-burst of light before the main flash to cause pupils to contract, reducing red-eye in portraits	Indoor portraits with subjects looking at the camera
Slow Sync (Rear)	⚡SLOW	Flash fires at the end of a long exposure — captures ambient light blur behind a sharp, flash-lit subject	Night portraits with background visible; artistic light trails
Slow Sync (Front)	SLOW⚡	Flash fires at the start of a long exposure — blur appears in front of the flash-frozen subject	Alternative slow sync for different creative effects
Flash Off	⚡ crossed	Flash will not fire even if it is raised	Quiet environments; when flash is distracting or forbidden

How to Change the Flash Mode

Step 1: Press OK to open the Super Control Panel.

Step 2: Navigate to the Flash Mode tile (it shows a lightning bolt icon).

Step 3: Press OK to enter the flash mode selection.

Step 4: Use the arrow buttons to highlight your preferred flash mode.

Step 5: Press OK to confirm.

WARNING: Close the flash when not in use

Leaving the flash raised when you do not need it drains the battery (the capacitor stays charged). It also risks catching on a camera bag or strap and bending the flash mechanism. Always push it closed when you are done using it.

TIP: Flash compensation

The OM-3's built-in flash can be set to fire more or less brightly than its automatic calculation suggests. This is called Flash Exposure Compensation. Adjust it via the SCP flash compensation tile or in the Shooting Menu. A value of -1 EV makes the flash darker (more natural-looking in portraits); +1 EV makes it brighter (for filling strong shadows).

5.10 Function Buttons (Fn1, Fn2, Fn3, and More)

Function buttons — labeled Fn1, Fn2, Fn3, etc. — are programmable shortcut buttons. Each one can be assigned to launch any one of over 60 different camera functions with a single press, putting your most-used settings at your fingertips without ever opening the main menu.

Location of Each Fn Button on the OM-3 Body

Button	Location on Body	Default Function
Fn1	Front of camera — left side of grip, below the Preview button	Preview (depth-of-field preview) — may vary by firmware
Fn2	Back of camera — right side, between the AEL button and the arrow pad	ISO sensitivity — opens ISO selection screen
Fn3	Top plate — between the Drive button and the hot shoe area	White Balance — opens WB selection
Fn4 / Record button	Top plate — the red Movie Record button can also be reassigned when not used for video	Video recording (default) — can be reassigned in Custom Menu B
OK button (center of arrow pad)	Back center of arrow pad cluster	Opens the Super Control Panel in live view. Confirms selections in menus.
Arrow pad UP	Top position of the arrow pad	Exposure Compensation shortcut (press UP to open EC scale)
Arrow pad DOWN	Bottom position of the arrow pad	Drive Mode shortcut in some firmware configurations
Arrow pad LEFT	Left position of the arrow pad	White Balance shortcut

Arrow pad RIGHT	Right position of the arrow pad	Flash Mode shortcut or ISO

NOTE: Exact defaults vary by firmware

The default assignments listed above are based on the OM-3's standard firmware configuration. Exact defaults may differ slightly between firmware versions. Always check your camera's current assignments in Custom Menu B before assuming a button does a specific thing.

The Full List of Functions You Can Assign to Any Fn Button

Any of the following functions can be assigned to any reassignable button on the OM-3. This is a comprehensive list — it is long by design, because the OM-3 is an extremely customizable camera:

- ISO — opens ISO selection or enables direct dial control of ISO
- White Balance — opens WB selection
- Drive Mode — opens drive mode selection
- Flash Mode — opens flash mode selection
- Exposure Compensation — opens EC scale
- Metering Mode — opens metering mode selection
- AF Mode — switches between S-AF, C-AF, and MF
- AF Area Mode — switches between target patterns
- Face/Eye Detection — toggle face and eye detection on/off
- Focus Peaking — toggle focus peaking highlight on/off
- Magnify — zooms the live view for manual focus checking
- Image Stabilization — toggle IBIS modes
- Picture Mode — opens picture mode selection
- Image Quality — opens RAW/JPEG selection
- Aspect Ratio — switches between 4:3, 3:2, 16:9, 1:1
- AEL Toggle — locks/unlocks exposure with each press
- AFL Toggle — locks/unlocks focus with each press
- One-Push WB — sets a custom white balance at that moment
- Histogram — toggles histogram overlay
- Level Gauge — toggles the electronic level
- Grid Display — toggles the grid overlay
- Zebra — toggles highlight clipping warning overlay
- Preview (depth of field) — held to close aperture for preview
- My Menu — opens your personal shortcut menu
- Pro Capture — activates Pre-Capture mode
- Live Composite — activates Live Composite long exposure mode

- Silent Mode — toggles electronic silent shutter
- Anti-Flicker — toggles the anti-flicker shooting feature
- Fn button off (disabled) — removes any function from the button

How to Reassign Any Fn Button — Exact Menu Path

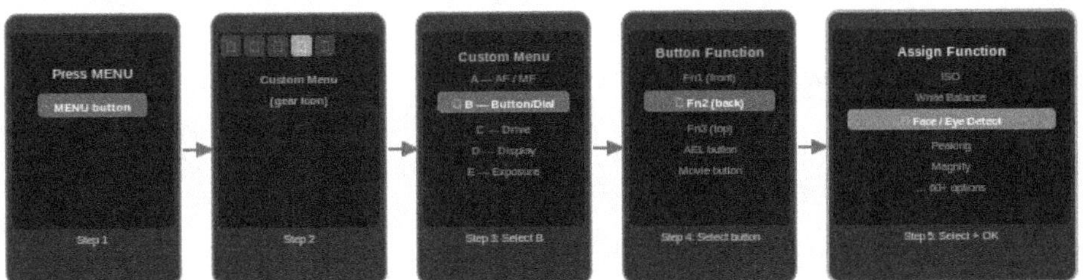

Figure 5.10 — Exact menu path for reassigning any Fn button: MENU → Custom Menu B → Button Function

Step 1: Press the MENU button on the back of the camera.

Step 2: Use the RIGHT arrow to navigate to the Custom Menu tab — it looks like a gear or cog icon.

Step 3: Press DOWN to enter the menu list under the Custom tab.

Step 4: Scroll DOWN to find the section labeled "B" (Button/Dial settings). Press OK or RIGHT to enter Custom Menu B.

Step 5: Scroll DOWN inside Custom Menu B until you find "Button Function" or "Fn Button Settings." Press OK or RIGHT to enter it.

Step 6: A list of assignable buttons appears: Fn1, Fn2, Fn3, AEL, Movie button, arrow pad directions, and others.

Step 7: Use UP/DOWN to highlight the button you want to reassign (for example, Fn2).

Step 8: Press OK or RIGHT to enter the function list for that button.

Step 9: A long scrollable list of available functions appears. Scroll UP/DOWN to find the function you want to assign.

Step 10: Highlight your desired function and press OK to confirm the assignment.

Step 11: The button is now reassigned. Press MENU to close and return to live view.

TIP: Build your own shooting shortcut set

> Think about the settings you change most often while shooting. If you frequently adjust ISO, AF mode, and white balance, assign those three functions to Fn1, Fn2, and Fn3 respectively. Now every setting change is one button press — no menus needed. This is how experienced photographers set up their cameras.

5.11 The OK Button and Arrow Pad (4-Way Controller)

Location

The Arrow Pad (also called the 4-way controller or D-pad) is a cluster of four directional buttons arranged in a cross pattern on the lower-right area of the camera back. In the center of this cross is the OK button. You operate all five of these with your right thumb.

The OK Button — What It Does

Context	What the OK Button Does
In Live View (shooting mode)	Opens the Super Control Panel (SCP) — your quick-access settings grid
Inside a menu	Confirms the currently highlighted selection and enters the selected item
Inside the SCP	Enters the selected SCP tile to open its full adjustment screen
During playback	May zoom into the currently displayed photo (check your settings)
During focus point selection	Resets the AF point to the center of the frame

The Four Arrow Buttons — What They Do

Arrow Button	In Live View / SCP	In Menus	Shortcut Function (default)
UP arrow	Moves cursor or AF point upward; scrolls list upward in SCP	Moves selection cursor up through menu items	Exposure Compensation — opens EC adjustment scale
DOWN arrow	Moves cursor or AF point downward; scrolls list downward in SCP	Moves selection cursor down through menu items	Drive Mode — opens drive mode selection in some configurations

LEFT arrow	Moves cursor or AF point to the left; navigates SCP left	Moves to previous item or tab; goes back one level in some menus	White Balance — opens WB selection
RIGHT arrow	Moves cursor or AF point to the right; navigates SCP right	Enters a submenu or sub-option (same as OK in many menus)	Flash — opens flash mode selection

Moving the AF Focus Point with the Arrow Pad

One of the most important uses of the arrow pad during shooting is to move the autofocus point around the frame so you can precisely choose where the camera focuses:

Step 1: In live view, make sure you are in a single-target or small-zone AF area mode (not all-target auto, which selects the focus point for you).

Step 2: Press any direction on the arrow pad. The AF frame (the green/white square on screen) moves in the direction you pressed.

Step 3: Continue pressing arrows to position the AF point over your subject — for example, your subject's eye.

Step 4: Half-press the shutter to focus at that exact point.

Step 5: To reset the AF point back to the center of the frame, press the OK button once.

TIP: Touch to move the AF point

You can also move the AF point simply by tapping the LCD screen at the location you want to focus. This is often faster than pressing the arrow pad multiple times, especially when the camera is at arm's length.

5.12 The MENU Button — Enter, Navigate, Exit

Location

The MENU button is on the right side of the back of the camera, above the AEL button. It is labeled MENU in small text. Press it with your right thumb.

What the MENU Button Does

Context	What Pressing MENU Does
From live view	Opens the main menu system at whatever tab was last active
Inside a menu — on a submenu or setting	Goes back one level to the parent menu
Inside a menu — at the top-level tab row	Closes the menu entirely and returns to live view
From playback	Returns to live view
From the SCP	Closes the SCP and returns to live view

How to Navigate the Full Menu System

The complete menu navigation workflow:

Step 1: Press MENU. The menu opens at the last-used tab.

Step 2: Press LEFT or RIGHT arrows to move between the five top-level tabs: Shooting (camera icon), Video (movie icon), Playback (triangle), Custom (gear), Setup (wrench).

Step 3: When the desired tab is active (highlighted), press DOWN to enter the list of items under that tab.

Step 4: Scroll through items using the UP/DOWN arrows or the rear dial.

Step 5: To enter a setting or submenu, press OK or the RIGHT arrow.

Step 6: To go back up a level, press MENU or the LEFT arrow.

Step 7: To change a value within a setting: use UP/DOWN or the dials, then press OK to confirm.

Step 8: To exit the menu entirely from any depth: press the shutter button halfway, or press MENU repeatedly until you return to live view.

TIP: My Menu shortcut

The OM-3 lets you create a personal shortcut menu called My Menu, which shows only the settings you access most often — without having to navigate through all five tabs. Set it up in the Setup Menu → My Menu. Once created, assign the Fn3 (or any Fn) button to open My Menu directly.

5.13 The Playback Button

Location

The Playback button is on the right side of the camera back, above the MENU button. It shows a right-pointing triangle (the universal play symbol). Press it with your right thumb.

What the Playback Button Does

Step 1: Press the Playback button once from live view. The most recently taken photo (or last photo on the SD card) appears on the LCD screen.

Step 2: Use the LEFT/RIGHT arrows to scroll backward and forward through your photos and videos.

Step 3: Use the rear dial to scroll more quickly through a large number of images.

Step 4: Double-tap the LCD or press the rear dial to zoom into the current photo for sharpness checking.

Step 5: In playback, press the INFO button to cycle through information overlays on the displayed image (histogram, shooting data, GPS data if available).

Step 6: Press the Playback button again, or half-press the shutter button, to exit playback and return to live view immediately.

What You Can Do in Playback Mode

Action	How to Do It
View next photo	Press RIGHT arrow or swipe right on LCD
View previous photo	Press LEFT arrow or swipe left on LCD
Zoom in	Pinch to zoom on LCD, or turn rear dial clockwise
Zoom out / fit to screen	Pinch together on LCD, or turn rear dial counter-clockwise
Move around a zoomed image	Use the arrow pad to pan left/right/up/down
Delete the current photo	Press the Delete button (separate button, described below)
Protect a photo from deletion	Press OK, then navigate to the Protect option
View shooting data for a photo	Press INFO to cycle through info overlays including histogram
Return to live view	Press Playback button again, or half-press the shutter

5.14 The Delete Button

Location

The Delete button is at the bottom of the right-side button cluster on the back of the camera, below the 4-way arrow pad. It shows a rubbish bin (trash can) icon. Press it with your right thumb during playback.

How to Delete a Single Photo

Step 1: Press the Playback button to enter playback mode.

Step 2: Use the arrow buttons to navigate to the photo you want to delete.

Step 3: Press the Delete button (bin icon). A confirmation dialog appears: "Delete this image? YES / NO." The cursor defaults to NO as a safety measure.

Step 4: Press the LEFT arrow to move to YES.

Step 5: Press OK to confirm deletion. The photo is permanently erased from the SD card. The next photo in the sequence appears.

How to Delete Multiple Photos at Once

Step 1: In playback mode, press the Delete button.

Step 2: The delete confirmation screen appears. Look for an option labeled "Delete Multiple" or "Select & Delete."

Step 3: Navigate to that option and press OK.

Step 4: A multi-select screen appears showing thumbnail images. Use the arrow pad to move between photos.

Step 5: Press OK on each photo you want to delete — a tick mark or trash icon appears on selected photos.

Step 6: When you have selected all the photos to delete, press the Delete button again.

Step 7: Confirm the deletion when prompted. All selected photos are permanently deleted.

WARNING: Deletion is permanent and cannot be undone

Once a photo is deleted from the SD card, it cannot be recovered through the camera. If you accidentally delete a photo you wanted to keep, data recovery software on a computer (such as Recuva or PhotoRec) may be able to recover it — but only if you stop using the card immediately and do not format it. The safest approach is to always review carefully before deleting.

How to Protect Photos from Accidental Deletion

If you want to prevent a photo from being deleted, you can protect it:

Step 1: Navigate to the photo in Playback mode.

Step 2: Press OK. A small menu may appear, or press MENU and navigate to the Playback Menu.

Step 3: Find the option labeled "Protect" and press OK.

Step 4: The photo is marked with a small lock icon. It cannot be deleted using the Delete button until the protection is removed.

Step 5: Note: protecting a photo does NOT prevent it from being erased by a full card format. Formatting always erases everything.

TIP: Review before you delete

Rather than deleting photos in the field, many photographers review their SD card on a computer first and delete in batch. This avoids accidentally erasing a photo that looks bad on the small camera screen but is actually good when viewed large.

Part 6 — The Menu System (Complete Step-by-Step Guide)

The OM-3's menu system contains every setting the camera offers — several hundred options across five major sections. This part of the guide covers all of them. Every setting is listed by its exact menu name, its factory default value, the available options, and a plain-English explanation of what it does and when you would want to change it.

Do not feel you need to read this section from start to finish in one sitting. Use it as a reference guide. When you encounter a menu item you have never seen before, find it here and read what it does. Over time, you will naturally learn the settings that matter most for your style of shooting.

NOTE: Menu items vary slightly by firmware version

The OM-3's menu contents may differ slightly between firmware versions. If a setting described here does not appear on your camera, it may be named slightly differently or located in a nearby sub-menu. Olympus/OM SYSTEM sometimes reorganize or rename settings in firmware updates. Always keep your firmware up to date (covered in Part 19).

6.1 How to Open and Close the Menu

Opening the Menu

Press the MENU button on the back of the camera. It is located to the right of the LCD screen, above the AEL button. The menu opens immediately at whatever tab was last active.

Closing the Menu

There are three ways to close the menu and return to live view:

- Half-press the shutter button — the fastest method. The menu closes instantly and the camera is ready to shoot.
- Press the MENU button when you are at the top-level tab row — this closes the menu.
- Press the Playback button — exits the menu and enters playback mode.

Going Back One Level

Press the MENU button while inside a submenu or setting to go back up one level. You can press MENU repeatedly to climb back through nested menus until you reach the top-level tabs, then press again to close.

6.2 How the Menu Is Organized — Tabs, Pages, and Submenus

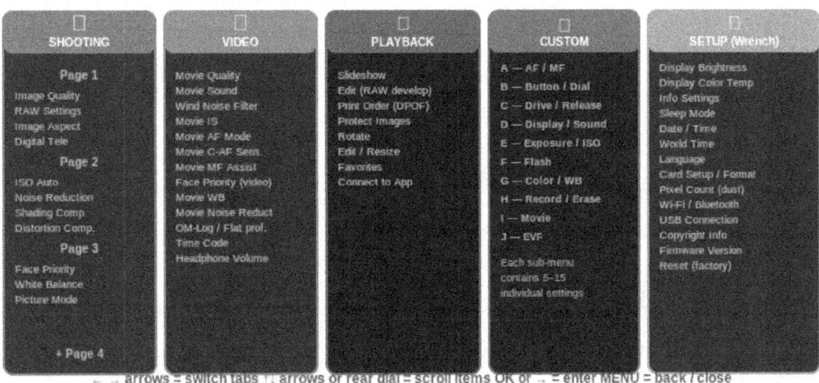

Figure 6.1 — The five menu tabs and their contents at a glance

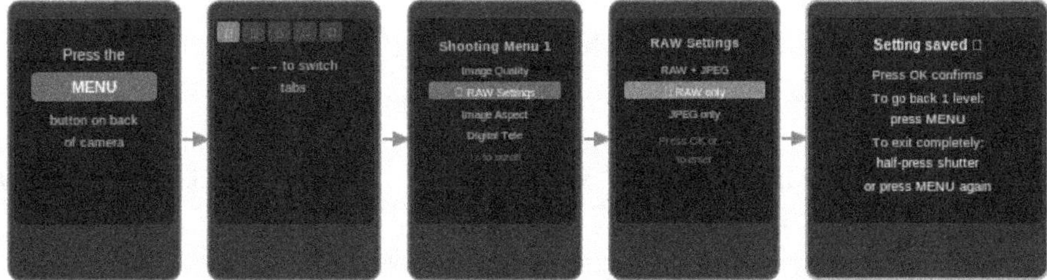

Figure 6.2 — How to open, navigate, change a setting, and exit the menu

The Five Tabs

The menu is divided into five sections, each accessed by a tab icon along the top of the screen. Use the LEFT and RIGHT arrows to switch between tabs. The active tab is highlighted.

Tab Icon	Tab Name	Contains
📷 **Camera icon**	Shooting Menu	All settings affecting how still photos are captured. Organized into 4 pages (sub-pages). The most frequently visited menu.
🎬 **Movie icon**	Video Menu	All settings specific to video recording — resolution, audio, stabilization, picture profiles.
▶ **Play icon**	Playback Menu	Settings for reviewing, editing, organizing, and printing your photos.

⚙ **Gear icon**	Custom Menu	Advanced customization of buttons, dials, autofocus behavior, display, and more. Organized into sub-sections A through J.
🔧 **Wrench icon**	Setup Menu	Camera-level configuration — date/time, language, Wi-Fi, card formatting, firmware, and factory reset.

Pages Within the Shooting Menu

The Shooting Menu is long enough that it is split across multiple pages, labeled 1 through 4 (or shown as a row of dots at the top of the screen). Scroll down past the last item on one page to move to the next page automatically.

Submenus

Many settings open into a submenu when you press OK or RIGHT. For example, pressing OK on "White Balance" opens a screen showing all WB options. Pressing OK on "Custom Menu" opens the A-through-J sub-section list. Navigate these the same way — UP/DOWN to scroll, OK or RIGHT to enter, MENU or LEFT to go back.

6.3 Shooting Menu (Camera Icon) — Every Setting Explained

SHOOTING MENU

Press MENU → select the Camera icon tab (first tab on the left)

Shooting Menu — Page 1

Setting Name	Default	Options	What It Does — Plain English Explanation
Image Quality	LF (Large Fine)	RAW / LF / LN / MF / MN / SF / SN / RAW+LF / RAW+LN / RAW+SF	Sets the file format and JPEG compression for saved photos. RAW saves the full unprocessed sensor data for editing later. LF = Large JPEG with Fine (low) compression — the highest quality JPEG. LN = Large JPEG with Normal compression (slightly smaller file). M and S sizes reduce pixel count. RAW+JPEG saves both simultaneously. For most users, RAW+LN is the best all-round choice.

RAW Settings	12-bit lossless	12-bit lossless / 12-bit lossy / Uncompressed	Determines the bit depth and compression of RAW files. 12-bit lossless gives the highest quality with moderate file size. 12-bit lossy is smaller but loses a tiny amount of colour detail. Uncompressed is the largest file. Unless you are a professional with specific workflow needs, keep this at 12-bit lossless.
Image Aspect	4:3	4:3 / 3:2 / 16:9 / 6:6 (1:1) / 3:4	Sets the proportional shape (aspect ratio) of the image frame. 4:3 is the native MFT sensor ratio — uses the full sensor. 3:2 matches 35mm film and is common for prints. 16:9 is widescreen. 1:1 is square for social media. 3:4 is a tall portrait format. Note: in RAW, the full 4:3 sensor data is always saved regardless of this setting — only the JPEG preview is cropped.
Digital Teleconverter	Off	Off / 1.4x / 2.0x	Digitally crops the center of the sensor to simulate a longer focal length. 1.4x makes a 100mm lens behave like 140mm; 2.0x like 200mm. This comes at the cost of reduced resolution because pixels are discarded. Only use this if you cannot get close enough physically and are willing to accept the lower resolution.
High Resolution Shot	Off	Off / Handheld / Tripod	Uses IBIS to shift the sensor by sub-pixel amounts and combines multiple exposures into a single 50-megapixel (or larger) image. Tripod mode provides the highest quality. Handheld mode works without a tripod but requires very still subjects. Not usable with moving subjects.
Drive / Self-Timer	Single	Single / SL / SH / Anti-shock / Silent / Timer	Sets the drive mode — identical to pressing the Drive button on top. See Part 5.8 for full descriptions of each mode.

		2s / Timer 12s / Custom / HDR / Bracketing / Pro Cap L / Pro Cap H	
Image Stabilization	IS1	IS1 / IS2 / IS3 / Off	Controls the 5-axis in-body image stabilization. IS1 stabilizes all directions (best for handheld stills). IS2 stabilizes up-down only (for panning shots — keeps horizontal freedom). IS3 stabilizes left-right only (for vertical panning). Off disables IBIS entirely (for use on motorized tripod heads or when using an IBIS-equipped lens alone).

Shooting Menu — Page 2

Setting Name	Default	Options	What It Does — Plain English Explanation
ISO Sensitivity	200	Low / 200 / 400 / 800 / 1600 / 3200 / 6400 / 12800 / 25600 / Hi-1 to Hi-5	Sets the base ISO. Lower = cleaner image, requires more light. Higher = brighter in dark conditions but more grain (noise). Hi-1 through Hi-5 are extreme extended ISOs beyond the native range and produce significant noise — use only when absolutely necessary.
ISO Auto (Low Limit)	200	Low / 200 / 400 / 800	When Auto ISO is active, this sets the lowest ISO the camera will choose. Keeping the minimum at 200 ensures the cleanest possible starting point. Set to Low if you want even cleaner results (though Low ISO can cause slightly more highlight clipping).
ISO Auto (High Limit)	3200	400 / 800 / 1600 / 3200 / 6400 / 12800 / 25600	When Auto ISO is active, this caps the highest ISO the camera will use. Set higher for dark environments where you accept more noise. Set lower (e.g. 1600) if noise is unacceptable in your work. For most

			situations, 3200 or 6400 is a good maximum.
ISO Auto (Min Shutter)	Auto	Auto / 1/8 – 1/2000	When Auto ISO is active, this sets the minimum shutter speed before the camera begins raising ISO. Auto lets the camera decide based on focal length. Setting a specific value (e.g. 1/250) ensures the camera raises ISO before allowing the shutter to go slower than that value — useful for guaranteeing motion-free shots.
Noise Filter	Low	Off / Low / Standard / High	Applies noise reduction processing to JPEG images (not RAW). Off does no processing — preserves detail but leaves noise visible. Low applies minimal smoothing. Standard is the balanced default. High aggressively smooths noise but can make images look waxy or lose fine texture detail. RAW shooters should leave this Off.
Noise Reduction (Long Exposure)	On	On / Off	When On, after a long exposure (typically 1 second or longer) the camera takes a second identical-length exposure with the shutter closed (a dark frame), then subtracts the heat-generated noise from your photo. This doubles the time per shot but dramatically cleans up long-exposure images. Turn Off if speed matters more than quality.
Shading Compensation	On	On / Off	Corrects corner darkening (vignetting) that occurs with some lenses, especially at wide apertures. Applied to JPEG files. RAW files contain the lens correction profile for manual application in editing software. Keep On for most situations.
Distortion Compensation	On	On / Off	Corrects barrel or pincushion lens distortion on JPEG files. Most zoom lenses have some distortion, especially at wide

			angles. Keep On for cleaner JPEGs. RAW files store the raw sensor data without correction applied — your editing software applies the lens profile.
Chromatic Aberration Compensation	On	On / Off	Removes colour fringing (usually purple or green edges) that occurs at high-contrast boundaries with some lenses. Applied to JPEG. Effective and worth keeping On.
Pixel Count (Diffraction Compensation)	Off	On / Off	Attempts to restore fine detail lost when shooting at very narrow apertures (f/11 and above), where diffraction reduces sharpness. Can add apparent sharpness to narrow-aperture JPEGs. Most effective when printing large. Leave Off unless you frequently shoot at f/11–f/22.

Shooting Menu — Page 3

Setting Name	Default	Options	What It Does — Plain English Explanation
Face Priority	Off	Off / On / Face+Eye (Right) / Face+Eye (Left) / Face+Eye (Auto)	Enables automatic detection of human faces and eyes. When On, the camera automatically places an AF frame on a detected face. Face+Eye modes prioritize locking onto a specific eye (or whichever eye is more prominent). Invaluable for portrait photography. When no face is detected, the camera reverts to the standard AF area mode.
White Balance	AWB	AWB / AWB Warm / Daylight / Shade / Overcast / Tungsten / Fluorescent (various types) / Flash / Underwater /	Sets the colour temperature correction. AWB is intelligent and works well in most conditions. Daylight (sun icon) is calibrated for direct sunlight (~5500K). Shade is warmer (~7500K) to compensate for cool shade light. Tungsten (~3000K) prevents orange casts under incandescent bulbs. Fluorescent options handle various tube types. CWB lets you set a custom white balance from a

		CWB (Custom) / K (Kelvin)	white/grey target. K lets you enter a precise Kelvin value.
WB Compensation	0,0	Amber-Blue ±7 / Green-Magenta ±7	Fine-tunes white balance along two colour axes. Move toward A (amber) to warm the image. Move toward B (blue) to cool it. Move toward G (green) or M (magenta) to correct colour casts. Useful for subtle adjustments when the preset WBs are close but not perfect.
Picture Mode	Natural	Natural / Vivid / Muted / Portrait / Monotone / ePortrait / Custom 1-4	Sets the colour and tone processing applied to JPEG images. Natural gives realistic, true-to-life colours. Vivid boosts saturation and contrast for punchy colours. Muted reduces saturation for a flat, neutral look suitable for post-processing. Portrait emphasises skin tones and softens contrast. Monotone removes colour. ePortrait applies portrait-optimizing processing including smoothing. RAW files are unaffected — select the profile in your RAW editor.
Picture Mode Settings	Various	Contrast / Sharpness / Saturation / Gradation / Colour filter (Mono)	Within each Picture Mode you can fine-tune contrast (−2 to +2), sharpness, saturation, and gradation (highlight/shadow curve). For Monotone, a colour filter option simulates film colour filters. Access by entering Picture Mode and pressing RIGHT on the chosen mode.
Gradation	Normal	Normal / Low Key / High Key / Auto	Controls the overall tonal curve of JPEG images. Normal is a standard S-curve. Low Key darkens shadows and mid-tones — suitable for moody, dramatic images. High Key brightens highlights and mid-tones — suitable for soft, airy images. Auto adapts to scene brightness.
Color Space	sRGB	sRGB / Adobe RGB	Determines the range of colours recorded in JPEG files. sRGB is the standard for screens, web, and consumer printing.

			Adobe RGB has a wider colour gamut — suited for professional printing workflows where the printer and editing software support it. RAW files contain full colour data regardless of this setting.
AF Mode	S-AF	S-AF / C-AF / MF / S-AF+MF / C-AF+TR	Sets the autofocus mode — same as the AF/MF lever but adds further options. S-AF (Single) focuses once when you half-press the shutter and holds until you release. C-AF (Continuous) constantly tracks and re-focuses on moving subjects. MF is full manual focus. S-AF+MF focuses automatically first, then allows manual adjustment. C-AF+TR adds subject tracking to continuous AF.
AF Area Mode	Single (small)	Single (small) / Single (large) / 9-zone / 25-zone / All (auto) / Custom zone	Determines the size and pattern of the autofocus target area. Single small is a precise single point. Single large covers a wider area. 9-zone and 25-zone use multi-point groups. All allows the camera to choose the focus point automatically — most hands-off. Custom zone lets you define a specific region of the frame as the AF area.

Shooting Menu — Page 4

Setting Name	Default	Options	What It Does — Plain English Explanation
Metering Mode	ESP	ESP (Evaluative) / Centre-Weighted / Spot / Highlight-Weighted	Determines how the camera measures light to calculate exposure. ESP (Electro-Selective Pattern) divides the scene into zones and weights them intelligently — best for most situations. Centre-Weighted averages the whole scene but gives more weight to the center. Spot measures a tiny circle at the AF point — precise metering of your exact subject. Highlight-Weighted meters to preserve the brightest

			highlights, ideal for concerts and stage lighting where clipping is unacceptable.
Exposure Compensation	0.0 EV	−5.0 to +5.0 EV in 1/3 or 1/2 stop steps	Intentionally brightens (+) or darkens (−) the exposure relative to the camera's meter reading. More convenient to set via the rear dial or AEL button, but also settable here. A setting here is persistent across power cycles until you reset it.
AE BKT (AE Bracketing)	Off / 3F 1.0EV	0.3 / 0.7 / 1.0 / 1.3 / 2.0 EV steps; 3, 5, or 7 frames	Configures automatic exposure bracketing. When active in Drive mode, the camera shoots a burst of frames at different exposures (e.g. -1EV, 0, +1EV). Used for HDR compositing or to ensure at least one correctly exposed shot in difficult lighting. Set the step size (how far apart the exposures are) and the number of frames here.
Flash Compensation	0.0 EV	−3.0 to +3.0 EV in 1/3 steps	Makes the flash fire more (+) or less (−) brightly than its auto calculation. Useful when the flash is too harsh and creates flat, unnatural results on faces (try −0.7 or −1.0) or when the flash is too weak to adequately illuminate a dark background (try +0.7 or +1.0).
Flash Mode	Auto	Auto / Red-Eye / Fill-In / Fill-In (Red-Eye) / Slow / Slow (Red-Eye) / Off	Sets the behaviour of the built-in flash — same as the SCP flash tile. See Part 5.9 for a full description of each mode.
Slow Limit (Flash Sync Speed)	1/60	1/30 / 1/60 / 1/100 / 1/125 / 1/180	In slow sync flash mode, this sets the slowest shutter speed the camera will use with flash. Lower values let in more ambient light for a natural background but risk camera shake. 1/60 is a reasonable balance for most indoor flash shooting without a tripod.

Anti-Flicker Shooting	Off	Off / On / Auto	Detects the flickering frequency of artificial lights (fluorescent or LED) and synchronizes the shutter release to the moment when the light is at its brightest peak. Prevents inconsistent exposure across frames in burst shooting under artificial light. Particularly useful for sports shot in arenas. Slightly reduces burst frame rate.
Trap Focus	Off	Off / On	When On, the camera fires the shutter automatically the moment a subject enters the focused distance — even without pressing the shutter button fully. Set your focus point manually, then wait. When the subject steps into that zone of focus, the camera fires. Useful for wildlife photography at a fixed point such as a bird feeder.
Live Bulb / Live Time	Off	Off / Live Bulb / Live Time	Activates a real-time preview mode for long exposures. Live Bulb shows the accumulating exposure on the LCD while the shutter is held open (updates every few seconds). Live Time opens the shutter on the first press and closes on the second — the LCD still updates progressively. Invaluable for star trail, light painting, and fireworks photography.
Live Composite	Off	Off / On	A unique OM SYSTEM feature. Takes a series of long exposures and composites them in real time, only adding pixels that are brighter than the previous frame. Perfect for light trails, lightning, and star trails — the background exposure stays constant while lights accumulate. Watch the composite build on the LCD in real time.

TIP: Shooting Menu quick access

You do not need to go through the full menu for most Shooting Menu settings. ISO, White Balance, Picture Mode, Flash Mode, Drive Mode, AF Mode, and Exposure Compensation are all accessible directly from the Super Control Panel (press OK from live view). Only use the Shooting Menu for settings not shown in the SCP.

6.4 Video Menu — Every Setting Explained

VIDEO MENU

Press MENU → select the Movie camera icon tab (second from left)

Setting Name	Default	Options	What It Does — Plain English Explanation
Movie Quality	4K 30p / FHD 30p	C4K 30p / C4K 24p / 4K 30p / 4K 24p / 4K 25p / FHD 60p / FHD 50p / FHD 30p / FHD 25p / FHD 24p / HD 30p	Sets the video resolution and frame rate. C4K is cinema 4K (4096x2160). 4K is standard 4K (3840x2160). FHD is Full HD (1920x1080). Higher resolution = sharper video but larger files. Higher frame rate = smoother motion AND the ability to slow down footage in post (FHD 60p can be slowed to 2x slow motion when delivered at 30p).
Movie Bit Rate	IPB (Normal)	ALL-I (High) / IPB (Normal) / IPB (Low)	Sets the compression method for video. ALL-I compresses each frame independently — highest quality, largest file, easiest to edit. IPB Normal compresses groups of frames together — good balance of quality and file size. IPB Low uses the most compression — smallest files but lowest quality. Use ALL-I for professional video work; IPB Normal for most uses.
Movie Sound	Stereo	Stereo / Mono / Off	Sets the microphone input mode. Stereo records left and right channels separately for spatial audio. Mono mixes both channels together. Off disables audio recording (video only). If using an

			external microphone, the camera may automatically detect it and switch to mono or stereo based on the mic type.
Movie Sound Level	Manual or Auto	Auto / Manual (−40 to 0 dB)	Controls the microphone input gain. Auto adjusts levels automatically — convenient but can cause pumping (level changes) in variable-volume environments. Manual lets you set a precise input level. Monitor with headphones to ensure the level is high enough to capture clear audio but low enough to avoid clipping (shown as red on the audio meters).
Movie Recording Level (L/R)	Center	Individual sliders for Left and Right channels	Fine-tunes the recording level of the left and right audio channels independently. Useful when using an external microphone where one channel is too loud or too quiet.
Wind Noise Filter	Off	Off / Low / Standard / High	Applies a low-cut (high-pass) filter to reduce rumbling wind noise picked up by the microphone. High cuts the most wind noise but also removes some low-frequency warmth from speech. Low is subtle. Keep Off if there is no wind; switch to Standard or High when outdoors in a breeze.
Movie IS	M-IS 1	M-IS 1 / M-IS 2 / Off	Controls image stabilization for video. M-IS 1 uses both sensor-based 5-axis IBIS and electronic stabilization for maximum steadiness. M-IS 2 uses IBIS only. Off disables stabilization. M-IS 1 provides the smoothest handheld video but applies a slight crop to the frame. M-IS 2 preserves the full frame with moderate stabilization. Use M-IS 1 for walking shots; M-IS 2 for mostly static handheld.

Movie C-AF Sensitivity	0 (Standard)	−2 (Slow) to +2 (Fast)	When recording video with C-AF, this sets how quickly the camera re-focuses when a subject moves. Negative values (slow) produce smooth, gradual focus pulls — more cinematic. Positive values (fast) track subjects aggressively but can cause abrupt focus hunting. For interview video, use −1 or −2 for smooth focus. For sports/action video, use 0 or +1.
Movie MF Assist	Off	Off / On	When On and using manual focus during video, pressing the OK button or a designated Fn button temporarily zooms the live view for precise manual focus adjustment, then automatically zooms back out after a few seconds without interrupting recording.
Face Priority (Movie)	Off	Off / On / Face+Eye (R/L/Auto)	Same as the still photo face detection setting but applied during video recording. When On, the camera continuously tracks faces and eyes throughout the recording, keeping subjects in sharp focus even when they move.
Movie White Balance	AWB	Same options as still photo WB	Sets white balance for video independently of the still photo WB setting. You can have AWB for stills and a fixed Daylight WB for video, for example. Fixed WB is strongly recommended for video because AWB can visibly shift mid-clip if the lighting changes, which is distracting in the final footage.
Movie Noise Reduction	Standard	Off / Low / Standard / High	Applies noise reduction to video footage. Higher settings reduce grain in low-light video but can create smooth, waxy-looking skin and reduce fine detail. Standard is appropriate for most uses.

			Off preserves maximum detail for post-processing.
Picture Mode (Movie)	Natural	Same as still photo Picture Mode options	Applies a colour and contrast profile to video. Natural and Muted are popular for video because they provide flat, neutral-looking footage that is easier to colour grade in post. Vivid creates punchy, saturated video with less flexibility for grading. OM-Log (see below) is for maximum dynamic range.
OM-Log / Flat Profile	Off	Off / OM-Log400	OM-Log400 is a flat, logarithmic picture profile that preserves maximum highlight and shadow detail in video — roughly 12+ stops of dynamic range. The footage looks flat and washed out straight from the camera but contains far more information for colour grading in software like DaVinci Resolve or Adobe Premiere. Only use OM-Log if you are comfortable with colour grading workflow.
Headphone Volume	10	0 – 20	Controls the volume output through the 3.5mm headphone jack on the side of the camera during video recording. Increase if the monitored audio is too quiet; decrease if it is painful. Does not affect the recorded audio level.
Time Code	Off	Off / On (various formats)	Embeds SMPTE time code into the video file metadata. Used in professional multi-camera production workflows where clips from multiple cameras need to be synchronised in an editing suite. Not needed for solo/consumer video work.
Movie Recording Limit	29:59	29:59 / Unlimited (where permitted)	Sets the maximum continuous recording duration. 29:59 minutes is the standard limit. Some cameras support unlimited recording in specific modes. Longer

recordings are automatically split into separate files.

TIP: Fix your white balance for video

Unlike still photos, a white balance shift mid-video clip is extremely noticeable and unprofessional. Always set a manual white balance (Daylight, Shade, or a Kelvin value) when recording video — never use AWB unless you intentionally want the white balance to shift as light changes.

6.5 Playback Menu — Every Setting Explained

▶ PLAYBACK MENU

Press MENU → select the triangle/play icon tab (third from left)

Setting Name	Default	Options	What It Does — Plain English Explanation
Slideshow	3 sec interval	Interval: 2s / 3s / 5s / 10s. BGM: Off / On. Repeat: Off / On	Plays through all photos on the SD card as a slideshow on the camera LCD. Set the display interval, background music (if a sound file is on the card), and whether the slideshow loops. Press OK or the shutter button to stop the slideshow.
Edit (RAW Development)	—	RAW + custom settings	Develop a RAW file into a JPEG image inside the camera without a computer. Select a RAW file in playback, choose this option, and the camera presents sliders for exposure, white balance, sharpness, noise reduction, colour mode, and more. Press OK when done to save a new JPEG alongside the original RAW. The RAW file is preserved unchanged. Useful for sharing a quick JPEG version of a RAW file without a computer.
Resize	—	Original size / 10MP / 8MP / 5MP / 3MP / 1.5MP	Saves a smaller JPEG copy of a photo. The original file is unchanged. Useful for creating a smaller version suitable for email or messaging. Select the photo in

			playback, enter this menu, choose the target size, and a new smaller file is saved.
Cropping	—	Select area on screen	Saves a cropped portion of a photo as a new JPEG file. Display the photo in playback, enter Cropping, use the touch screen or arrow pad to select the area to keep, and press OK to save the cropped version. The original file is unchanged.
RAW Retouch	—	Shadow adjustment / Noise reduction / Distortion / Various	Applies specific corrections to a saved RAW file and saves the result as a JPEG. Offers targeted adjustments such as shadow lifting, removing chromatic aberration, applying distortion correction, or changing white balance — all in-camera without software.
Art Filter Bracketing	—	Select filter combination	Applies multiple Art Filters to a single JPEG image and saves each filtered version as a separate file. Useful for quickly seeing how a photo looks in different artistic styles.
Protect	Off	Off / On (lock icon)	Marks selected photos with a protection lock. Protected photos cannot be deleted using the Delete button. They CAN still be erased by a card format. Use to prevent accidentally deleting your best shots while culling in the field. Select a photo, enter this menu, and toggle protection on or off.
Rotate	—	0° / 90° CW / 90° CCW / 180°	Rotates the display orientation of a saved photo and saves the new orientation in the file's metadata. The actual pixel data is not rotated — only the display instruction. Most editing software honours this metadata automatically.
Erase (Delete Multiple)	—	Select images / All images	Deletes multiple photos in one operation. Select this option, tick the photos you want to delete, then confirm. Faster than

			deleting one by one when culling a large number of shots.
Print Order (DPOF)	—	Select photos, number of prints	Creates a Digital Print Order Format instruction embedded in the SD card. When you take the card to a photo printing kiosk or compatible printer, it reads the DPOF order and automatically prints the selected photos at the specified quantities.
Favorites	—	Tag / Remove tag	Marks selected photos as favorites with a small star icon. Favorites can be filtered for display — useful for separating your best shots from the rest while reviewing in the field. Does not affect the file — just adds metadata.
Connection to Smartphone (Share)	—	Select and transfer	Transfers selected photos from the camera to the connected OM SYSTEM app on your smartphone via Wi-Fi. Select the photos you want to share, enter this option, and the transfer begins. The camera must first be connected to the app via Bluetooth (covered in Part 2.4).
Edit Filename	—	Custom prefix (up to 3 characters)	Allows you to change the letter prefix used in new filenames (the letters before the 4-digit number, e.g. changing P to IMG or OMD). Custom prefixes can help identify which camera shot which files when merging images from multiple cameras.
Pixel Mapping	—	Start / Cancel	Runs a camera self-test to identify and map out any stuck pixels (individual sensor pixels that always output the wrong value). Takes about 3 seconds. Run this if you see consistent, fixed bright or dark dots in the same location in all your photos.

6.6 Custom Menu (Gear Icon) — Every Submenu Explained

⚙ CUSTOM MENU

Press MENU → select the Gear icon tab (fourth from left) → enter sub-sections A through J

The Custom Menu is the most powerful part of the OM-3's menu system. It contains advanced settings for every aspect of the camera's behaviour. It is organised into ten sub-sections labeled A through J. Each sub-section groups related settings together.

To reach any Custom Menu setting: Press MENU → navigate to the Gear icon tab → press DOWN to enter the list → scroll to the sub-section letter → press OK or RIGHT to enter it → scroll to the specific setting.

Custom Menu A — Autofocus and Manual Focus Settings

Setting Name	Default	Options	What It Does — Plain English Explanation
AF Mode	S-AF	S-AF / C-AF / MF / S-AF+MF / C-AF+TR	Same as the Shooting Menu AF Mode setting — sets the primary focus behaviour. See Shooting Menu Page 3 for full descriptions.
AEL/AFL Mode	Mode 1	Mode 1 / Mode 2 / Mode 3 / Mode 4	Determines the behaviour of the AEL/AFL button. Mode 1: half-shutter focuses in S-AF, AEL button locks exposure. Mode 2: half-shutter meters only (no AF), AEL button focuses. Mode 3: half-shutter is inactive for AF, AEL button focuses and locks. Mode 4: (C-AF) AEL locks focus while held, shutter focuses continuously. Choose Mode 3 to set up back-button focus.
Full-Time AF (C-AF)	Off	Off / On	When On in C-AF mode, the camera continuously focuses even before you half-press the shutter. Reduces shutter lag for moving subjects because the lens is always tracking. Increases battery drain. When Off, C-AF only activates when you half-press.
AF Targeting Pod	Off	Off / On	Enables precise AF point selection by touching the LCD screen while looking through the EVF. When On, touching the

			LCD moves the AF point to the touched area while your eye stays at the viewfinder. A touch-sensitive strip for precise control without moving the camera.
Pre-AF	On	Off / On	When On, the camera runs a continuous low-power AF scan even before you half-press the shutter. This further reduces shutter lag by partially pre-focusing before you shoot. Slightly increases battery consumption. Leave On for most situations.
AF Illuminator	On	Off / On	Controls whether the AF Assist Lamp on the front of the camera (the small orange light) fires to illuminate dark scenes and help the autofocus system find contrast. Turn Off if the lamp disturbs your subject (e.g. wildlife, concerts, sleeping infants).
Shutter AF	On	Off / On	Determines whether half-pressing the shutter button activates autofocus. On is the default — half-press focuses. Off disables half-press focusing, so the shutter button only fires the shutter. Combined with AEL/AFL Mode 3, this enables full back-button focus (all focusing done via the AEL button only).
AF Area Selection Mode	Single (small)	Single (small) / Single (large) / 9-zone / 25-zone / All / Custom zone	Same as Shooting Menu AF Area Mode — sets the AF target pattern. Accessible here for deeper configuration alongside related AF settings.
Home Position (AF area)	Center	Any saved position	Saves a custom AF point position as the Home position. Press the OK button during shooting to instantly return the AF point to this saved position (e.g. always snap back to center frame).

Focus Ring Direction	Normal	Normal / Reverse	Reverses the direction of the focus ring rotation on Olympus MFT lenses for manual focus. Some photographers prefer clockwise rotation to focus closer (matching DSLR conventions); others prefer counter-clockwise. Set to your preference.
Focus Peaking	Off	Off / On (White / Red / Yellow)	Enables focus peaking — a highlight overlay that colours the edges of in-focus areas during manual focus. The colour of the peaking highlight can be set to white, red, or yellow based on which is most visible against your subject and background.
MF Magnify (Magnification)	7x	3x / 5x / 7x / 10x / 14x	Sets the zoom level when the magnified view is activated (for checking manual focus sharpness). 7x or 10x is sufficient for most work. 14x is extreme — useful for micro-photography or astrophotography.
C-AF Tracking Sensitivity	0	−2 (sticky) to +2 (loose)	Sets how aggressively C-AF tracks and re-acquires subjects. At −2, the camera locks onto the initial subject and holds it even if something briefly passes in front. At +2, the camera immediately transfers focus to new subjects. Use −1 or −2 for birds in flight where you want to keep focus on the bird even when branches briefly occlude it; use 0 for sports where the main subject can change.
Focus Limiter (Start Distance)	0.2m	Various distances per lens	Restricts the range within which the lens hunts for focus during AF. Setting a minimum focus distance prevents the lens from searching at close distances when you are shooting distant subjects (and vice versa). Reduces hunting time and speeds up AF lock. Not all lenses support this via the menu.

Custom Menu B — Button and Dial Settings

Setting Name	Default	Options	What It Does — Plain English Explanation
Button Function (Fn1-Fn3, AEL, etc.)	Various defaults	60+ assignable functions per button	Reassigns any function button or the AEL button to a different action. See Part 5.10 for the complete list of assignable functions and the step-by-step reassignment procedure.
Dial Function	Various	P: EC+Av / S: Tv+Av / M: Av+Tv / etc.	Determines what each dial (front and rear) controls in each shooting mode. The default assignments are intuitive for most users, but you can swap them if you prefer the aperture on the rear dial and shutter speed on the front dial, for example.
Lever Function (Fn Lever)	Mode 1	Mode 1 (standard) / Mode 2 (alternative assignments)	Some OM SYSTEM cameras have a function lever that switches between two complete sets of button assignments. Selecting Mode 2 activates an entirely different set of custom button functions — useful for rapidly switching from one shooting configuration to another.
Movie Record Button	Movie REC	Movie Record / Assignable	Allows the red movie button to be reassigned to a non-video function. If you rarely shoot video, you might assign it to High Resolution Mode, Live Composite, or another feature. Reassigning it removes the direct video record shortcut.
Half-Press Release Priority	AF	AF / Release	Determines what happens when you half-press and the camera has not yet confirmed focus. AF priority means the shutter will not fire until focus is confirmed. Release priority fires the shutter immediately regardless of focus status. AF priority is safer for most shooting. Release priority is used when capturing a decisive moment matters more than perfect sharpness.

Release Timing Priority	Normal	Normal / Anti-Shock	Adds a slight delay between the electronic shutter signal and the mechanical shutter opening to eliminate any vibration from shutter actuation. Equivalent to Anti-Shock drive mode but as a persistent setting rather than a drive mode selection.
Dial Direction	Normal	Normal / Reverse	Reverses the rotation direction of the front or rear dial for increasing/decreasing values. Some photographers find it more intuitive to turn the dial one way vs. the other. Adjust to your preference.
IS Lock (IS Lever)	Off	Off / On	When an IS Lock button or lever is available (on certain lenses), this setting activates it. When IS Lock is On, the stabilization system holds still (does not compensate for intentional panning) — useful when you want to completely freeze the frame before a precision shot on a tripod.

Custom Menu C — Release and Drive Settings

Setting Name	Default	Options	What It Does — Plain English Explanation
Sequential Low Frame Rate	5 fps	1 / 2 / 3 / 4 / 5 fps	Sets the frame rate for Sequential Low (SL) burst mode. Lower rates (1-2 fps) are useful when you want multiple shots of a slower-moving subject without filling the card too fast. 5fps is the maximum for SL.
Sequential High Frame Rate	15 fps	10 / 15 / 20 / 30 fps (varies by shutter mode)	Sets the frame rate for Sequential High (SH) burst mode. Higher frame rates with the electronic shutter can reach 20-30 fps. 15fps with mechanical shutter is sufficient for most sports. Higher rates fill the buffer and SD card very quickly.
Anti-Shock Delay	0.125s	0 / 0.125 / 0.25 / 0.5 / 1 / 2 / 4	Sets the delay between pressing the shutter and the shutter actually opening

		/ 8 / 16 / 30.5 sec	in Anti-Shock mode. A longer delay allows more vibration to settle before the exposure begins. For macro and telephoto work, 0.25-0.5 seconds is usually sufficient. For extreme telephoto or long exposures, 1-2 seconds is recommended.
Pro Capture (Pre-Capture frames)	14 frames	4 / 8 / 14 / 20 / 25 / 35 frames (varies)	Sets how many pre-capture frames are buffered before you fully press the shutter in Pro Capture mode. More frames means you capture more action that occurred before you pressed — but the buffer fills faster and requires a fast SD card.
Exposure Smoothing	Off	Off / On	When On, gradually transitions between exposure settings during burst shooting to produce a smoother sequence of images when the light changes between frames. Useful for sports under artificial lighting where exposure can jump between frames.
BULB Exposure Timer	Off	Off / 1 – 900 sec	In Bulb mode, when set to a specific time, the camera automatically closes the shutter after the specified number of seconds without you needing to release the shutter button. Useful for unattended long exposures at night.
Self-Timer Custom	12s / 1 shot	Delay 1-30s / Shots 1-10	Configures the Custom Self-Timer drive mode. Set the delay before the first shot and the number of shots to take. Useful for group photos where you need time to run into frame, and then want multiple shots for a better result.

Custom Menu D — Display and Sound Settings

Setting Name	Default	Options	What It Does — Plain English Explanation

LCD Brightness	0 (Normal)	−7 to +7	Adjusts the brightness of the rear LCD screen. Increase in bright sunlight for better visibility. Decrease indoors or at night to save battery and preserve your night vision. 0 is calibrated for accurate colour representation. Deviating from 0 may make colours appear inaccurate on screen even if the recorded file is correct.
EVF Brightness	0 (Auto)	Auto / −7 to +7	Adjusts the brightness of the Electronic Viewfinder. Auto adjusts to ambient light. Manual settings override this. Keep at 0 or Auto for accurate representation.
LCD Colour Temperature	0	−7 (cool) to +7 (warm)	Shifts the colour temperature of the LCD display toward warmer (amber) or cooler (blue) tones. This affects how your photos look on screen but does NOT affect the recorded files. Adjust if the LCD colour appears obviously wrong compared to your calibrated monitor.
Live View Boost	Off	Off / On	When On, the camera brightens the live view display in very dark conditions to make composition easier, even if the resulting photo will be correctly exposed at a lower brightness. Useful when composing in dimly lit environments. The brighter display is a preview aid only — the actual exposure is unaffected.
Info Settings (Live View)	Various	Select which overlays appear in each INFO mode	Customizes which information overlays appear in each of the five INFO display modes (accessible by pressing the INFO button). You can choose whether the histogram, level gauge, exposure scale, shooting data, and other elements appear in each mode. See Part 3.5 for a description of each INFO mode.
Grid Display	Off	Off / Grid 1 (3×3) / Grid 2 (6×4) / Grid 3	Overlays a grid on the live view for composition guidance. Grid 1 (3×3) is the classic rule-of-thirds grid. Grid 2 is a finer

		(custom diagonal) / Grid 4 (square)	grid for precision alignment. Grid 3 adds diagonal lines for triangular composition. Grid 4 adds a centered square for symmetrical composition.
Highlight & Shadow Alert	Off	Off / On (highlights) / On (shadows) / On (both)	Enables a flashing overlay on the LCD during playback that highlights overexposed (blown) areas in red and underexposed (crushed) areas in blue. Useful for quickly identifying exposure problems. Does not affect the recorded file.
Histogram Display	Off	Off / Live / Blinking	Controls how the histogram appears. Live shows it constantly in a corner of the viewfinder. Blinking only shows it when highlights are clipping. Combine with the INFO button to toggle it on demand. See Part 3.5 for histogram interpretation.
Sleep Mode	1 min	1 / 3 / 5 / 10 min / Off	Sets the time after which the camera enters sleep mode (screens off, processing halted) to conserve battery. Half-pressing the shutter wakes the camera instantly. Set longer if you find the camera sleeping too frequently during slow-paced shoots. Set shorter to extend battery life during long shooting days.
Power Off Delay (EVF)	3 sec	1 / 3 / 5 / 10 sec	After the eye sensor detects that your eye has left the EVF, this delay controls how long the EVF stays on before switching off. A short delay (1 sec) conserves battery. A longer delay (5-10 sec) prevents the EVF from turning off if you briefly lower the camera.
Beep Settings	Beep On / Focus Beep On	Off / Quiet / Loud (separately for focus confirm and shutter)	Controls the camera's audible beeps. Focus confirm beep sounds when S-AF locks focus. Shutter sound plays when the electronic shutter fires (since the electronic shutter itself is silent). Disable beeps for quiet environments such as

			concerts, ceremonies, or wildlife photography.
Volume Settings	10	0 – 20 (playback volume)	Sets the speaker volume for audio playback through the built-in speaker during video review.

Custom Menu E — Exposure and ISO Settings

Setting Name	Default	Options	What It Does — Plain English Explanation
Exposure Step	1/3 EV	1/3 EV / 1/2 EV	Sets the increments for aperture, shutter speed, and ISO adjustments. 1/3 EV gives finer control. 1/2 EV makes each dial click a larger jump — some photographers prefer fewer steps. Most professional users keep this at 1/3 EV for maximum precision.
EV Compensation Step	1/3 EV	1/3 EV / 1/2 EV	Sets the step size for Exposure Compensation adjustments — same logic as above but specifically for the EC scale.
ISO Auto (Step)	1 EV	1/3 EV / 1 EV	Sets how the camera steps through ISO values when Auto ISO is active. 1/3 EV gives smoother ISO transitions (less visible jump in noise). 1 EV is the standard. 1/3 EV can help when recording video where a sudden ISO jump is visible.
Bulb Mode Monitor	30 sec	15 / 30 / 60 / 120 sec	In Bulb mode, sets how often the Live Bulb preview on the LCD updates to show the accumulating exposure. More frequent updates (15 sec) use slightly more battery but let you monitor the exposure more closely. 30 seconds is the practical balance.
Exposure Shift	0.0 EV	-1.0 to +1.0 EV	Permanently offsets the camera's exposure meter by the specified amount. If your OM-3 consistently over- or under-exposes compared to your preference, use this to correct it across all modes.

			Different from EC — Exposure Shift moves the meter's zero point itself, not the EC offset from it.
Metering Timer	8 sec	4 / 8 / 16 / 30 sec / Hold	After you half-press the shutter and release, the exposure reading is held on screen for this duration before resetting. A longer timer gives you more time to recompose after metering. Hold keeps the reading indefinitely until the camera sleeps or you take a shot.
Aperture for Diffraction	f/8	f/5.6 / f/8 / f/11 / f/16 / Off	Works with the Pixel Count / Diffraction Compensation setting. Sets the aperture value at which diffraction compensation processing begins. Below this aperture, no processing is applied. At or above it, the correction is applied to JPEG files. Set to match the aperture where your lens typically begins softening due to diffraction (usually f/11 or f/16 for MFT lenses).

Custom Menu F — Flash Settings

Setting Name	Default	Options	What It Does — Plain English Explanation
Flash Compensation Step	1/3 EV	1/3 EV / 1/2 EV	Sets the adjustment increment for flash exposure compensation — identical to the standard EV step setting but applied to flash output.
RC (Radio-Controlled / Optical Wireless) Flash	Off	Off / RC Mode	Activates the optical wireless flash control system, turning the built-in flash into a commander (controller) that signals external OM SYSTEM RC-compatible flash units positioned off-camera. In RC mode the built-in flash fires a small non-illuminating trigger signal and groups of external flashes respond. Essential for multi-light studio-style setups without

			cables. Multiple flash groups (CH1-3) can be set to different power levels.
RC Channel	1	1 / 2 / 3 / 4	Sets the wireless communication channel between the commander flash (built-in) and remote flash units. All flashes in the system must be on the same channel. Multiple channels allow multiple independent wireless systems to coexist nearby without interfering.
Flash Exposure Meter Coupling	TTL-AUTO	TTL-AUTO / Manual	Sets whether flash exposure is calculated through-the-lens (TTL-AUTO, where the camera meters the flash output and adjusts it automatically) or Manual (you set the flash power level directly as a fraction of full power — e.g. 1/2, 1/4). TTL-AUTO is convenient. Manual is more consistent and predictable in a controlled environment.
Sync Order (2nd Curtain)	1st Curtain	1st Curtain / 2nd Curtain	Determines when during the exposure the flash fires. 1st Curtain fires at the moment the shutter opens — motion blur appears ahead of the subject. 2nd Curtain fires at the moment before the shutter closes — motion blur trails naturally behind the subject, which looks more intuitive and cinematic. For most flash work use 1st Curtain. For creative motion photography use 2nd Curtain.
Flash Slow Limit	1/60	1/30 / 1/60 / 1/100 / 1/125 / 1/180 / Off	Identical to the Shooting Menu slow limit setting — sets the slowest shutter speed usable with flash in automatic modes. Accessible here for convenience alongside other flash settings.
Manuals Flash Level	1/1 (full)	1/1 / 1/2 / 1/4 / 1/8 / 1/16 / 1/32 / 1/64	When Flash Exposure Meter Coupling is set to Manual, sets the flash output as a fraction of full power. 1/1 is maximum output. 1/64 is the minimum — very gentle fill light. Lower outputs reduce

			recycling time and extend flash battery life.

Custom Menu G — Colour and White Balance Settings

Setting Name	Default	Options	What It Does — Plain English Explanation
WB Auto (Warm Keep)	Off	Off / On	When On, Auto White Balance (AWB) in tungsten/incandescent light retains more of the warm amber tone of the light rather than correcting it to neutral white. Produces more natural-looking indoor photos where you want the warmth of candles or incandescent bulbs to show. When Off, AWB aggressively corrects to neutral white.
WB Bracketing	Off	Off / 2F / 3F (in various EV steps)	Saves multiple versions of each photo with different white balance adjustments simultaneously. Each shutter press produces 2 or 3 JPEG files at different WB values — for example, one cool, one neutral, one warm. Useful when you are unsure of the correct WB and want options without reshoot.
Colour Space	sRGB	sRGB / Adobe RGB	Same as the Shooting Menu colour space setting — accessible here for convenience alongside other colour settings. See Shooting Menu Page 3 for explanation.
Picture Mode (Custom 1-4)	Custom	Configure parameters for up to 4 custom modes	Allows you to create up to four fully customized picture modes with your own settings for contrast, sharpness, saturation, gradation, colour filter (mono), and more. Once configured, they appear in the Picture Mode list. Useful for photographers who want a consistent personal look applied to all JPEGs.
Monotone (Colour Filter)	None	None / Yellow / Orange / Red / Green	When using Monotone picture mode, applies a simulated colour filter that affects how different colours in the

			original scene translate to grey tones. A Red filter darkens blue skies and brightens red subjects (classic landscape effect). A Green filter brightens foliage and skin tones.
Gradation (Custom)	Normal	Normal / Low Key / High Key / Auto	Sets the tonal curve applied to JPEGs — identical to the Gradation setting in the Shooting Menu but accessible here alongside other colour and tone settings.

Custom Menu H — Record and Erase Settings

Setting Name	Default	Options	What It Does — Plain English Explanation
RAW + JPEG Separate Folder	Off	Off / On	When On, RAW files and JPEG files are saved to separate sub-folders on the SD card, making them easier to sort when copying to a computer. Folder names are automatically organized. Keep Off unless you specifically need this organization in your workflow.
Create New Folder	—	Create	Creates a new image folder on the SD card. Cameras save files to a folder (e.g. 100OLYMP). You can create a fresh folder to start a new sequence — useful for separating shoots on the same card. The new folder number increments automatically.
File Name Settings	PXXXX	Choose prefix characters	Sets the prefix letters used in image file names (the letters before the 4-digit number). The factory default is usually P or IM depending on firmware. Changing this to something distinctive (like your initials) helps identify your files when mixing images from multiple cameras.
Dualcard Recording Mode	—	(Not applicable — OM-3 has one card slot)	The OM-3 has only one SD card slot. This setting is not present or is greyed out.

erase Confirmation	No first	Yes first / No first	Determines which option (Yes or No) is pre-selected in the delete confirmation dialog. 'No first' is the default safety setting — you must move to Yes before confirming deletion. 'Yes first' makes deletion slightly faster but risks accidental erasure.
Quick Erase (Single Image)	Off	Off / On	When On, pressing the Delete button during single-image playback deletes the photo immediately without showing a confirmation dialog. Speeds up the culling process significantly. Use with care — there is no undo.
RAW Edit Save	Save to card	Save to card / Save to same folder	When editing a RAW file in-camera and saving the result as a JPEG, determines where the new JPEG is saved — at the root of the card or in the same folder as the original RAW. Keep at same folder for tidier file organisation.
Eye-Fi Connected	Disable	Disable / Enable	For use with Eye-Fi wireless SD cards — controls whether the camera communicates with the card's built-in Wi-Fi. Most users will not have an Eye-Fi card and should leave this Disabled.

Custom Menu I — Movie-Specific Settings

Setting Name	Default	Options	What It Does — Plain English Explanation
Movie Effect	On	Off / On	When Off, movie recording uses whatever settings are configured in the Movie Menu independently of still photo settings. When On, certain effects such as Art Filters applied to still photos are also applied to video. Keep On for casual video work; turn Off for professional video where you want full independent control.

Movie Digital IS (Crop)	Off	Off / On	Enables additional electronic image stabilization for video by using a central crop of the sensor (which provides more stabilization margin). When On, a slight crop is applied — the field of view narrows slightly. Combined with M-IS 1, this gives very smooth handheld video.
Movie AF Mode (C-AF specific)	C-AF	C-AF / C-AF+TR / MF	Sets the specific autofocus behaviour used during video recording. C-AF+TR adds subject tracking — the camera identifies and follows a subject even if they leave and re-enter the frame. Useful for active vloggers and documentary situations.
C-AF Movie Lock On	0 (Medium)	−2 (Loose) to +2 (Tight)	Controls how aggressively C-AF during video holds onto a tracked subject versus switching to a new subject if another person or object enters the frame. −2 holds the current subject very firmly. +2 readily switches to new subjects. Use negative values for interviews (stay on the speaker) and positive values for events where the action moves to different people.
Movie Flicker Reduction	Off	Off / Auto	Same as Anti-Flicker for stills, applied to video recording under artificial lighting. When On, the camera detects the AC power cycle frequency (50Hz or 60Hz) of fluorescent or LED lights and synchronizes frame capture to minimize flickering bands in the footage. Essential for indoor shooting under artificial light.
Headphone Volume (Movie)	10	0 – 20	Duplicate of the Video Menu headphone volume setting — accessible here for convenience.
Time-Lapse Movie	Off	Interval / Frames / Start time	Configures the time-lapse movie recording mode. Set the interval between frames (e.g. every 5 seconds),

			the total number of frames to capture, and optionally a start delay. The camera assembles the frames into a movie automatically. Not the same as interval shooting (which saves individual files) — this saves directly as a video file.
Video Control (Stop at end)	Off	Off / On	When On, video recording stops automatically when the SD card is nearly full, preventing a write error. When Off, recording continues until the card is completely full, which can sometimes cause the last few seconds of video to be corrupted.

Custom Menu J — Electronic Viewfinder (EVF) Settings

Setting Name	Default	Options	What It Does — Plain English Explanation
EVF Style	Style 1	Style 1 / Style 2	Switches the EVF display layout. Style 1 overlays shooting information on top of the live image. Style 2 places a band of information below the image area, keeping the image itself cleaner and unobstructed. Choose based on which layout you prefer for viewing.
EVF / Monitor Switch	Auto	Auto / Monitor Only / EVF Only / Auto (LV)	Controls how the camera switches between the LCD screen and the EVF. Auto uses the eye sensor. Monitor Only keeps the LCD permanently on. EVF Only keeps the viewfinder permanently on. Auto (LV) uses the eye sensor but allows manual override with the LV button. See Part 3.3 for full details.
EVF Brightness	Auto	Auto / −7 to +7	Controls the brightness of the EVF display independently of the LCD. Auto adjusts to ambient light via a light sensor near the eyepiece. Manual override allows fine-tuning.

EVF Colour Temperature	0	−7 (cool) to +7 (warm)	Shifts the EVF display colour temperature for personal preference. Does not affect recorded images. Useful if the EVF appears too blue or too orange compared to the actual scene or to your LCD.
Auto Monitor Off (EVF)	3 sec	1 / 3 / 5 / 10 sec	When using the EVF, this sets how long the LCD stays off after your eye leaves the viewfinder before it switches back on. A longer time prevents the LCD from flashing on and off rapidly if your eye briefly moves away.
Diopter Adjustment	Physical dial	N/A — adjusted with the small dial beside the eyepiece	The diopter adjustment for the EVF is done physically using the small ridged wheel to the right of the eyepiece, not through this menu. This entry in the menu is for reference only or may not appear.
EVF High Luminance	Off	Off / On	When On, the EVF runs at its maximum brightness level continuously. Useful in very bright outdoor conditions where the standard auto-brightness level is still insufficient. Uses significantly more battery. Only activate when necessary.
Eye Start AF	Off	Off / On	When On, the camera begins focusing automatically as soon as the eye sensor detects your eye near the viewfinder. Reduces lag between looking through the EVF and having a focused image ready. Slightly increases battery consumption.

TIP: Custom Menu J and battery life

The EVF's Auto Brightness and Eye Start AF features, when active simultaneously, use the eye sensor continuously and can drain the battery faster than you might expect. If battery life is a priority, set EVF to EVF-Only or Monitor-Only mode and disable Eye Start AF when you do not need instantaneous EVF switching.

6.7 Setup Menu (Wrench Icon) — Every Setting Explained

SETUP MENU

Press MENU → select the Wrench icon tab (fifth/last tab on the right)

Setting Name	Default	Options	What It Does — Plain English Explanation
Display Brightness	0 (Normal)	−7 to +7	Adjusts the brightness of the rear LCD screen for easier viewing in different ambient light conditions. Higher values (positive) make the screen brighter for outdoor use. Lower values (negative) reduce brightness for indoor or dark environments to save battery and preserve your night vision. The neutral position (0) is calibrated for colour-accurate display.
EVF Luminance	Auto	Auto / Manual (−7 to +7)	Adjusts the brightness of the electronic viewfinder independently of the LCD. Auto mode adjusts dynamically based on the ambient light sensor near the eyepiece. Use manual override if Auto is too bright or too dim for your preference.
Info Settings	Default set	Select overlays per INFO mode	Determines what information is displayed in each of the five INFO button display modes. You can configure each mode to show or hide the histogram, level gauge, shooting data strip, exposure scale, grid, and other overlays. Customise these to match your workflow.
Live View Boost	Off	Off / Mode 1 / Mode 2	Amplifies the live view image in dark environments so you can compose shots that would otherwise be nearly invisible on screen. Mode 1 is moderate brightening. Mode 2 is maximum amplification. Neither mode affects the actual exposure of the recorded photo.

Sleep Mode	1 min	1 / 3 / 5 / 10 min / Off	Sets the inactivity timer after which the camera enters sleep mode. In sleep mode the screens switch off to conserve battery. Half-press the shutter to wake immediately. Set to longer times if the camera sleeps too frequently. Set to Off if you want the camera always ready but accept faster battery drain.
Power Off Delay (EVF)	3 sec	1 / 3 / 5 / 10 sec	After you lower the camera from your eye, this delay determines how long the EVF waits before turning off. A short delay (1 sec) saves power. A longer delay (10 sec) prevents the EVF from turning off and on if you briefly look away.
Date and Time	Set at first power-on	Year / Month / Day / Hour / Minute / Clock format (12h/24h) / Date format	Sets the camera's internal clock. The time is embedded into every photo and video file's metadata (EXIF). Keep this accurate — incorrect timestamps make organizing photos by date unreliable. To change: enter this setting, use LEFT/RIGHT to move between fields, UP/DOWN to change values, OK to save.
World Time	Home	Home city / Alternate city (for travel)	Sets the time zone. The camera stores two time zone slots — Home and Alternate (Travel). When you travel, switch to the Alternate slot and select your destination city. The clock adjusts automatically. Cities are listed with their UTC offset. When you return home, switch back to Home. This preserves both settings without re-entry.
Language	Set at first power-on	30+ languages	Sets the display language for all menus and screen text. Scroll through the list to find your preferred language. The camera immediately switches all text to the new language upon confirmation.
Monitor (LCD) Style	Style 1	Style 1 / Style 2	Changes the overall layout of information on the LCD screen. Style 1 overlays

			information on the live image. Style 2 uses a dedicated information band below the image. A matter of personal preference.
Card Setup	—	Format / Card Info	Contains two items. Format erases and reinitialises the SD card (see Part 2.3 for the full explanation and procedure). Card Info displays the card type, capacity, and remaining space — press it to view, not to change anything.
Pixel Mapping	—	Start / Cancel	Runs a short test (about 3 seconds) to detect and map stuck pixels on the camera sensor. Stuck pixels appear as fixed bright or dark dots in the same position in all photos. Run this if you notice such artifacts. Most users never need to use this.
Wi-Fi / Bluetooth	—	Bluetooth On/Off / Private Connection / Wi-Fi Settings / QR Code / Reset Wireless	Controls all wireless communication. Enable Bluetooth to allow pairing with the OM SYSTEM app. Private Connection creates a dedicated one-to-one link with your smartphone. Wi-Fi Settings shows the camera's IP address and network name. QR Code displays a scannable code for quick app connection. Reset Wireless clears all wireless pairings. See Part 2.4 for full pairing instructions.
USB Connection Mode	Auto	Auto / Storage / MTP / Tethering / Charging	Determines what the camera does when a USB-C cable is connected. Auto detects the intent based on what is connected. Storage presents the SD card to the computer as a removable drive for file copying. MTP (Media Transfer Protocol) uses a driver for media management on Windows. Tethering enables remote control and live view via software such as Capture One or OM Workspace. Charging powers the battery without triggering a data connection.

USB Charging	On	Off / On	When On, the camera charges the battery via the USB-C port whenever a cable is connected to a USB power source, even if the camera is powered off. When Off, USB connection is used for data only. Leave On unless your USB data connection is being disrupted by the charging detection.
Copyright Settings	—	Artist name / Copyright owner	Embeds copyright and creator information into every photo's EXIF metadata. Enter your name as the artist and your copyright notice as the owner (e.g. Copyright 2025 [Your Name]). This information travels with the file and appears in any application that reads EXIF metadata — useful for professional photographers tracking image ownership.
My Menu (Custom Shortcut Menu)	—	Add / Remove / Reorder settings	Creates a personal shortcut menu that gives you instant access to your most-used settings without navigating through multiple tabs. Add any setting from any menu section to My Menu. Access My Menu by assigning a Fn button to 'My Menu.' See Part 18 for full configuration instructions.
Firmware Version	—	Display only	Displays the current firmware version installed on the camera body and (if a compatible lens is attached) the lens firmware version. Use this to confirm whether you are running the latest firmware. Compare against the OM SYSTEM website. See Part 19 for the firmware update procedure.
Reset (Factory Reset)	—	Reset / Cancel	Resets all camera settings to the original factory defaults. This is a full reset — all your custom button assignments, saved custom modes, menu settings, and wireless pairings are erased. Only use this for troubleshooting a persistently

misbehaving camera, or when passing the camera to another person. After a reset, the first-time setup wizard runs again the next time you power on.

WARNING: Factory Reset erases all customization

A full factory reset cannot be undone. Before resetting, take photos of your key settings on your smartphone screen so you can re-enter them afterward. Pay particular attention to: Custom Menu A-J settings, Custom Mode C1/C2/C3 configurations, Fn button assignments, My Menu items, and Wi-Fi/Bluetooth pairings.

TIP: Create a My Menu for daily use

After working through this chapter, identify the 5-8 settings you change most frequently during a typical shoot. Add them to My Menu (Setup Menu → My Menu → Add Settings). Assign a Fn button to open My Menu. Now all your most-used settings are just one button press away — far faster than navigating the full menu system.

Part 7 — The Focus System

Sharp focus is the foundation of a technically successful photograph. The OM-3 has one of the most advanced focus systems in any mirrorless camera at its price level — combining fast phase-detection and contrast-detection autofocus, face and eye tracking, a powerful manual focus mode with visual aids, and the extraordinary Pro Capture system that records frames before you press the shutter.

This part of the guide explains every element of the focus system from the ground up. You will learn the difference between each AF mode, how to choose the right AF area for your subject, how to use Face and Eye Detection, how Touch AF works on the LCD, and how to use manual focus effectively with the built-in aids. We finish with a complete explanation of Pro Capture — one of the most unique and useful features on the OM-3.

7.1 AF Modes: S-AF, C-AF, and MF

The OM-3 offers three fundamental focus modes, each suited to a different type of subject and shooting situation. The mode determines HOW the camera focuses — not WHERE in the frame it focuses (that is the AF Area Mode, covered in Section 7.2).

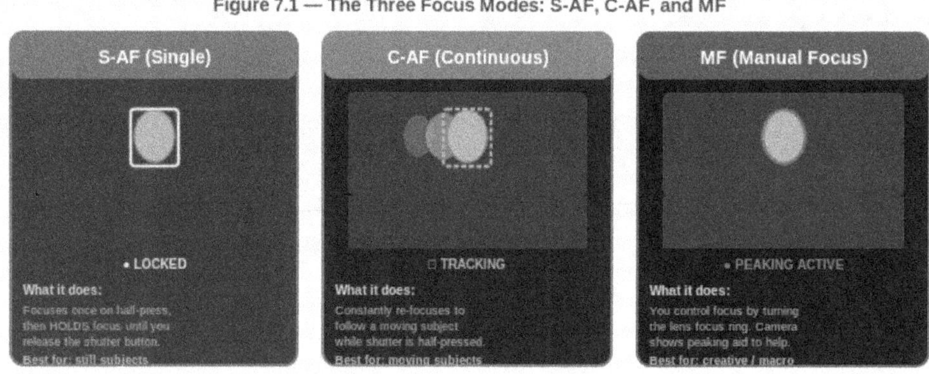

Figure 7.1 — S-AF locks and holds focus; C-AF continuously tracks; MF puts you in full control

S-AF — Single Autofocus

What It Does

In S-AF mode, the camera focuses once when you half-press the shutter button. When the AF system finds and confirms focus on your subject, the AF frame turns green and a short beep sounds (if enabled). The focus distance is then locked — it will not change even if your subject moves. It stays locked for as long as you keep the shutter button half-pressed. The moment you release and press again, it focuses again from scratch.

When to Use S-AF

Situation	Why S-AF Works Well
Portraits of a person sitting or standing still	Lock focus on the eye once, reframe for your preferred composition, shoot.
Landscape photography	Lock focus at the ideal hyperfocal distance, then shoot multiple frames of the same scene.
Architecture and buildings	Static subjects — no need for continuous tracking. S-AF is faster and more decisive.
Product photography on a table	Perfect stillness — S-AF locks reliably and stays locked indefinitely.
Street photography of stationary subjects	Signs, market stalls, textures — lock and reframe freely.

How to Switch to S-AF

There are three ways to select S-AF:

Step 1: Slide the AF/MF lever on the front of the camera (right side of lens mount) to the top position (AF). Then press the MENU button → navigate to Shooting Menu Page 3 → AF Mode → select S-AF → press OK.

Step 2: Or open the Super Control Panel (press OK) → navigate to the AF Mode tile → press OK → select S-AF → press OK.

Step 3: Or if you have assigned an Fn button to AF Mode, press that button and scroll to S-AF.

C-AF — Continuous Autofocus

What It Does

In C-AF mode, the camera continuously re-focuses on your subject for as long as you keep the shutter button half-pressed. If your subject moves toward or away from the camera, the lens adjusts its focus distance to stay sharp on that subject. When you fully press the shutter, the camera captures the photo at whatever the current best-focus distance is.

C-AF is the preferred mode for any subject that is moving — sports, wildlife, children, moving vehicles, or anything where the distance between you and your subject is changing. The OM-3's C-AF system is particularly strong, using predictive tracking algorithms to anticipate where a moving subject will be at the exact moment of exposure.

When to Use C-AF

Situation	Why C-AF Works Well
Birds in flight	Subject moves constantly — C-AF tracks beak-to-tail continuously across the frame.
Football / basketball / athletics	Athletes change direction rapidly — C-AF adapts instantly.
Children running and playing	Unpredictable, fast movement — C-AF stays on them without refocusing between shots.
Cars / motorbikes approaching	Continuous distance change — C-AF adjusts every frame.
Dogs or cats running toward you	Fast movement, often in dim light — C-AF with high ISO handles both.

C-AF+TR — Continuous AF with Subject Tracking

An enhanced version of C-AF is C-AF+TR (Tracking). In this mode, once the camera locks onto a subject, it identifies that specific subject and continues to follow it even if it leaves and re-enters the frame, or if another object briefly passes in front of it. To activate tracking, select C-AF+TR from the AF Mode options, then half-press the shutter — the camera identifies and locks onto the nearest suitable subject and begins tracking it.

> **TIP: C-AF Tracking Sensitivity**
>
> In Custom Menu A, the C-AF Tracking Sensitivity setting controls how tightly the camera holds onto a tracked subject. Setting it to -1 or -2 makes the camera hold the original subject very firmly, even if another person walks in front of it. Setting it to +1 or +2 makes the camera readily hand off tracking to new subjects. For birds in flight, use -1 or -2. For events where many people are moving, use 0.

MF — Manual Focus

What It Does

In MF mode, the autofocus motor is completely disengaged. You control the focus by physically rotating the focus ring on the lens barrel — the ring closest to the camera body on most MFT lenses. The camera does not focus for you at all. Two visual aids help you judge sharpness: focus peaking (coloured edge highlights on sharp areas) and magnified view (covered in detail in Section 7.5).

When to Use MF

- Macro / close-up photography — AF can hunt endlessly in macro range; MF gives you precise control.
- Astrophotography — the camera cannot find contrast in a dark sky; focus manually on a bright star.
- Through glass (zoo, aquarium, car window) — AF locks onto the glass instead of the subject; MF ignores it.
- Low-contrast subjects — white walls, fog, mist — where AF struggles to find edges to contrast-detect on.
- Video — to create intentional focus pulls between subjects in a smooth, cinematic way.
- Precise control — when you know exactly what distance you want in focus regardless of the subject.

S-AF+MF — The Best of Both Worlds

A special combined mode called S-AF+MF is available. In this mode the camera autofocuses when you half-press the shutter. Once focus is confirmed and locked, you can then fine-tune focus by rotating the lens focus ring — without losing the AF lock. This is excellent for portrait work where you want the camera to find the face automatically but then adjust the focus slightly for the exact eye you want sharpest.

Step 1: Select S-AF+MF from the AF Mode options (Shooting Menu Page 3 → AF Mode or via SCP).

Step 2: Half-press the shutter — the camera autofocuses and the AF frame turns green.

Step 3: While keeping the shutter half-pressed, turn the lens focus ring to fine-tune.

Step 4: When satisfied, full-press the shutter to shoot.

7.2 AF Area Modes

While the AF Mode (S-AF, C-AF, MF) determines HOW the camera focuses, the AF Area Mode determines WHERE in the frame the camera looks for its subject to focus on. The OM-3 offers six distinct AF area modes, each suited to different shooting scenarios.

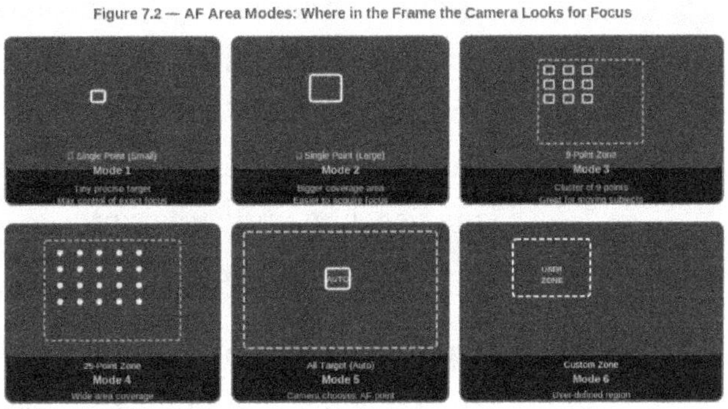

Figure 7.2 — The six AF area modes: from a tiny precise point to full-frame automatic selection

The Six AF Area Modes Explained

AF Area Mode	What It Looks Like on Screen	What It Does	Best For
Single Point (Small)	A tiny green/white square that you position anywhere in the frame	The camera only looks for focus at the single small point. Extremely precise — only what is directly under the tiny square will be in focus.	Precise portrait work (one specific eye), through-fence or through-gap shots, macro photography, any situation requiring surgical precision.
Single Point (Large)	A larger green/white square, moveable around the frame	Same as Single Small but the target area is larger — easier to place on a subject and more tolerant of small subject movements. Slightly less precise.	General portrait work, documentary, street photography with a defined subject area.
9-Point Zone	A cluster of 9 smaller AF points in a square group, moveable as a unit	The camera uses all 9 points simultaneously, focusing on whatever is detected within the zone. The zone can be moved around the frame. Good balance of precision and coverage.	Moving subjects within a confined area, subjects that move slightly between shots, sports with a defined action zone.
25-Point Zone	A larger cluster of 25 AF points across a wide area	Similar to 9-point but with wider coverage. The camera uses the most contrast-rich area within the 25-point zone. Less precise but very tolerant of subject movement.	Fast-moving subjects with unpredictable paths, wildlife bursting into action, children running.
All Target (Auto)	The full frame is enclosed in a dashed	The camera automatically selects which AF point or points to use based on the entire scene. It prioritises	Quick snapshots, passing the camera to someone unfamiliar with AF settings, general

	rectangle — all points active	the nearest subject, the most contrasty subject, and detected faces (if Face Detection is on). Fully hands-off.	family and travel photography where precision is less critical than speed.
Custom Zone	A user-defined rectangle in any location and size in the frame	You define a specific rectangular zone on screen. The camera focuses only within that zone, regardless of what is outside it. Configure the zone size and position in Custom Menu A.	Recurring scenarios where your subject always appears in a specific part of the frame — e.g. a finish line, a doorway, a bird feeder.

How to Select and Change the AF Area Mode

There are three ways to change the AF Area Mode:

Method 1 — Via the Super Control Panel (Fastest)

> **Step 1:** Press OK to open the Super Control Panel.
>
> **Step 2:** Navigate to the AF Area tile — it shows a small frame-within-frame icon.
>
> **Step 3:** Press OK to enter the AF Area Mode selection screen.
>
> **Step 4:** A visual representation of each mode appears. Use the arrow pad to highlight the mode you want.
>
> **Step 5:** Press OK to confirm. The new AF area pattern immediately appears on the live view screen.

Method 2 — Via the Shooting Menu

> **Step 1:** Press MENU → navigate to the Shooting Menu (camera icon) → scroll to Page 3.
>
> **Step 2:** Select AF Area Mode and press OK or RIGHT.
>
> **Step 3:** Scroll through the options and press OK on your choice.

Method 3 — Assign to a Fn Button

Assign AF Area Mode to a function button (Fn1, Fn2, or Fn3) via Custom Menu B → Button Function. Then a single press of that button opens the AF Area selection screen directly.

How to Move the AF Point Using the Arrow Pad

When using Single Point (small or large) or Zone modes, the AF point or zone can be repositioned anywhere in the frame:

> **Step 1:** Ensure you are in live view with Single Point or a Zone AF area mode selected.
>
> **Step 2:** Press the LEFT, RIGHT, UP, or DOWN arrow button on the 4-way pad. The AF point or zone moves in that direction.
>
> **Step 3:** Continue pressing arrows to position the AF target over your subject — for example, your subject's left eye.
>
> **Step 4:** Half-press the shutter to confirm focus at that exact point.
>
> **Step 5:** To instantly snap the AF point back to the center of the frame, press the OK button once.

How to Move the AF Point Using the Touchscreen

If you prefer not to use the arrow pad, you can simply tap the LCD screen at the location you want to focus:

- Single tap — the AF point jumps to the tapped location immediately.
- This works in both landscape and portrait orientations.
- This also works while looking through the EVF — if Touch AF Pad is enabled in Custom Menu A, touching the LCD moves the AF point even when your eye is at the viewfinder.
- Tap the very center of the screen to return to center, or press OK on the arrow pad.

> **TIP: AF point memory**
>
> In Custom Menu A you can save a specific non-center AF point position as your Home Position. Then pressing the OK button during shooting snaps the AF point back to your saved custom position (rather than the center). Useful if you always shoot with the focus point at a specific off-center location.

7.3 Face and Eye Detection

Face and Eye Detection is one of the most powerful autofocus tools on the OM-3. When enabled, the camera's processor continuously scans the live view frame for human faces. When it detects one, it places a white detection frame around it and prioritises focusing on that face — and specifically on the nearest detectable eye.

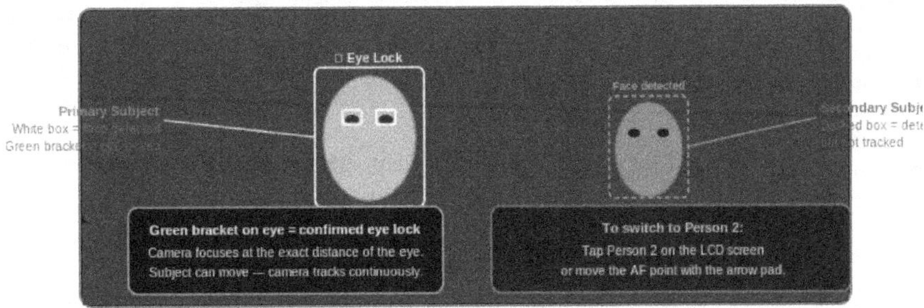

Figure 7.3 — Face detection (white box around face), eye lock (green bracket on eye), secondary subject detected (dashed box)

How to Turn On Face and Eye Detection — Exact Menu Path

Face and Eye Detection can be turned on in two ways:

Method 1 — Via the Super Control Panel

Step 1: Press OK to open the Super Control Panel.

Step 2: Navigate to the AF Area Mode tile and press OK.

Step 3: In the AF Area selection screen, look for an option labeled Face Priority or Face+Eye. Select it and press OK.

Method 2 — Via the Shooting Menu

Step 1: Press MENU.

Step 2: Navigate to the Shooting Menu (camera icon, first tab).

Step 3: Press DOWN to enter the menu list.

Step 4: Scroll DOWN to Page 3 of the Shooting Menu.

Step 5: Find the item labeled Face Priority and press OK or RIGHT to enter it.

Step 6: The options are: Off / On / Face+Eye (Right) / Face+Eye (Left) / Face+Eye (Auto).

Step 7: Highlight your preferred option and press OK.

Step 8: Press MENU to close.

The Face Priority Options Explained

Option	What It Does
Off	Face and Eye Detection is disabled. The camera uses the standard AF Area mode without any awareness of faces or eyes.
On (Face Priority)	The camera detects faces and prioritises focusing on the detected face. It does not specifically target the eye — the whole face area is the focus target.

Face+Eye (Right)	Detects faces and specifically locks autofocus onto the detected subject's right eye. If the right eye is not visible, the camera falls back to the left eye, then the whole face.
Face+Eye (Left)	Detects faces and specifically locks autofocus onto the detected subject's left eye. Falls back to right eye, then whole face if left eye is not visible.
Face+Eye (Auto)	Detects faces and automatically chooses the nearer or more prominent eye to lock onto. This is the recommended setting for most portrait work — the camera makes the best decision automatically.

What You See on Screen When Face Detection Is Active

Understanding the visual indicators helps you know what the camera is doing:

What You See	What It Means
White rectangle around a face	The camera has detected a face. It is being tracked but is not yet the primary focus target.
Green rectangle around a face	This face is the primary focus target. The camera will focus here when you half-press the shutter.
Green small brackets on an eye	The camera has identified and locked autofocus onto a specific eye. This is the most precise form of detection — the focus distance is set exactly to the eye's distance from the camera.
White small brackets on an eye	Eye detected but not yet locked. May appear briefly before the green lock is confirmed.
Orange or yellow face box	Focus lock on this face was successful but the face has partially moved outside the expected area — the camera is trying to reacquire.
No face boxes at all	No faces detected in the current frame. The camera falls back to the standard AF area mode.

How Face and Eye Detection Works in Practice

Step 1: Enable Face+Eye (Auto) via the Shooting Menu or SCP.

Step 2: Point the camera at a person. Within a fraction of a second, a white rectangle appears around their face.

Step 3: Half-press the shutter. The face box turns green, and a small bracket appears on the near eye. This is the AF lock confirmation.

Step 4: The subject can now move — the camera tracks the face and maintains focus on the eye continuously (in C-AF mode) or until you release and re-press (in S-AF mode).

Step 5: If multiple people are in the frame, all detected faces show white boxes. The camera automatically selects the primary subject (usually the nearest face or the one most centered). Tap a different face on the LCD to switch tracking to that person.

Step 6: When no face is in the frame, the camera uses the standard AF area mode as a fallback. The transition is seamless.

NOTE: Face detection with masks and glasses

The OM-3's face detection system works well with glasses but may struggle with face masks covering the lower half of the face. When masks are worn, Face Priority without Eye mode (the On option rather than Face+Eye) typically performs better because it targets the whole face area rather than looking specifically for eyes.

TIP: Use Face+Eye for video interviews

When filming a talking-head interview or vlog, enable Face+Eye (Auto) and set AF Mode to C-AF. The camera will keep the speaker's eyes in continuous focus even when they turn their head, look down at notes, or move slightly toward or away from the camera. This eliminates focus hunting during video recording.

7.4 Touch AF on the LCD

The OM-3's LCD is a fully capacitive touchscreen that allows you to interact with autofocus directly by touching the screen. Touch AF offers three different gestures, each producing a different result:

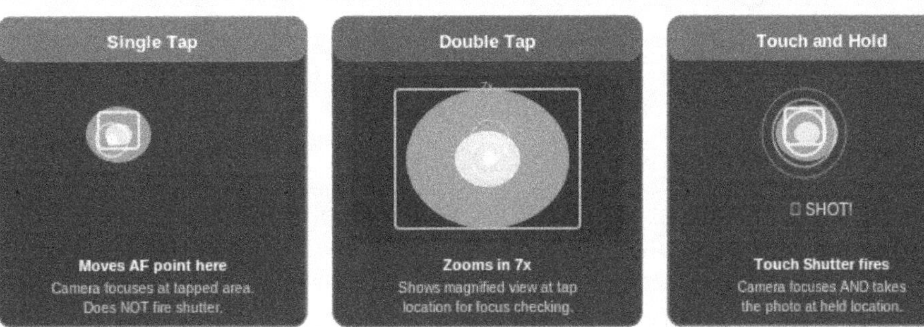

Figure 7.4 — Single tap moves the AF point; double-tap zooms in; touch and hold fires the shutter

Touch AF Gesture Reference

Gesture	What Happens	When to Use It
Single tap on any area	The AF point moves instantly to the tapped location. The camera focuses at that point on the next half-press of the shutter. Does NOT fire the shutter.	Repositioning the focus point quickly without using the arrow pad. Most common Touch AF use. Great when the camera is on a tripod and you want to shift focus between subjects.
Double tap on any area	The live view zooms in to approximately 7x magnification at the tapped location. Useful for checking fine focus manually or precisely repositioning the AF point at pixel level.	Manual focus verification, checking whether a subject's eye is truly sharp before shooting a series, or repositioning the AF point with extreme precision.
Touch and hold (long press)	Activates Touch Shutter. The camera focuses at the held location AND automatically fires the shutter — all from a single touch gesture. No physical shutter button press required.	One-handed self-portraits, smartphone-style photography, shooting from awkward angles where you cannot reach the shutter button, quick discreet shots.

Enabling and Disabling Touch AF

Step 1: Press MENU.

Step 2: Navigate to Custom Menu D (Display / Sound).

Step 3: Find Touch Screen Settings or Touch Control.

Step 4: You will see sub-options for Live View Touch AF and Playback Touch. Toggle each independently.

Step 5: Off disables touch entirely. On enables both touch AF point movement and touch shutter.

Step 6: You can also disable only the Touch Shutter (to prevent accidental shots when the camera is at your eye) while keeping Touch AF point movement active.

Touch AF While Looking Through the EVF

The OM-3 supports a feature called Touch AF Pad (or Touch Pad AF) in Custom Menu A. When enabled, you can use the LCD as a touchpad while your eye is at the EVF — touching anywhere on the LCD surface moves the AF point in the corresponding direction on the EVF display. This gives you smooth, intuitive AF point positioning without removing your eye from the viewfinder.

Step 1: Go to MENU → Custom Menu A → AF Targeting Pod (or Touch Pad AF) → set to On.

Step 2: Raise the camera to your eye and look through the EVF.

Step 3: With your thumb, touch and slide on the LCD surface. The AF point on the EVF moves correspondingly.

Step 4: Half-press the shutter to focus at the repositioned point.

TIP: Disable touch shutter when shooting with the EVF

If you frequently use the EVF with your cheek or nose near the LCD, you may accidentally trigger the Touch Shutter. Go to Custom Menu D → Touch Screen Settings → disable Touch Shutter Only while leaving Touch AF Point active. This prevents accidental shots while keeping the convenient touch-to-focus-point feature.

7.5 Manual Focus Assists: Focus Peaking and Magnified View

When using Manual Focus (MF), the camera cannot tell you what is in focus — only your eyes can. But two powerful visual aids make manual focusing fast, accurate, and reliable: Focus Peaking overlays coloured highlights on the sharpest areas, and the Magnified View zooms in to give you a pixel-level check of sharpness.

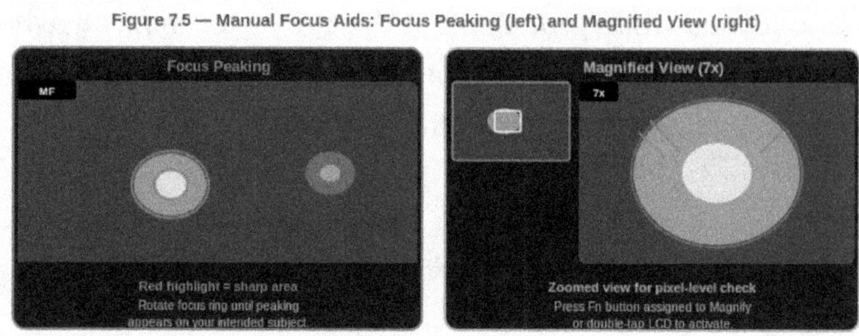

Figure 7.5 — Focus Peaking (left): coloured edges show what's sharp. Magnified View (right): pixel-level sharpness check

Focus Peaking — Coloured Edge Highlights

What Focus Peaking Is

Focus Peaking is a real-time overlay that analyses the live view image for high-contrast edges — which indicates sharpness — and highlights those edges with a coloured outline. When you rotate the lens focus ring, the coloured highlights move from one area of the frame to another, showing you exactly which plane of the scene is currently in sharp focus.

How to Enable Focus Peaking

Step 1: Go to MENU → Custom Menu A → scroll to Focus Peaking.

Step 2: Press OK or RIGHT to enter the Peaking settings.

Step 3: Set Peaking to On.

Step 4: Choose the Peaking Colour — White, Red, or Yellow. Red is the most visible against blue-sky backgrounds; White works well for most scenes; Yellow is good for dark subjects.

Step 5: Press OK and MENU to close.

Step 6: Alternatively, assign Focus Peaking to an Fn button (Custom Menu B → Button Function → Peaking) for instant toggle.

How to Use Focus Peaking Effectively

Step 1: Switch the AF/MF lever to MF.

Step 2: Enable Focus Peaking (as above) — coloured highlights appear on whatever is currently in focus.

Step 3: Look at the live view screen or EVF. If the subject you want in focus shows coloured highlights on its edges, it is already in the focus zone.

Step 4: If your subject has no peaking highlights, rotate the focus ring on the lens slowly. Watch where the coloured highlights appear and sweep across the frame.

Step 5: Stop rotating when the coloured highlights appear strongly on your intended subject.

Step 6: For fine-tuning, use the Magnified View (see below) to confirm pixel-level sharpness.

Step 7: Half-press the shutter to freeze the display (peaking highlights disappear briefly during capture), then full-press to shoot.

Peaking Colour	When to Use It
Red	Most universally visible. Works well against blue skies, green foliage, and blue/green backgrounds. Choose this as your default.
White	Best for dark subjects or high-contrast scenes. Can be hard to see against very bright or snowy backgrounds.
Yellow	Works well against dark or colourful subjects. Useful for portraits against a rich blue or red background where red peaking would blend with the background colour.

WARNING: Peaking is an approximation, not a guarantee

Focus Peaking highlights high-contrast edges, which is a good indicator of sharpness — but it is not the same as a sharpness test. Subjects with very fine texture (silk fabric, out-of-focus backgrounds) can sometimes show false peaking highlights. Always confirm critical sharpness with the Magnified View before shooting a final frame.

Magnified View — Zooming In to Check Sharpness

What the Magnified View Is

The Magnified View instantly zooms the live view display to 3x, 5x, 7x, 10x, or 14x magnification at the current focus point. At high magnification you can see individual pixels — making it the most reliable way to confirm that your manual focus is exactly where you want it before taking the shot.

How to Activate the Magnified View

Step 1: Assign the Magnify function to a Fn button: MENU → Custom Menu B → Button Function → select your Fn button → select Magnify → OK.

Step 2: In MF mode, press your assigned Fn button. The live view immediately zooms to the preset magnification level.

Step 3: The small inset image (picture-in-picture) in the corner of the magnified view shows the full frame so you can see context.

Step 4: Rotate the focus ring to bring your subject into sharp focus at the magnified view.

Step 5: Press the same Fn button again (or half-press the shutter) to zoom back out to full-frame view.

Step 6: Shoot.

Setting the Magnification Level

Step 1: Go to MENU → Custom Menu A → MF Magnify (or MF Assist Magnification).

Step 2: Choose your preferred zoom level: 3x / 5x / 7x / 10x / 14x.

Step 3: 7x is the practical sweet spot for most manual focus work. 10x or 14x is useful for astrophotography or extreme macro work.

Step 4: Press OK and MENU to save.

TIP: Combine peaking and magnify

Use peaking to get close to focus quickly — rotate the ring until peaking appears on your subject. Then activate the Magnified View to confirm and fine-tune at pixel level. This two-step process is faster than using magnify alone (where you have to search for the focus point from scratch) and more accurate than using peaking alone.

Additional MF Assist: Focus Distance Indicator

Some OM SYSTEM lenses display a focus distance indicator on screen when MF is active. This shows the current focus distance in metres or feet as a number or a scale. This is useful for zone focusing (where you pre-focus at a specific distance and shoot any subject at that range without focusing), and for focus breathing reference in video work.

7.6 Pro Capture Mode

Pro Capture is one of the most distinctive and practically useful features on the OM-3. It solves a fundamental problem in action photography: by the time you react to a decisive moment and fully press the shutter, the moment has already passed. Pro Capture eliminates this problem by continuously buffering frames BEFORE you press — so when you do press, the camera can reach back in time and include those pre-captured frames in your final burst.

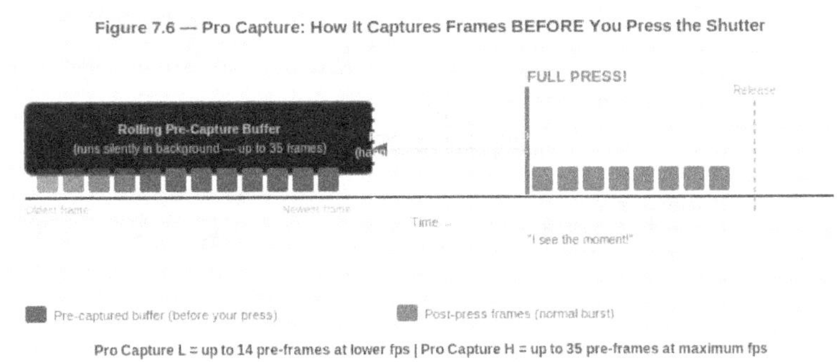

Figure 7.6 — Pro Capture stores frames before your press. When you press, both pre-captured and post-press frames are saved.

What Pro Capture Does — Plain English

Imagine you are photographing a kingfisher sitting on a branch over a river. You know it is about to dive — but you do not know exactly when. With normal burst shooting, you press the shutter when you see it begin to dive, but the critical frame — the moment the feet leave the branch, the body arcing into the dive — has already happened before your finger hit the button.

With Pro Capture, the camera is silently buffering up to 35 frames every second while you hold the shutter button half-pressed and wait. When the kingfisher begins to dive, you press fully. The camera saves all the pre-buffered frames (which include the beginning of the dive) PLUS continues shooting after your press. The result is a complete sequence of the dive — including frames that happened before you consciously pressed.

Pro Capture L vs Pro Capture H — The Difference

	Pro Capture L	Pro Capture H

Frame rate	Up to 15 fps (uses mechanical shutter)	Up to 30–50 fps (uses electronic shutter at maximum speed)
Pre-capture frames	Up to 14 frames stored before full press	Up to 35 frames stored before full press
Shutter type	Mechanical — standard shutter click sound	Electronic — fully silent, no mechanical movement
Rolling shutter	No rolling shutter artifacts	May show some rolling shutter distortion with very fast horizontal motion
Flash compatibility	Compatible with flash	NOT compatible with flash (electronic shutter cannot sync with flash)
Best for	Most action photography, bird landing shots, sports sequences — balanced speed and quality	Extreme speed situations: bird in flight, insects, hummingbirds, peak-of-action moments where 30+ fps is needed
SD card requirement	UHS-I U3 minimum	UHS-II V60/V90 recommended for sustained burst

How to Activate Pro Capture — Exact Steps

Method 1 — Via the Drive Button (Fastest)

Step 1: Press the DRIVE button on top of the camera.

Step 2: The drive mode selection screen appears. Use the arrow pad to scroll through the options.

Step 3: Find Pro Cap L (Pro Capture Low speed) or Pro Cap H (Pro Capture High speed) and highlight it.

Step 4: Press OK to confirm.

Step 5: The drive mode indicator in the live view display changes to show the Pro Capture icon.

Method 2 — Via the Super Control Panel

Step 1: Press OK to open the SCP.

Step 2: Navigate to the Drive Mode tile.

Step 3: Press OK to enter the drive mode options.

Step 4: Scroll to Pro Cap L or Pro Cap H.

Step 5: Press OK to confirm.

How to Configure Pro Capture Settings

You can adjust how many pre-capture frames are stored before your press:

Step 1: Go to MENU → Custom Menu C → Pro Capture (Pre-Capture Frames).

Step 2: Options typically range from 4 / 8 / 14 / 20 / 25 / 35 frames depending on the mode.

Step 3: Choose the number of pre-capture frames you want. More frames = longer reach back in time, but requires faster SD card and larger buffer.

Step 4: Press OK and MENU to close.

How to Use Pro Capture — Step by Step in the Field

Step 1: Select Pro Capture L or H via the Drive button or SCP.

Step 2: Compose your shot with the camera aimed at the scene where the action will occur. For birds, aim at the branch or perch where the bird is waiting.

Step 3: Half-press the shutter button and hold it there. This begins the pre-capture buffer silently in the background. The camera starts storing frames continuously — but nothing is saved to the SD card yet.

Step 4: Wait for the decisive moment — the bird begins to fly, the diver enters the water, the sprinter explodes off the blocks.

Step 5: At the moment you see (or anticipate) the peak action, press the shutter button fully down. Do not hesitate.

Step 6: The camera saves all pre-buffered frames (back as far as the number of frames you configured) PLUS continues shooting the standard burst forward from your press.

Step 7: Release the shutter button when the action is over.

Step 8: Review the sequence in playback — you will find the decisive moment captured with frames that occurred before you consciously pressed the button.

Pro Capture Tips and Best Practices

Topic	Recommendation

SD card speed	Use a UHS-II V60 or V90 rated card for Pro Capture H. Pro Capture L works reliably with a UHS-I U3 card. A slow card will cause the buffer to fill quickly and write speeds to back up, reducing the burst duration.
Battery consumption	The pre-capture buffer runs continuously during your half-press. This drains the battery faster than normal shooting. Carry a spare battery when using Pro Capture for extended sessions.
Focus mode pairing	Pair Pro Capture with C-AF for moving subjects — the camera tracks the subject continuously while buffering frames. For static subjects about to move (kingfisher on a branch), S-AF + half-press lock works well.
How long to half-press before the action	Half-press several seconds before you expect the action. The buffer is continuously refreshed — older frames are dropped as new ones are added. You don't waste anything by waiting longer.
File management	Each Pro Capture activation produces a burst of potentially 35+ images. Cull aggressively in post to keep only the best frames. Use your camera's rating or protect feature to flag keepers immediately after the shoot.
Electronic shutter and banding	Pro Capture H uses the electronic shutter, which can show banding stripes under fluorescent lighting. If you see horizontal bands across burst frames shot indoors, switch to Pro Capture L (mechanical shutter).

TIP: Pro Capture for musicians, performers, and athletes

Pro Capture is not just for birds and wildlife. It is equally powerful for capturing the peak expression of a singer, the exact moment a gymnast is fully extended in a jump, or the spray of water at a swimmer's entry. Any situation where the decisive moment is unpredictable and lasts only a fraction of a second benefits enormously from Pro Capture.

Part 8 — Exposure Controls

Exposure is the single most important technical concept in photography. Get it right and your photo captures exactly what you saw — the right brightness, the right mood, the right detail in both the bright and dark areas of the scene. Get it wrong and no amount of post-processing will fully rescue a badly exposed image.

The OM-3 gives you complete control over every aspect of exposure — from fully automatic to fully manual. This part of the guide explains what exposure is in plain language, then covers each exposure control in depth: ISO, aperture, shutter speed, exposure compensation, AE lock, and the four metering modes. For each control you will find the plain-English concept, the exact steps for changing it on the OM-3, and real-world guidance on when and why to use it.

8.1 What Is Exposure? (Plain English)

Exposure is simply how much light reaches the camera's sensor when you take a photo. Too much light and the photo looks washed out and pale — this is called overexposure. Too little light and the photo looks dark and murky — this is underexposure. A well-exposed photo shows natural brightness with detail visible in both the lightest and darkest areas of the scene.

You control how much light reaches the sensor using three physical variables, each of which also affects your photo creatively beyond just its brightness. These three variables are called the Exposure Triangle:

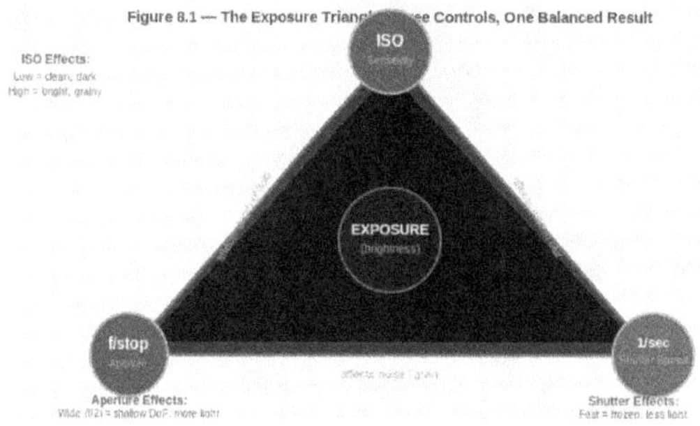

Figure 8.1 — The Exposure Triangle: ISO, Aperture, and Shutter Speed must balance together

The Three Pillars of Exposure

Variable	Controls	Creative Side Effect	Where on the OM-3
ISO	How sensitive the sensor is to light. Higher ISO = brighter image from the same amount of light.	Noise / grain in the image. Low ISO = clean. High ISO = visible grain.	Front dial (M mode), SCP, or ISO button shortcut
Aperture (f-stop)	The size of the opening inside the lens. Wider opening = more light through the lens.	Depth of field — how much of the scene is in focus. Wide aperture (f/2) = blurry background. Narrow aperture (f/16) = everything sharp.	Front dial in A and M modes
Shutter Speed	How long the sensor is exposed	Motion rendering. Fast shutter = frozen motion.	Rear dial in S and M modes

	to light. Longer = more light.	Slow shutter = motion blur.

All three work together. If you make one change — say, narrowing the aperture to get a sharper background — the amount of light entering the camera decreases. To compensate, you can increase ISO (make the sensor more sensitive), slow the shutter speed (let more time for light to collect), or both. This balancing act is the fundamental skill of photography.

> **NOTE: The camera balances for you in semi-automatic modes**
>
> In Aperture Priority (A) mode, you set the aperture and the camera adjusts shutter speed automatically to compensate. In Shutter Priority (S) mode, you set shutter speed and the camera adjusts aperture. In Program (P) mode, the camera sets both. Only in Manual (M) mode do you set all three yourself.

8.2 ISO — How to Change It and What It Affects

ISO is a number that describes how sensitive your camera's sensor is to light. The OM-3's native ISO range runs from ISO 200 up to ISO 25600, with extended High settings beyond that. A lower ISO number means the sensor is less sensitive — it needs more light to produce a bright image. A higher ISO means the sensor amplifies what little light is available — but that amplification also amplifies noise (grain).

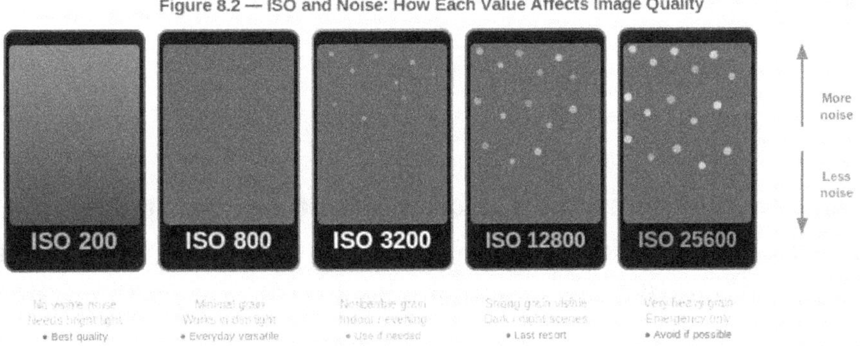

Figure 8.2 — ISO and noise: clean results at low ISO, progressively more grain at high ISO values

What Each ISO Value Means for Your Photo

ISO Value	Noise Level	Light Needed	Best Situations
ISO 200 (Low)	None visible — maximum quality	Bright light required (outdoors sunny day)	Bright sunlight, golden hour, studio with powerful flash, tripod landscape

ISO 400	Virtually none	Good light (overcast day, bright shade)	Cloudy day outdoors, bright indoor with window light
ISO 800	Very slight grain at 100% view	Moderate light (dim indoors)	Indoor events with adequate lighting, evening outdoors
ISO 1600	Noticeable at 100% but acceptable in print	Low light (indoor evening, restaurant)	Indoor sports, social events, dim restaurants
ISO 3200	Clearly visible grain in smooth areas	Very low light (candlelight, dark church)	Night street photography, concerts, dark indoor venues
ISO 6400	Strong grain, some colour noise	Near-dark conditions	Astrophotography foregrounds, dark performance venues
ISO 12800	Heavy grain, reduced detail	Very dark — minimal available light	Emergency low-light situations where a grainy shot is better than no shot
ISO 25600 and Hi settings	Extreme grain, degraded colour	Essentially darkness	Last resort only — expect painterly, impressionistic results rather than sharp detail

TIP: The lowest ISO is always cleanest

Whenever light conditions allow, use the lowest ISO setting that still gives you the shutter speed you need. If you are on a tripod in good light, ISO 200 gives you the cleanest possible image. Only raise ISO when the alternative is a blurry photo from a shutter speed that is too slow.

How to Adjust ISO Manually — Exact Steps

Method 1 — Front/Rear Dial with ISO Shortcut (Fastest)

Step 1: In live view, press and hold the OK button briefly — or if an Fn button has been assigned to ISO, press that Fn button.

Step 2: The ISO selection screen appears, showing a scale of ISO values.

Step 3: Turn the front dial or rear dial to move through the ISO values.

Step 4: The live view brightness updates in real time as you change ISO.

Step 5: Once you reach your desired ISO value, release or press OK to confirm.

Method 2 — Via the Super Control Panel

Step 1: Press OK to open the Super Control Panel.

Step 2: Navigate to the ISO tile (upper right area of the SCP grid).

Step 3: Turn the front or rear dial to change the ISO value directly — the tile updates in real time.

Step 4: Or press OK on the tile to open a full ISO selection screen.

Step 5: Half-press the shutter to exit the SCP and return to live view.

Method 3 — Via the Shooting Menu

Step 1: Press MENU → Shooting Menu (camera icon) → scroll to ISO Sensitivity on Page 2.

Step 2: Press OK to enter the ISO selection.

Step 3: Use UP/DOWN arrows to select the value.

Step 4: Press OK to confirm. Press MENU to close.

Setting Up Auto ISO — Exact Menu Path

Auto ISO lets the camera automatically select the ISO value within a range you specify. This is extremely useful in changing light conditions — the camera keeps the shutter speed and aperture where you want them and raises or lowers ISO as needed.

Step 1: Press MENU → Shooting Menu → Page 2.

Step 2: Find ISO Auto (Low Limit) and press OK. Set the minimum ISO the camera will use. ISO 200 is the standard minimum — do not set it lower unless you specifically need it.

Step 3: Find ISO Auto (High Limit) and press OK. Set the maximum ISO you are willing to accept. For general use, ISO 3200 or 6400 is a practical maximum. For low-light event photography, ISO 6400 or 12800 gives more flexibility.

Step 4: Find ISO Auto (Min Shutter) and press OK. This is the slowest shutter speed the camera will use before it starts raising ISO. Set this to the minimum shutter speed you need to avoid motion blur. For handheld portraits, try 1/125. For sports, 1/500 or faster. Set to Auto to let the camera decide based on focal length.

Step 5: To activate Auto ISO: in the ISO selection (SCP or ISO button), scroll past the numbered values until you reach the AUTO option, then select it.

Step 6: The display will show AUTO or A-ISO where the ISO number normally appears.

TIP: Auto ISO with Manual mode

In Manual mode with Auto ISO active, you set both aperture and shutter speed yourself, and the camera automatically adjusts only the ISO to achieve correct exposure. This gives you full creative control over depth of field and motion rendering while the camera handles the exposure calculation automatically. Many professional photographers use exactly this combination.

Checking the Current ISO During Shooting

The current ISO value is always shown in the top row of the live view display on both the LCD and EVF. Look for the number next to the letters ISO — for example ISO 800 or ISO 3200. If Auto ISO is active, it shows AUTO or the current auto-selected value (which updates as light changes). You never need to enter a menu to see the current ISO — it is always visible on screen.

8.3 Aperture — How to Adjust in A and M Mode

Aperture is the adjustable opening inside your lens that controls how much light passes through to the sensor. It is measured in f-numbers (f-stops). The f-number scale is counterintuitive at first: a smaller f-number means a LARGER opening (more light), and a larger f-number means a SMALLER opening (less light).

Beyond controlling light, aperture has a profound creative effect: it controls depth of field — the zone of the image that appears acceptably sharp. A wide aperture (low f-number like f/1.8 or f/2.8) produces a shallow depth of field where only your subject is sharp and the background blurs into a smooth, out-of-focus wash. A narrow aperture (high f-number like f/11 or f/16) produces a deep depth of field where both near and far objects appear sharp.

The F-Stop Scale — A Quick Reference

F-Stop	Opening Size	Light Admitted	Depth of Field Effect

f/1.4 – f/2	Very wide	Maximum light	Extremely shallow — only a thin slice of the scene is sharp. Beautiful background blur (bokeh).
f/2.8 – f/4	Wide	Lots of light	Shallow — subject sharp, background noticeably blurred. Ideal for portraits.
f/5.6 – f/8	Medium	Moderate light	Moderate — subject and nearby background fairly sharp. Sharpest point of most lenses.
f/11 – f/16	Narrow	Less light	Deep — most of the scene near to far is acceptably sharp. Ideal for landscapes.
f/22 and above	Very narrow	Minimum light	Very deep — everything near and far is sharp. But diffraction reduces overall sharpness at very small apertures.

How to Change Aperture in Aperture Priority (A) Mode

Step 1: Turn the Mode Dial to A (Aperture Priority).

Step 2: The aperture value is displayed in bold white on screen (e.g. f/5.6), meaning it is under your control.

Step 3: Rotate the FRONT DIAL (the ridged wheel around or behind the shutter button) with your right index finger.

Step 4: Roll the front dial LEFT (toward you) to open the aperture — the f-number decreases (e.g. from f/8 to f/5.6 to f/4).

Step 5: Roll the front dial RIGHT (away from you) to narrow the aperture — the f-number increases (e.g. from f/4 to f/5.6 to f/8).

Step 6: Watch both the aperture value and the shutter speed on screen. As you open the aperture the camera automatically selects a faster shutter speed to compensate. As you narrow it the shutter slows.

Step 7: Check the exposure scale at the bottom of the frame. If the shutter speed the camera chooses is too slow (shown in red or blinking), raise ISO or widen the aperture.

How to Change Aperture in Manual (M) Mode

Step 1: Turn the Mode Dial to M.

Step 2: Both shutter speed and aperture are shown in bold white — both are under your control.

Step 3: Rotate the FRONT DIAL to change aperture (same direction as in A mode above).

Step 4: Watch the exposure scale — move it to zero for metered correct exposure, or deliberately to one side for a brighter or darker result.

Step 5: The REAR DIAL controls shutter speed in M mode — use both dials simultaneously for full manual control.

TIP: The sharpest aperture for most MFT lenses

Most Micro Four Thirds lenses are optically sharpest around f/5.6 to f/8. Wide open (f/1.4, f/1.8) the edges may be slightly soft. Very narrow (f/16, f/22) diffraction reduces overall sharpness. For the maximum detail in your images — landscapes, architecture, product shots — try f/5.6 to f/8 as your default starting point.

REAL-WORLD EXAMPLE: Portrait with blurry background

You are photographing a friend against a colourful garden background. You want the friend sharp but the flowers behind them to blur beautifully.

Set Mode Dial to A. Turn the front dial to your widest aperture — f/2.8 if your lens opens that wide, or f/4. Point at your subject's eye, half-press to focus, then full-press to shoot. The background blurs into soft coloured shapes. If the background is still too recognizable, move closer to your subject or use a longer focal length.

REAL-WORLD EXAMPLE: Landscape with near and far in focus

You are photographing a mountain scene. You want the wildflowers in the foreground AND the distant peaks both to be sharp.

Set Mode Dial to A. Turn the front dial to f/11. Put the camera on a tripod (the shutter will slow down). Focus one-third into the depth of the scene using the focus point. Shoot. Both the flowers and the mountains are sharp because f/11 gives you deep depth of field.

8.4 Shutter Speed — How to Adjust in S and M Mode

Shutter speed is how long the camera's shutter stays open when you take a photo. During that time, light hits the sensor and is recorded. A fast shutter speed means the shutter opens and closes very quickly — less total light reaches the sensor but any moving subject appears frozen sharp. A slow shutter speed means the shutter stays open longer — more total light enters but any moving subject (or a moving camera) appears blurred.

The Shutter Speed Scale — A Quick Reference

Shutter Speed	Duration	Motion Effect	Typical Use
1/8000 sec	Extremely short	Freezes even the fastest motion completely	Waterdrop photography, extreme sports, birds at peak speed
1/2000 – 1/1000 sec	Very short	Freezes fast motion — wings, running athletes	Bird flight, motorsport, football, fast wildlife
1/500 – 1/250 sec	Short	Freezes most everyday motion	Walking people, casual sports, general handheld photography
1/125 – 1/60 sec	Moderate	Risk of motion blur from fast subjects; handheld minimum for many lenses	Stationary subjects, controlled movement, image stabilization helps
1/30 – 1/15 sec	Somewhat slow	Motion blur on anything moving; camera shake risk — use tripod or IS	Panning shots (subject sharp, background blurred), creative blur
1/4 – 1 sec	Slow	Strong motion blur; silky water effect	Waterfalls, fountains, nightscapes with light movement
2 – 30 sec	Very slow	Light trails, star movement visible	Star photography, fireworks, light painting, empty streets
Bulb (B)	As long as you hold	As long as you want	Star trails, multi-minute exposures, creative long exposures

How to Change Shutter Speed in Shutter Priority (S) Mode

Step 1: Turn the Mode Dial to S (Shutter Priority).

Step 2: The shutter speed is displayed in bold white on screen (e.g. 1/500), meaning it is under your control. The aperture is grey — the camera sets it automatically.

Step 3: Rotate the REAR DIAL (the scroll wheel on the upper right of the camera back) with your right thumb.

Step 4: Roll the rear dial RIGHT (clockwise when viewed from above) to increase the shutter speed (faster — e.g. from 1/60 to 1/125 to 1/250).

Step 5: Roll the rear dial LEFT (counter-clockwise) to decrease the shutter speed (slower — e.g. from 1/250 to 1/125 to 1/60).

Step 6: Watch the aperture — the camera automatically adjusts it to maintain correct exposure. If the aperture value blinks red, the camera cannot achieve correct exposure at that shutter speed (usually because it is too fast for the available light and the aperture is already at its maximum). Slow the shutter speed or raise ISO.

How to Change Shutter Speed in Manual (M) Mode

Step 1: Turn the Mode Dial to M.

Step 2: Rotate the REAR DIAL to change shutter speed.

Step 3: Rotate the FRONT DIAL to change aperture simultaneously.

Step 4: Watch the exposure scale — when the marker is at zero the camera's meter considers the exposure correct.

The Reciprocal Rule — Minimum Handheld Shutter Speed

There is a traditional guideline in photography called the reciprocal rule: when shooting handheld (without a tripod), your shutter speed should be at least 1 divided by your effective focal length. With a 50mm equivalent focal length, the minimum safe handheld shutter speed is 1/50 second. With a 200mm equivalent, it is 1/200 second.

The OM-3's 5-axis IBIS (image stabilization) extends this safety margin significantly — typically by 5 to 7 stops. This means you can handhold much slower shutter speeds than the rule suggests. However, IBIS only stabilizes camera shake — it cannot help with a moving subject. For moving subjects you still need a fast shutter regardless of IBIS.

TIP: Set the minimum shutter in Auto ISO

If you are using Auto ISO, set the ISO Auto Minimum Shutter Speed (Shooting Menu Page 2) to a value that guarantees sharp handheld shots with your lens. For a 25mm lens (50mm equivalent on MFT), try 1/60 or 1/80 as your minimum. The camera will raise ISO before allowing the shutter to drop below this speed.

REAL-WORLD EXAMPLE: Silky waterfall effect

You want to photograph a waterfall so the water appears as smooth, silky white ribbons rather than frozen droplets.

> *Put the camera on a tripod. Set Mode Dial to S. Turn the rear dial to 1 second (shown as 1" on screen). Set ISO to 200. Use a remote shutter release or the 2-second self-timer to avoid camera shake when pressing. Review the result — if the water is not silky enough, try 2 seconds. If it is completely white with no texture, try 1/4 second.*

8.5 Exposure Compensation

Exposure Compensation (EC) is a tool that lets you intentionally override the camera's automatic exposure calculation to make the photo brighter or darker than the meter suggests. You keep the shooting mode (P, A, or S) and let the camera handle the exposure math — but you push the result in the direction you want.

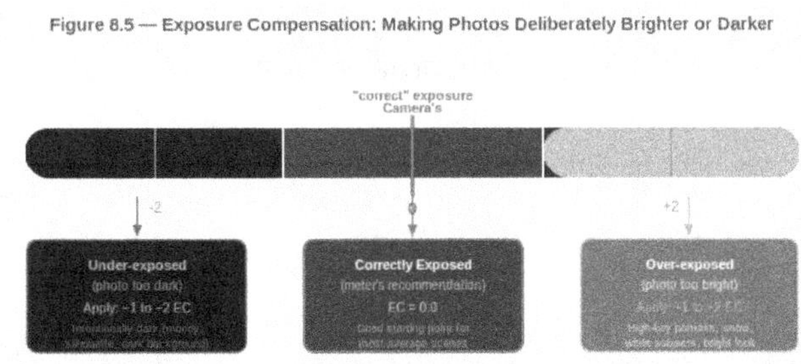

Figure 8.5 — The Exposure Compensation scale: negative values darken, positive values brighten

What Exposure Compensation Does

The camera's light meter is calibrated to render every scene as middle grey — approximately 18% reflectance. This works perfectly for an average scene with a balanced mix of light and dark tones. But for scenes that are predominantly bright (snow, white walls, a bride's dress) or predominantly dark (a black cat, a dark forest, a night scene), the meter gets it wrong:

- A snow scene: The meter sees all that white and tries to make it grey — the photo comes out dark and dull. Apply +1 to +2 EC to restore the snow to its true bright white.
- A backlit subject: The bright background fools the meter into underexposing your subject — they appear as a silhouette. Apply +1 to +2 EC to bring detail back into their face.
- A night scene with a small bright subject: The dark surroundings fool the meter into overexposing the subject. Apply -1 to -2 EC to bring the scene back to its intended darkness.
- A creative choice: You want a high-key airy portrait — apply +1 EC. You want a moody low-key dramatic shot — apply -1 or -2 EC.

How to Apply Exposure Compensation on the OM-3 — Exact Steps

Method 1 — Rear Dial Direct (Fastest in P and A modes)

> **Step 1:** In P or A mode, the rear dial often controls Exposure Compensation directly without pressing any additional button.

Step 2: Roll the rear dial to the RIGHT to increase EC (brighter: +0.3, +0.7, +1.0, +1.3 etc.).

Step 3: Roll the rear dial to the LEFT to decrease EC (darker: -0.3, -0.7, -1.0 etc.).

Step 4: Watch the exposure scale on screen — the marker moves away from zero to show the offset you have applied.

Step 5: The EC value (e.g. +1.0 or -0.7) appears on screen in the top row of information.

Method 2 — AEL Button + Rear Dial (Universal Method)

Step 1: Press and hold the AEL button (on the back of the camera, right of the LCD, above the arrow pad).

Step 2: While holding AEL, roll the rear dial RIGHT (brighter) or LEFT (darker).

Step 3: Release the AEL button. The EC value stays applied.

Step 4: This method works in all semi-automatic modes (P, A, S).

Method 3 — Arrow Pad UP Shortcut

Step 1: Press the UP arrow on the 4-way pad. The Exposure Compensation scale appears as a pop-up on screen.

Step 2: Use the LEFT/RIGHT arrows (or the rear dial) to move the marker left (darker) or right (brighter).

Step 3: Press OK to confirm, or simply half-press the shutter to shoot with the new EC value.

Resetting Exposure Compensation to Zero

Exposure Compensation persists between shots until you reset it. After finishing with a scene that needed EC, always return it to ±0.0. To reset quickly: use whichever method above moves the dial, and bring the marker back to the zero center position. Or press OK on the EC scale and select 0.0.

WARNING: EC stays applied between shots

If you apply +1.5 EC for a bright scene and forget to reset it before photographing a normally lit scene, all subsequent photos will be overexposed. Always check the EC value displayed on screen before moving to a new subject. If the display shows anything other than ±0.0, your EC is still active.

When to Use Positive EC (+) and When to Use Negative EC (−)

Scene Type	What the Meter Does	EC to Apply	Why
Bright snow or white sand beach	Underexposes (makes it grey)	+1.0 to +2.0 EV	Restore the white to its natural brightness
Subject against bright window (backlit)	Underexposes subject face	+1.0 to +2.0 EV	Bring detail back into the shadowed face
White wedding dress	Underexposes (tries to grey the white)	+0.7 to +1.3 EV	Keep the dress detail and brightness
Sunrise / sunset sky	Overexposes (tries to brighten the dark sky)	-0.7 to -1.0 EV	Keep the vivid drama of the coloured sky
Dark subject on dark background	Overexposes (tries to brighten the darkness)	-1.0 to -2.0 EV	Preserve the intentional low-key mood
Portrait in even soft light	Usually correct	0 EV (no change)	Meter works well for average skin tones in neutral light
Concert performer under spotlight	Overexposes performer (tries to balance dark surroundings)	-0.7 to -1.3 EV	Prevent the spotlight-lit face from blowing out
High-key airy fashion photo	Correct but you want brighter	+1.0 to +2.0 EV	Creative choice — intentionally bright and ethereal look

TIP: Use the histogram to confirm

The exposure compensation scale on screen shows the theoretical offset from the meter's reading. The histogram shows you the actual brightness distribution of what the camera would capture. Use the EC scale to apply your adjustment, then check the histogram to confirm the result is what you intended. See Part 3.5 for histogram interpretation.

8.6 AE Lock — Locking Exposure Separately from Focus

Auto Exposure Lock (AEL) freezes the camera's exposure reading at whatever value it currently shows on the meter. Once locked, you can reframe the shot, point at a completely different part of the scene, or even change your composition dramatically — and the exposure stays exactly where you locked it. This is one of the most useful techniques for handling challenging lighting situations.

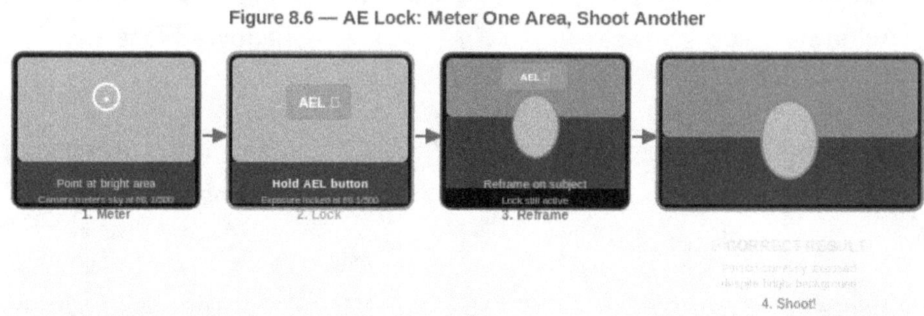

Figure 8.6 — AE Lock: meter a correctly lit area, lock the reading, reframe on your subject, shoot

When to Use AE Lock

Situation	Without AE Lock	With AE Lock
Subject against bright background	Camera re-meters when you point at subject — underexposes the subject	Meter the background, lock it, reframe on subject — balanced exposure
Moving between light and shadow	Camera constantly re-meters — exposure jumps between frames	Lock to a consistent reading — uniform exposure across the series
Spot metering a specific tone	If you reframe after spot metering, camera meters the new composition	Spot meter the critical tone, lock it, reframe freely
Architectural photography with mixed outdoor/indoor light	Camera struggles between the bright window and dark interior	Meter the exterior, lock, include interior — choose intentional balance

How to Use AE Lock — Step by Step

Step 1: Point the camera at the area of the scene you want to use as your metering reference — this might be your subject's face, a grey card, the sky, or another area that represents the exposure level you want.

Step 2: Half-press the shutter button to take a metering reading. The exposure values settle on screen.

Step 3: Without lifting your shutter finger from the half-press, press and hold the AEL button with your right thumb. The AEL button is on the back of the camera, to the right of the LCD screen, above the center of the arrow pad. It is labeled AEL or marked with an asterisk (*).

Step 4: You will see a small AEL indicator or star symbol (*) appear in the display. This confirms the exposure is locked.

Step 5: While continuing to hold the AEL button, reframe the shot to your preferred composition — the exposure remains at the locked value.

Step 6: Full-press the shutter to take the photo. The photo is exposed at the locked value regardless of what is now in the frame.

Step 7: Release the AEL button. The lock is released and normal metering resumes.

AE Lock vs Exposure Compensation — When to Use Which

Tool	What It Does	When to Use It
AE Lock	Holds the current metering reading — temporary, released when you release AEL button	One-off shots with unusual lighting; moving between compositional variations of the same scene; precise metering of a specific subject area
Exposure Compensation	Permanently offsets the meter reading by a set amount — persists across all subsequent shots until reset	Consistently bright or dark scenes where all photos need the same adjustment; shooting conditions that require ongoing correction like snow scenes or backlit subjects

TIP: AE Lock toggle mode

By default, AE Lock is active only while you hold the AEL button. You can switch it to toggle mode in Custom Menu A — one press locks, a second press unlocks. Toggle mode is useful when you need both hands to operate the camera (on a tripod with a remote shutter) and cannot hold the AEL button through the exposure.

8.7 Metering Modes

The metering mode determines how the camera measures the light in a scene to calculate the exposure. Different metering modes look at different areas of the frame and weight them differently. Choosing the right metering mode for your scene is a fundamental part of getting correct exposure without excessive use of exposure compensation.

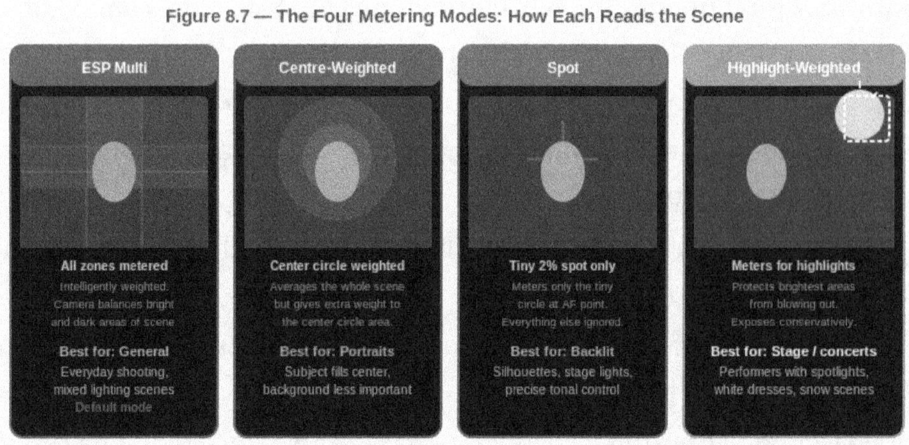

Figure 8.7 — The four metering modes: ESP (all zones), Centre-Weighted, Spot, and Highlight-Weighted

ESP Metering (Multi / Evaluative) — The Default

ESP stands for Electro-Selective Pattern. It is the default metering mode on the OM-3 and the most intelligent. The camera divides the entire frame into multiple zones, measures the brightness of each zone, and applies a sophisticated algorithm to produce a balanced exposure — taking into account the overall scene brightness, the position of the AF point, whether a face has been detected, and the contrast between highlights and shadows.

Aspect	Detail
What it measures	The entire frame divided into multiple zones, weighted toward the AF point and detected faces
Accuracy	Excellent for most scenes — handles 80-90% of everyday situations correctly without any adjustment
Best for	General photography, mixed lighting, landscapes, events, everyday shooting
When it struggles	Scenes with extreme contrast (very bright background, dark subject) or intentionally non-standard exposures
Recommended adjustment	Use Exposure Compensation when the result looks wrong — typically +1 to +2 for backlit subjects, -0.5 to -1 for night scenes

Centre-Weighted Metering

Centre-Weighted metering averages the brightness across the entire frame but gives significantly more weight — roughly 60-75% — to a circular area in the center of the frame. The corners and edges of the frame have less influence on the exposure calculation.

Aspect	Detail
What it measures	The whole frame, but with strong emphasis on the central circle area
Accuracy	Very reliable when your subject fills the center of the frame
Best for	Portraits where the face is centered, classical compositions with centered subjects, predictable studio situations
When it struggles	Off-center subjects — the bright or dark area in the center skews the reading for a subject that is not there
Historical note	This was the standard metering method for film cameras. Many experienced photographers who learned on film prefer it for its predictability

Spot Metering — Maximum Precision

Spot metering reads the light from an extremely small area — roughly 2% of the total frame area — centered on the current AF point. Everything outside this tiny circle is completely ignored by the meter.

Aspect	Detail
What it measures	Only the tiny circle at the AF point — approximately 2% of the frame
Accuracy	Extremely precise — reads exactly the tone you aim it at
Best for	Backlit subjects where you want the subject correctly exposed regardless of background; stage and concert performers under spotlights; wildlife against bright sky; any scene with extreme tonal contrast
When it struggles	Requires skill — if you aim the spot at the wrong area you get completely wrong exposure. Not ideal for fast-moving subjects where the spot may land on the background

Technique	Move the AF point onto your subject, take the reading, then use AE Lock to lock the exposure before reframing. Or use Spot metering with a grey card as a metering reference.

REAL-WORLD EXAMPLE: Stage performer under a spotlight

You are photographing a singer on a dark stage. The performer is brightly lit by a spotlight but the rest of the stage is black. ESP metering will try to brighten the whole scene — the performer's face will blow out.

Switch to Spot metering. Move the AF point to the performer's face. Half-press the shutter — the meter reads only the face, exposed correctly. Apply -0.3 to -0.7 EC to protect the highlights. Now the face is perfectly exposed regardless of the surrounding darkness.

Highlight-Weighted Metering — Protecting Your Highlights

Highlight-Weighted metering is unique to the OM SYSTEM. Instead of trying to achieve a balanced average exposure, it specifically identifies the brightest areas of the scene and exposes to prevent them from clipping (blowing out to pure white with no recoverable detail). The result is a slightly darker overall exposure that protects the most critical highlight information.

Aspect	Detail
What it measures	Scans the entire frame and identifies the brightest zones; meters conservatively to protect those highlights
Accuracy	Excellent for highlight-critical subjects — but may require + EC for subjects that are not the highlight
Best for	Wedding photography (protecting the dress), concerts and performances (spotlight preservation), automotive photography with shiny surfaces, photography of white or silver objects
When it struggles	Scenes without strong highlights — in flat, even lighting it may underexpose unnecessarily
Practical advantage	Eliminates the need to frequently apply negative EC for scenes with bright highlights — the meter does it automatically

How to Change the Metering Mode — Exact Steps

Method 1 — Via the Super Control Panel (Fastest)

Step 1: Press OK to open the Super Control Panel.

Step 2: Navigate to the Metering Mode tile — it shows an icon that looks like a circle with a dot (ESP), concentric circles (Centre-Weighted), a small dot (Spot), or a bracket/star (Highlight).

Step 3: Press OK to enter the metering selection screen.

Step 4: Use the arrows to highlight your preferred metering mode.

Step 5: Press OK to confirm and return to the SCP.

Step 6: Half-press the shutter to return to live view.

Method 2 — Via the Shooting Menu

Step 1: Press MENU → Shooting Menu (camera icon) → scroll to Page 4.

Step 2: Find Metering Mode and press OK or RIGHT.

Step 3: Select your preferred mode from the list.

Step 4: Press OK to confirm. Press MENU to close.

Quick Metering Mode Decision Guide

Scene	Recommended Metering Mode	Reason
General everyday photography	ESP (Multi)	Intelligent, handles most scenes well with minimal adjustment
Portrait with centered subject	Centre-Weighted	Reliable and predictable for faces filling the center of frame
Backlit subject, subject against bright sky	Spot + AE Lock	Read exactly the subject's tone, ignore the bright background
Stage performer, spotlight subject	Spot or Highlight-Weighted	Prevent bright lights from blowing out
Snow scene, white subject	ESP with +1 to +2 EC, or Highlight-Weighted	Camera underexposes white — EC or Highlight mode corrects it
Studio with controlled lighting	Centre-Weighted or Spot	Consistent, predictable lighting reward precise metering
Landscape with even sky and foreground	ESP (Multi)	Balanced scenes are exactly what ESP is designed for

Night street photography with bright lights	Spot or Highlight-Weighted	Prevents lamp and neon signs from clipping

TIP: Set metering mode to your Fn button

Metering mode is something many photographers change often — switching between ESP for general use and Spot for a backlit subject. Assign Metering Mode to an Fn button (Custom Menu B → Button Function) for instant one-press access without opening any menu.

Part 9 — White Balance

White balance is one of the most powerful and frequently overlooked controls in photography. When it is set correctly, colours in your photos look natural and accurate — white objects appear white, skin tones look healthy, and the overall mood of the scene is preserved faithfully. When it is wrong, even a technically perfect photo can look amateur: a portrait bathed in unpleasant orange from an indoor lamp, or a landscape turned cold and clinical by an incorrect blue cast.

The OM-3 offers a complete set of white balance tools — from fully automatic to completely manual and everything in between. This part of the guide explains what white balance is in plain English, walks through every preset option with its recommended use case, and shows you how to set a custom white balance for the most demanding and accurate situations.

9.1 What Is White Balance? (Plain English)

Different light sources produce light of different colours. A candle flame produces very warm, orange light. A midday sun produces clean, nearly white light. The shade on a clear blue-sky day produces cool, blue-tinted light. Fluorescent tubes produce a greenish cast. Each of these light sources has a colour temperature — measured in a unit called Kelvin (K).

The important thing to understand is this: the human visual system automatically and subconsciously corrects for these differences. When you walk from bright sunshine into a room lit by incandescent bulbs, your eyes very quickly adapt and the bulb light appears white and normal. The camera does not do this automatically — it records the light as it actually is. Without correction, the indoor photo looks orange because the light actually is orange-coloured.

White balance is the camera's way of applying the same correction your eyes do automatically. By telling the camera what kind of light you are shooting in, it applies the mathematically opposite colour shift to neutralise the cast — subtracting orange to make indoor tungsten light look white, adding orange to make cool shade light look neutral. The result is that white objects appear white, and all other colours look natural.

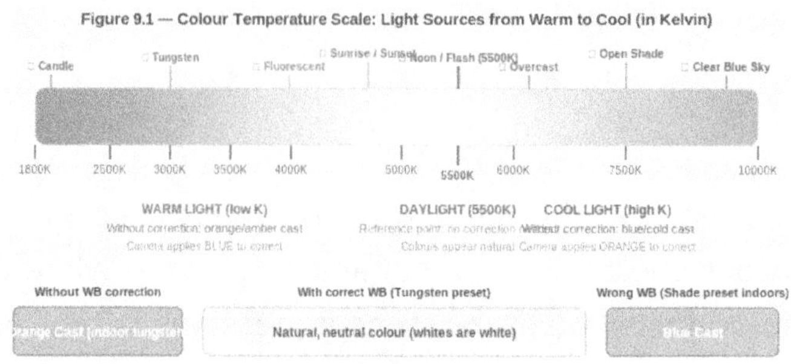

Figure 9.1 — The colour temperature scale from warm (orange) to cool (blue). The three strips show the effect of wrong WB (orange cast), correct WB (neutral), and opposite wrong WB (blue cast).

The Kelvin Scale — How It Works

The Kelvin scale measures colour temperature. Confusingly, it runs in the opposite direction from what you might expect — higher numbers are cooler (bluer) and lower numbers are warmer (more orange). Here is the key range:

Kelvin Value	Light Source	Colour Appearance
1,800 – 2,000 K	Candle flame	Very warm, deep orange-red
2,700 – 3,000 K	Tungsten / incandescent bulbs	Warm, clearly orange-yellow
3,200 – 3,500 K	Halogen lamps, warm LED	Warm yellow, less orange than tungsten
4,000 – 4,500 K	Cool white fluorescent / cool LED	Neutral with slight green tinge
5,000 – 5,500 K	Noon sunlight / electronic flash	Clean, neutral white — the reference standard
5,500 – 6,000 K	Overcast sky / cloudy daylight	Slightly cool, slightly blue-grey
7,000 – 8,000 K	Open shade, blue sky reflected	Noticeably cool, blue-tinged
9,000 – 12,000 K	Clear blue sky, snow shadows	Very cool, distinctly blue

Why White Balance Matters for JPEG vs RAW Shooters

File Format	White Balance Behaviour

JPEG	White balance is baked permanently into the JPEG file when it is saved. If you get it wrong, the colour cast is very difficult to correct later without degrading quality. For JPEG shooters, correct white balance in-camera is essential.
RAW	White balance information is stored as metadata alongside the raw sensor data, but is NOT permanently applied to the pixel values. You can change the white balance to any value you like in post-processing (Lightroom, Capture One, OM Workspace) with zero quality loss. For RAW shooters, in-camera WB matters less — though getting it right saves post-processing time.
RAW + JPEG	The JPEG has WB baked in. The RAW file allows full WB freedom in post. Many photographers use a close WB preset for the JPEG preview and correct precisely in post from the RAW.

TIP: RAW shooters: still set WB thoughtfully

Even if you shoot RAW and plan to correct WB in post, setting a reasonable WB in-camera ensures the LCD review image looks accurate — so you can judge the scene correctly on the spot. If your LCD preview shows a strong colour cast, you may misjudge exposure or miss colour-related problems until you get to the computer.

9.2 Auto White Balance (AWB)

Auto White Balance is the default white balance mode on the OM-3 and the starting point for most photographers. In AWB mode, the camera's processor analyses the colours present in the scene and attempts to determine what the neutral (white) reference should be. It then applies a correction to shift the image toward neutral.

How AWB Works in Practice

The camera's AWB algorithm looks for clues in the image — large areas of neutral colour, skin tones, recognised scene types — and uses them to estimate the colour temperature of the light. In most everyday conditions, AWB produces very good results:

- Sunny outdoors: AWB reads the neutral daylight and makes minimal correction. Result: accurate natural colours.
- Overcast / cloudy: AWB detects the slightly cool cast and warms the image slightly. Result: neutral, natural colours.

- Mixed lighting (a room with window light and lamps): AWB tries to balance the conflicting light sources. Result: reasonable, though not perfect — slight cast may remain.
- Pure tungsten indoor light: AWB detects the strong orange cast and adds blue correction. Result: mostly neutral white, though some warmth may remain depending on scene content.

Strengths and Limitations of AWB

AWB Strengths	AWB Limitations
Completely hands-off — no thought required	Can shift between shots in the same scene if the light changes even slightly
Adapts instantly to changing lighting conditions	Inconsistent across a burst sequence under mixed lighting — adjacent frames may have different WB
Works very well in mixed daylight conditions	Struggles with unusual light sources (sodium vapour street lights, fire, stage gel colours)
Best starting point for beginners	Can remove the intentional warmth of golden hour that you may want to preserve
Produces consistent results in flat, even studio-style lighting	Video shot on AWB may visibly shift WB mid-clip if you pan across different light sources

AWB Warm — Retaining Warmth in Incandescent Light

The OM-3 offers a variant of AWB called AWB Warm (sometimes shown as AWB W or AWB Keep Warm). Unlike standard AWB which aggressively neutralises the orange cast of incandescent and tungsten light, AWB Warm intentionally retains some of the warmth — producing images that look naturally warm under indoor lamplight rather than colour-corrected cold-and-white.

This setting is ideal for candlelit restaurant photography, fireplace scenes, or any situation where the warm golden-amber quality of the light is part of the atmosphere you want to preserve. To enable it: MENU → Custom Menu G → WB Auto (Warm Keep) → On.

How to Change White Balance — Method Overview

White balance can be changed via three routes. The fastest is the Super Control Panel:

> **Step 1:** Press OK to open the Super Control Panel (SCP).

Step 2: Navigate to the White Balance tile — it shows the letters AWB or the current WB icon (sun, cloud, etc.) in the upper-right area of the SCP grid.

Step 3: Press OK to open the full WB selection screen.

Step 4: Use the arrow pad to scroll through and highlight your preferred WB option.

Step 5: Press OK to confirm and return to the SCP.

Step 6: Half-press the shutter to return to live view. The WB icon updates in the top row of the display.

NOTE: WB shortcut button

On the OM-3, the LEFT arrow on the 4-way pad is often pre-assigned as a direct White Balance shortcut. Press it from live view and a WB selection pop-up appears immediately — no need to open the SCP. If this shortcut does not work on your camera, assign it in Custom Menu B → Button Function → Arrow Left → White Balance.

9.3 Preset White Balance Options — Each Explained with a Use Case

The OM-3 offers a full set of white balance presets, each calibrated for a specific type of light source. These presets produce more consistent results than AWB because they do not vary from shot to shot — once you select a preset, every photo in that session uses exactly the same colour correction.

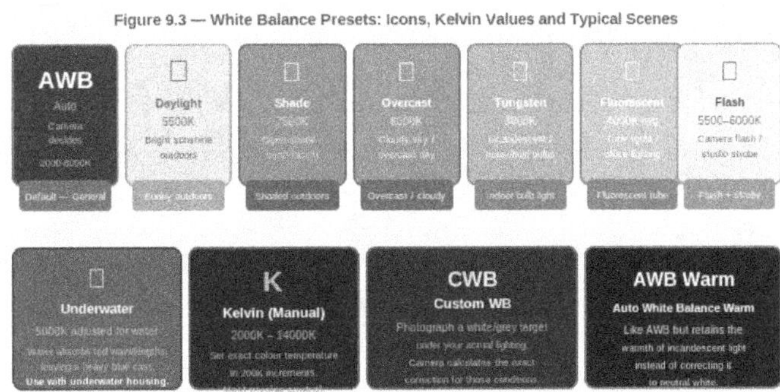

Figure 9.3 — All WB presets: icons, Kelvin values, best-use situations and additional K and CWB options

AWB — Auto White Balance (2000K–8000K, varies)

Already covered in detail in Section 9.2. This is the fully automatic mode. The camera analyses the scene and picks the correction that it calculates will produce a neutral result. Best for: quick shooting where the lighting is predictable and you do not need shot-to-shot consistency.

AWB Warm — Auto White Balance with Warmth Preserved

A variant of AWB that intentionally retains some of the orange-amber warmth of incandescent and tungsten lighting. The camera still corrects most of the orange cast — just not all of it. The result feels natural and cosy rather than sterile and over-corrected.

- Kelvin range: approximately 2700K–5500K (shifts with scene, but preserves warmth at the lower end)
- Best for: candlelit portraits, indoor lamp lighting where you want the warmth to show, fire photography
- Not for: situations where you need clinical neutral accuracy

Daylight / Sunny (Sun Icon) — 5500K

The Daylight preset is calibrated for direct sunlight at or around noon — the closest thing to a universally neutral light source. At 5500K, daylight is the reference standard against which most lighting and photography equipment is calibrated. When you shoot in direct sunshine with the Daylight preset, no correction is applied — the camera simply records the scene as-is.

- Kelvin value: 5500K (fixed)
- Appearance: warm and natural in direct sun; slightly cool in overcast shade
- Best for: outdoor photography in direct sunlight, outdoor portraits in sun, any bright midday outdoor scene
- Not for: indoor tungsten light (result: very strong orange cast), shade (result: slight blue cast)

> **REAL-WORLD SCENARIO: Outdoor portrait in sunshine**
>
> *You are photographing a friend on a sunny beach at noon. Set WB to Daylight (sun icon). The camera applies no correction because the light is already neutral. Skin tones, clothing colours, and the sea all look exactly as they do to your eyes. No colour cast. Switch to AWB and compare — the result may be subtly different if the scene has unusual dominant colours.*

Shade (Tree Icon) — 7500K

Open shade on a clear sunny day is surprisingly cool and blue. This happens because objects in shade are lit primarily by the blue sky overhead rather than by the sun directly. The shade preset adds a warming correction — shifting the image toward amber-orange — to counteract this blue-sky influence.

- Kelvin value: approximately 7500K (adds warm correction to counteract cool shade)
- Appearance: warm and natural when used in genuine open shade; strongly orange/warm if used in sunlight
- Best for: outdoor portraits in open shade, subjects lit by bounced skylight, north-facing locations in the northern hemisphere

- Creative use: deliberately apply Shade preset in golden-hour sunlight to intensify the warm glow for a more dramatic sunset look

Overcast (Cloud Icon) — 6000K

On an overcast cloudy day the sun is hidden but the overall sky acts as a large, soft light source. The light is slightly cooler and more diffused than direct sunlight. The Overcast preset adds a small warming correction to keep colours looking natural rather than slightly cold.

- Kelvin value: approximately 6000K
- Appearance: natural and neutral under thick cloud cover
- Best for: portrait photography on overcast days (the diffused light is flattering), outdoor events and weddings on cloudy days
- Not for: indoor lighting

> **NOTE: Overcast is ideal for portrait work**
>
> Overcast light is beloved by portrait photographers because clouds act like a giant natural diffuser — eliminating harsh shadows, reducing contrast on faces, and producing beautiful, even skin tones. Combined with the Overcast WB preset, cloudy days often produce the most flattering portraits. Do not wait for sunshine.

Tungsten / Incandescent (Lightbulb Icon) — 3000K

Old-style incandescent light bulbs and tungsten studio lights produce very warm, orange light at around 3000K. Without correction this gives photos a strong orange-amber cast. The Tungsten preset adds a heavy blue correction to neutralise this and make whites appear white under bulb light.

- Kelvin value: approximately 3000K
- Appearance: neutral and clean under genuine tungsten/incandescent bulbs; strongly blue if used outdoors in daylight
- Best for: rooms lit by traditional incandescent bulbs, tungsten studio lighting (though studio has its own exact K value), hotel room lamps
- Modern LED bulbs: many warm-white LEDs are around 2700K-3200K and respond well to the Tungsten preset. But cool-white LEDs may be 5000K+ and need no correction.

> **REAL-WORLD SCENARIO: Indoor family photo under household lamps**
>
> *You are photographing a family gathered in a living room lit by standard household bulb lamps. The walls look orange on your LCD, and skin tones have an unhealthy warm cast. Set WB to Tungsten. Instantly the orange cast disappears, walls look white, and skin tones look natural. If the result looks slightly blue, try the Overcast preset instead — some modern warm LEDs are not as warm as tungsten and need less correction.*

Fluorescent (Strip Light Icon) — Multiple Sub-Types

Fluorescent tube lights are complex light sources. Unlike tungsten and daylight which sit cleanly on the colour temperature scale, fluorescent lights have what photographers call a discontinuous spectrum — they emit light at specific wavelengths that are spaced out, rather than across all wavelengths evenly. This produces a characteristic green cast that a simple warm-cool correction cannot fully fix.

The OM-3 offers several fluorescent sub-types because there are different kinds of fluorescent tubes with different colour characteristics:

Fluorescent Sub-Type	Typical Environment	Approx. Kelvin
Daylight Fluorescent	Modern cool-white tubes (hospitals, offices, shops)	6500K
Natural Fluorescent	Neutral-balance tubes	5000K
Cool White Fluorescent	Older office strip lighting	4200K
Warm White Fluorescent	Warm-toned tube lighting	3500K
Warm Fluorescent	Very warm indoor tube lighting	3000K

If you are unsure which sub-type matches your fluorescent environment, start with Cool White Fluorescent for typical office/public space tubes, or Natural Fluorescent for modern retail and office lighting. Review the result on the LCD and adjust if a colour cast remains.

- Best for: offices, supermarkets, gyms, schools, public buildings, hospitals
- Note: LED panel lights are increasingly replacing fluorescent tubes in offices. Many LED panels are rated at 4000K or 5000K and may respond better to AWB or a Daylight/Overcast preset than to the Fluorescent presets.

Flash (Lightning Bolt Icon) — 5500–6000K

The Flash white balance preset is calibrated specifically for the colour temperature of electronic flash (speedlights, strobe heads, and ring flashes). Modern flash units are typically rated at 5500K to 6000K — very close to natural daylight, but not identical. Using the Flash preset instead of Daylight when shooting with flash produces slightly better colour accuracy, particularly with skin tones.

- Kelvin value: approximately 5500–6000K (varies slightly by flash manufacturer and power level)

- Best for: portrait photography with on-camera or off-camera flash, product photography with studio strobes
- Tip: if using flash outdoors in daylight, the Daylight preset often works just as well as the Flash preset since both are calibrated near 5500K

Underwater (Wave Icon)

Water progressively absorbs different wavelengths of light as depth increases. Red light is absorbed first, then orange, then yellow — so at even moderate depth, the natural scene appears strongly blue-green. The Underwater white balance preset adds a strong warm (orange-red) correction to compensate for this water filtration effect.

- Best for: use with the OM-3 inside a compatible underwater housing during snorkelling or scuba photography
- Important: the OM-3 itself is splash-resistant and weather-sealed, but it is NOT rated for full submersion without a dedicated underwater housing. Do not submerge the bare camera.
- Note: the Underwater preset is most useful in the 2–10 metre depth range. In very shallow water (under 1 metre) where red light is still plentiful, Daylight or AWB may actually be more accurate.

K — Kelvin Manual (2000K–14000K)

The K setting lets you manually enter a precise Kelvin colour temperature value rather than relying on a preset. You scroll through values in 200K increments from 2000K to 14000K.

- How to access: in the WB selection screen, scroll to K and press OK. A Kelvin value selector appears — use the rear dial or arrow keys to scroll to the value you want.
- Best for: professional photographers who know their lighting environment's exact colour temperature (studio strobes are usually rated with their K value), or for creative use where you want precise control
- Example values: 2800K for tungsten, 3200K for halogen, 5500K for flash, 7000K for shade
- Creative use: setting a very low K value (e.g. 2500K) outdoors produces an intentionally cold, blue look. Setting a high K value (e.g. 8000K) outdoors produces an intentionally warm, golden look.

> **TIP: Use K value for consistent video**
>
> For video work, the Kelvin manual setting is especially valuable. Once you know the K value of your set lighting (e.g. 5600K for daylight-balanced LED panels), entering it directly ensures perfectly consistent colour temperature across the entire recording with no risk of AWB shifts mid-clip.

9.4 Custom White Balance — Step-by-Step Setup

Custom White Balance (CWB) is the most accurate white balance method available. Instead of relying on a preset approximation or the camera's automatic guess, Custom WB involves photographing a neutral reference target (a grey card or a white sheet of paper) under your actual lighting conditions. The camera then analyses that image and calculates the precise colour correction needed to make the grey card appear perfectly neutral — and applies that correction to all subsequent photos.

The result is colour accuracy that no preset or auto setting can match, because it is calibrated to the exact, specific light in your specific scene at that specific moment. If the light source is an unusual colour (aged fluorescent tubes with a greenish tint, a coloured wall reflecting onto your subject, mixed daylight and tungsten), Custom WB corrects for all of it simultaneously.

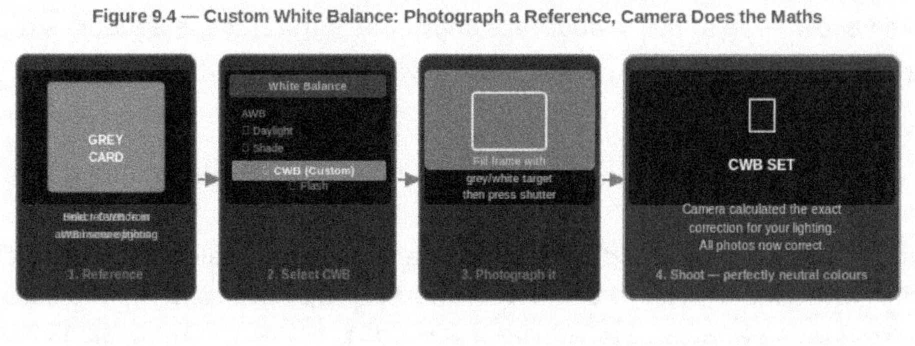

Figure 9.4 — Custom WB: photograph a grey reference card under your actual light, camera calculates the exact correction

What You Need for Custom WB

- A neutral grey card or white balance reference card — available at any camera shop for a few dollars. An 18% grey card is the professional standard. A clean white sheet of paper is a usable alternative but is less accurate because paper can have a slight blue (optical brightener) or off-white tint.
- The card must be placed in the same light that will illuminate your subject — do not hold it in sun if your subject is in shade.
- The card should fill a large portion of the frame — ideally 60-80% of the image area. The lens does not need to be focused.

How to Set Custom hite Balance — Exact Steps

Step 1: Place your grey card (or hold it so that it is lit by the same light as your subject). The card can be held by you or by an assistant — it just needs to be in the right light.

Step 2: Point the camera at the grey card. Fill most of the frame with the card. You do not need the card to be in focus — it can be blurry.

Step 3: Press MENU → Shooting Menu (camera icon) → scroll to White Balance → press OK to enter WB selection.

Step 4: In the WB selection screen, scroll through the options until you reach CWB (Custom WB). Highlight it but DO NOT press OK yet.

Step 5: Look for a SET or SHOOT option — the exact wording varies by firmware, but you will see an option to capture the reference image. Press the button indicated (often the OK button or the shutter button while CWB is highlighted).

Step 6: The camera takes a white balance reading from the grey card currently in frame. The screen may flash briefly or display a confirmation message.

Step 7: If the camera asks you to confirm, press OK to accept the new custom WB value.

Step 8: The CWB setting is now stored. Press MENU to close.

Step 9: From now on, when CWB is selected as your white balance, all photos use this custom correction. Your grey card, under this specific light, will appear perfectly neutral grey in all photos.

NOTE: CWB persists until you overwrite it

The Custom WB value you set stays stored in memory even after the camera is turned off. The next time you power on and select CWB, it will still use the same stored correction. If the light changes (you move to a different room, the sun moves significantly, the light source is turned off), you must take a new CWB reading. The old stored value will be wrong for the new light.

Alternative Method — Setting CWB from an Existing Photo

The OM-3 also allows you to set a Custom WB from a photo already saved on your SD card. This is useful if you forgot to set CWB during the shoot but photographed a grey card at any point during the session:

Step 1: Enter Playback mode (press the Playback button).

Step 2: Navigate to the photo that shows the grey card.

Step 3: Press MENU → Playback Menu → RAW Retouch or look for 'WB Compensation from Image' option.

Step 4: Some firmware versions offer a 'Custom WB from this image' function directly in the Playback Menu — highlight it and press OK.

Step 5: The camera calculates the custom WB from the grey card in the selected image and stores it as the new CWB value.

Step 6: Return to shooting mode and select CWB.

TIP: Grey card for video

For professional video work, have your subject or assistant hold the grey card in frame at the start of a scene, record a few seconds of it, then remove it and shoot normally. In post-production, use that grey card footage to set the white balance reference in your editing software. This achieves the same accuracy as in-camera CWB but gives you more flexibility in post.

9.5 White Balance Fine-Tuning (Amber/Blue, Green/Magenta Axes)

After selecting any white balance preset or mode (AWB, Daylight, Shade, CWB, or any other), you can apply an additional fine-tuning adjustment to shift the colour in any direction. This is done on a two-axis colour grid inside the camera, giving you very precise control over the final colour rendering.

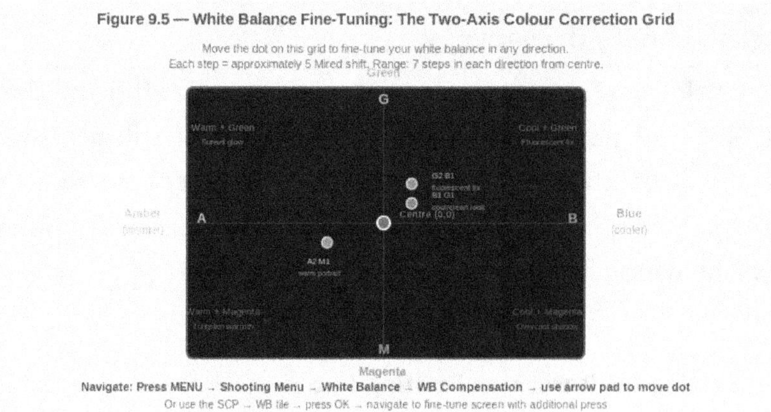

Figure 9.5 — The WB fine-tuning grid: two axes (Amber-Blue and Green-Magenta), adjustable up to 7 steps in each direction

Understanding the Two Axes

The fine-tuning grid has two axes:

Axis	Direction	What It Does	Measured In
Horizontal Axis (A–B)	Left = Amber (A) / Right = Blue (B)	Shifts the colour temperature warmer (left) or cooler (right). This is the primary colour temperature correction axis — similar to adjusting the Kelvin value.	Steps 1–7 in each direction (7A = very warm, 7B = very cool)

Vertical Axis (G–M)	Up = Green (G) / Down = Magenta (M)	Corrects for the green or magenta colour cast that some artificial light sources produce. Fluorescent lights typically need a magenta correction (move down). Some LED lights may need a green correction (move up).	Steps 1–7 in each direction (7G = very green, 7M = very magenta)

How to Access the WB Fine-Tuning Grid — Exact Steps

Step 1: Press MENU → Shooting Menu (camera icon) → scroll to White Balance → press OK.

Step 2: In the WB selection screen, choose your desired WB preset (e.g. AWB or Daylight) — but do not press OK yet.

Step 3: With the preset highlighted, press the RIGHT arrow or the INFO button — this enters the fine-tuning screen for that specific WB preset. (The exact button varies by firmware — look for a small grid icon or fine-tune indicator on screen.)

Step 4: The fine-tuning grid appears. A red dot sits in the center at position (0, 0) — no adjustment applied.

Step 5: Use the UP, DOWN, LEFT, and RIGHT arrows on the 4-way pad to move the red dot in any direction.

Step 6: Moving LEFT (toward A): warms the image — adds amber.

Step 7: Moving RIGHT (toward B): cools the image — adds blue.

Step 8: Moving UP (toward G): adds a green tint.

Step 9: Moving DOWN (toward M): adds magenta (useful for correcting fluorescent green cast).

Step 10: Press OK to confirm the adjustment and return to the WB selection screen.

Step 11: Press MENU to close. Your fine-tuning offset will now be applied on top of the selected WB preset for all subsequent shots.

How Fine-Tuning Interacts with WB Presets

Each WB preset stores its own separate fine-tuning offset. This means you can set a +A2 M1 fine-tuning for your Daylight preset (to warm portraits in direct sun slightly) and separately set a G2 fine-tuning for your Fluorescent preset (to correct for green fluorescent cast) — and they will not interfere with each other. When you switch presets, the fine-tuning for that specific preset is applied automatically.

Practical Fine-Tuning Recipes

Situation / Goal	Suggested Adjustment	Result
Skin tones look slightly too red / magenta in portraits	Move 1–2 steps toward G (green)	Reduces the reddish-pink tone in skin, more natural complexion
Skin tones look slightly green or sallow	Move 1–2 steps toward M (magenta)	Adds warmth and flushes the green out of skin tones
Scene feels slightly too cold / clinical despite correct WB preset	Move 1–2 steps toward A (amber)	Adds subtle warmth to the overall image
Scene feels slightly too warm / orange despite correct WB preset	Move 1–2 steps toward B (blue)	Adds subtle cooling to the overall image
Fluorescent light leaves a green cast even with Fluorescent preset	Move 1–3 steps toward M (magenta)	Corrects the residual green cast that many fluorescent tubes leave
LED panel light has a slight green or yellow cast	Move 1–2 steps toward M, then 1 step toward B	Corrects the mixed green-warm cast of some LED panels
Golden hour portrait — want even more warmth than the Shade preset gives	Move 2–3 steps toward A	Intensifies the golden warm light for a more dramatic sunset feel
Overcast portrait — want a cooler, moody desaturated look	Move 1–2 steps toward B and 1 step toward G	Creates a cool, clean, slightly editorial look

White Balance Bracketing — Testing Multiple WB Values at Once

The OM-3 supports White Balance Bracketing (WB Bracketing), which shoots a single frame but automatically saves multiple versions of the JPEG file with different white balance fine-tuning values applied. This lets you try several WB corrections simultaneously without reshoot.

Step 1: Go to MENU → Custom Menu G → WB Bracketing.

Step 2: Choose the number of frames (2 or 3) and the step size (how far apart the variations are in Mired).

Step 3: Shoot. The camera saves 2 or 3 JPEG files from the single capture — one at your current WB, one or two shifted versions.

Step 4: Review all three versions in playback and select the best one.

TIP: Use WB Bracketing when you are unsure

If you are in a mixed-lighting environment where no single WB preset looks perfect and you cannot set a custom WB at that moment, enable WB bracketing with 3 frames and a 2-step spread. This gives you three slight variations to choose from after the shoot. The RAW file is saved only once — only the JPEGs are multiplied.

White Balance Best Practices — Summary

Shooting Context	Recommended WB Approach
Casual photos, changing conditions, outdoors	AWB or AWB Warm — fast and reliable in most situations
Consistent outdoor portrait sessions	Daylight in sun, Overcast when clouds cover the sun
Indoor event photography under mixed lights	AWB (accept some variation) or CWB from a grey card for precision
Studio photography with strobe lights	Flash preset, or K value matching your strobe's rated temperature
Tungsten / halogen indoor lighting	Tungsten preset (3000K)
Office / public space fluorescent lighting	Fluorescent (Cool White) preset + possible M fine-tuning
Video — scripted or controlled environment	K value (exact Kelvin), NEVER AWB for video
Underwater photography	Underwater preset, or CWB from a grey card

Maximum accuracy in any light	Custom WB from a grey card — applies to any light source
RAW shooter who corrects in post	AWB for convenience; adjust precisely in Lightroom / Capture One

Part 10 — Image Quality and Format

Every time you press the shutter, the OM-3 records your photo as a digital file on the SD card. The decisions you make about file format, size, and shape affect how large the file is, how much editing freedom you have afterward, how many photos fit on the card, and how your images look when printed or shared online.

This section covers four choices: the format (JPEG, RAW, or both), the size and compression level of JPEG files, the aspect ratio (the shape of the frame), and the exact steps for changing all of these settings on the OM-3.

10.1 JPEG vs. RAW vs. RAW+JPEG — What Each Means, Which to Choose

The most important image quality decision you will make is which file format to use. The OM-3 can save your photos in three ways: as a JPEG, as a RAW file, or as both simultaneously. Understanding the difference between these formats is essential for making the right choice for your photography.

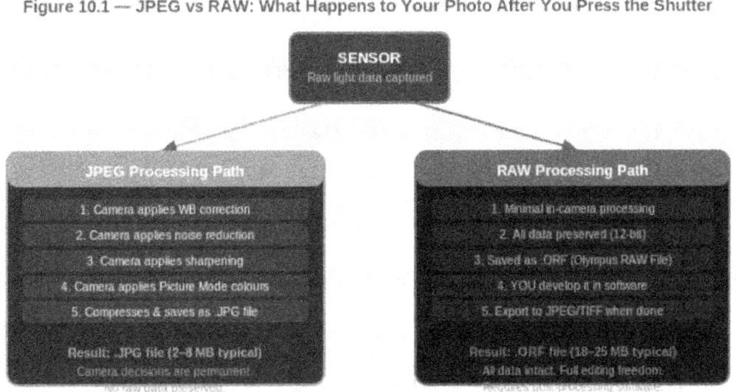

Figure 10.1 — After you press the shutter, JPEG goes through in-camera processing; RAW preserves all data for you to develop later

JPEG — The Processed, Ready-to-Share Format

JPEG (Joint Photographic Experts Group) is the most common image format in the world. It is what your phone camera saves, what you see on social media, and what most online platforms accept. On the OM-3, when you shoot JPEG, the camera performs a complete processing pipeline immediately after you press the shutter:

- Applies your chosen White Balance setting — permanently baking the colour correction into the file.
- Applies your chosen Picture Mode (Natural, Vivid, Monotone, etc.) — permanently applying those colours and tones.
- Applies noise reduction, lens corrections, sharpening, and distortion compensation.
- Compresses the resulting image using JPEG compression — reducing the file size by discarding some data.

- Saves the final compressed image as a .JPG file on your SD card.

The entire process happens in less than a second. The result is a file that is immediately ready to share — no post-processing required. But the decisions are permanent: you cannot change the white balance, picture mode, or noise reduction after the fact because the raw sensor data has been discarded.

RAW — The Unprocessed, Full-Data Format

A RAW file is not an image in the traditional sense. It is a record of the raw electrical data from every pixel on the sensor, captured before any in-camera processing is applied. On the OM-3, RAW files are saved in the Olympus/OM SYSTEM proprietary format with the extension .ORF (Olympus Raw File).

RAW files are larger than JPEGs — typically 18 to 25 megabytes on the OM-3, compared to 3 to 8 megabytes for a Large JPEG. But they contain information that simply does not exist in a JPEG:

- All 12 bits of tonal information per channel (versus 8 bits in JPEG) — giving you roughly 4,000 levels of brightness instead of 256. This makes highlights and shadow recovery far more effective.
- The raw white balance data — allowing you to change the white balance to any value in post with zero quality loss.
- Uncompressed colour data — no JPEG compression artefacts or quality loss from the camera.
- Full latitude for noise reduction — you can apply more sophisticated noise reduction in software than the camera can apply in-camera.

To view or use a RAW file, you need RAW processing software such as Adobe Lightroom, Capture One, or OM SYSTEM's own free OM Workspace application. You develop (process) the RAW file in the software, making all the decisions about white balance, exposure, noise reduction, and colour — and then export a final JPEG or TIFF for sharing or printing.

RAW + JPEG — Both Files Simultaneously

In RAW+JPEG mode, the OM-3 saves two separate files for every shot: a full RAW .ORF file AND a JPEG processed according to your current camera settings. This gives you the best of both worlds — the JPEG is immediately usable for sharing, while the RAW file is there if you need to edit any shot more extensively.

The downside is storage: RAW+JPEG uses approximately three times more card space than JPEG alone, and the camera writes more data per shot, which slightly affects the burst buffer capacity.

Choosing Between JPEG, RAW, and RAW+JPEG

Format	File Size (approx)	Post-Processing Needed?	Editing Freedom	Best For

JPEG Large Fine (LF)	5–8 MB per photo	No — immediately usable	Limited — WB, tone, NR decisions are permanent	Casual photography, events where speed matters, situations where you do not have time to edit, sharing directly from camera
RAW (.ORF)	18–25 MB per photo	Yes — requires RAW software	Complete — change any setting in post with no quality loss	Professional work, landscape and portrait photography where quality is paramount, any situation where you may need to rescue an exposure or white balance error
RAW + JPEG (LF)	23–33 MB per photo (both files)	No for JPEG, optional for RAW	Complete (from RAW file)	The safest and most flexible choice — use the JPEG for quick sharing and fall back on the RAW for serious edits. Recommended for most users who have sufficient storage.
RAW + JPEG (LN)	21–29 MB per photo	No for JPEG, optional for RAW	Complete (from RAW file)	Same as above but with a slightly smaller JPEG companion — useful when card space is limited

TIP: Start with RAW+LN if you are unsure

If you are new to RAW processing and are not sure which format to use, RAW+LN (RAW plus Large Normal JPEG) is a very good default. The JPEG is immediately shareable and the RAW file is there if you ever want to edit a photo more seriously. As you become more comfortable with RAW processing, you can switch to RAW only to save space.

NOTE: RAW files need OM Workspace or Lightroom

If you choose to shoot RAW, you will need software to open the .ORF files. OM SYSTEM's own OM Workspace application is free and available at omsystem.com. Adobe Lightroom Classic and Lightroom (subscription), Capture One, and DxO PhotoLab also fully support OM-3 RAW files. Standard Windows Photos or Apple Photos may not show RAW files correctly without a codec update.

WARNING: JPEG quality settings also matter

Not all JPEGs are equal. The OM-3 offers different JPEG sizes (Large, Medium, Small) and compression levels (Fine, Normal). A Small Normal JPEG from the OM-3 is far lower quality than a Large Fine JPEG — even though both are JPEG files. Always verify your JPEG quality settings are appropriate before shooting. See Section 10.2.

10.2 Image Size and Compression Settings

When shooting JPEG (either JPEG-only or the JPEG part of RAW+JPEG), you choose both the pixel dimensions (Size: Large, Medium, or Small) and the compression ratio (Quality: Fine or Normal). These two settings together determine how large the JPEG file is and how much detail is preserved.

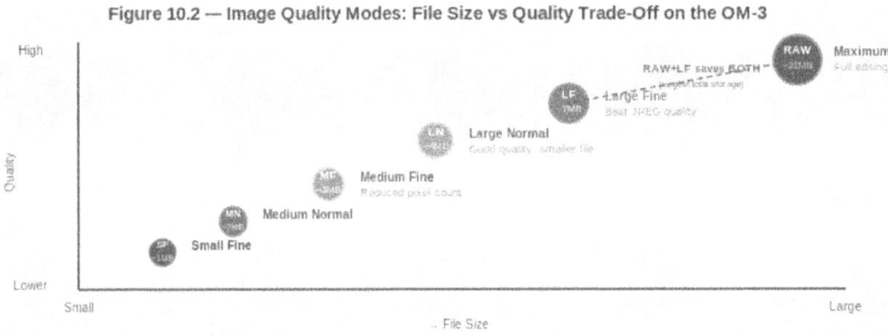

Figure 10.2 — Image quality modes plotted by file size vs quality. RAW sits at maximum quality; smaller JPEGs trade quality for storage space.

Image Size — How Many Pixels

Size refers to the pixel dimensions of the saved image. The OM-3's sensor has approximately 20 megapixels in 4:3 ratio. The three size options work as follows:

Size Code	Pixel Dimensions (4:3)	Megapixels	Max Print Size at 300 DPI	File Size (Fine JPEG)
Large (L)	4608 × 3456 pixels	~20 MP	15.3 × 11.5 inches (A3+ quality)	5–8 MB

Medium (M)	3200 × 2400 pixels	~8 MP	10.7 × 8.0 inches (A4 quality)	2–4 MB
Small (S)	1280 × 960 pixels	~1.2 MP	4.3 × 3.2 inches (snapshot size)	0.5–1 MB

For almost all purposes, use Large (L). The extra pixels give you the ability to crop heavily without losing quality, to print at large sizes, and to produce more detailed images. Medium is useful if you need smaller files for a specific purpose — such as website use or filling a card during a very long event. Small is only appropriate for thumbnails or placeholder images.

Compression — Fine vs Normal

Compression determines how much the JPEG algorithm squeezes the image data to reduce file size. The OM-3 offers two levels:

Compression	Code	File Size	Image Quality	When to Use
Fine	F (e.g. LF = Large Fine)	Larger (5–8 MB for Large)	Highest JPEG quality — minimal compression artefacts, smooth gradients, fine detail preserved	Any situation where image quality matters. Always use Fine unless you have a specific reason to accept lower quality.
Normal	N (e.g. LN = Large Normal)	Smaller (3–5 MB for Large)	Good quality — some compression artefacts visible at 100% zoom in smooth areas (sky, skin), but acceptable for most uses	When card space is limited and you need more shots, or when you know the final output will be viewed at small sizes (web thumbnails, social media at standard resolution)
Super Fine (SF)	SF (if available)	Very large (8–12 MB for Large)	Minimal compression, closest JPEG to RAW quality	When maximum JPEG quality is needed without shooting RAW — product photography, client work

> **TIP: Always shoot Large Fine as your default JPEG setting**
>
> Unless you have a specific reason to reduce image size or quality, set your JPEG to Large Fine (LF). Storage is cheap — you can always buy a larger card. But you cannot go back and re-capture a moment at higher quality after the fact. LF is the correct default for 99% of situations.

The Full Quality Code Reference

The OM-3 displays image quality as a code in the live view display and in the SCP. Here is the full code reference so you can understand at a glance what your camera is currently set to:

Display Code	Full Name	Approximate File Size	Notes
RAW	RAW only (.ORF)	18–25 MB	No JPEG companion. Maximum editing freedom.
RAW+LF	RAW + Large Fine JPEG	23–33 MB (both files)	Best quality + JPEG for sharing. Most popular professional choice.
RAW+LN	RAW + Large Normal JPEG	21–30 MB (both files)	Slightly smaller JPEG companion. Good all-round choice.
RAW+SF	RAW + Small Fine JPEG	18–26 MB (both files)	Very small JPEG companion — useful when you just need a tiny preview JPEG.
LF	Large Fine JPEG	5–8 MB	Highest quality JPEG, no RAW. Best for events and situations without time to edit.
LN	Large Normal JPEG	3–5 MB	Good quality JPEG, slightly smaller file. Acceptable for most purposes.
MF	Medium Fine JPEG	2–4 MB	Reduced pixel count. For when you genuinely do not need 20MP.
MN	Medium Normal JPEG	1–3 MB	Reduced size and quality. Web and small print use.

SF	Small Fine JPEG	0.5–1 MB	Very small file. Thumbnail / reference use only.
SN	Small Normal JPEG	0.3–0.6 MB	Smallest possible file. Almost never used.

10.3 Aspect Ratio Settings (4:3, 3:2, 16:9, 1:1, 3:4)

Aspect ratio is the proportional shape of the image frame — the relationship between its width and its height. The OM-3 offers five aspect ratio options, each producing a differently shaped image. Understanding which to use requires thinking about where the image will be displayed or printed.

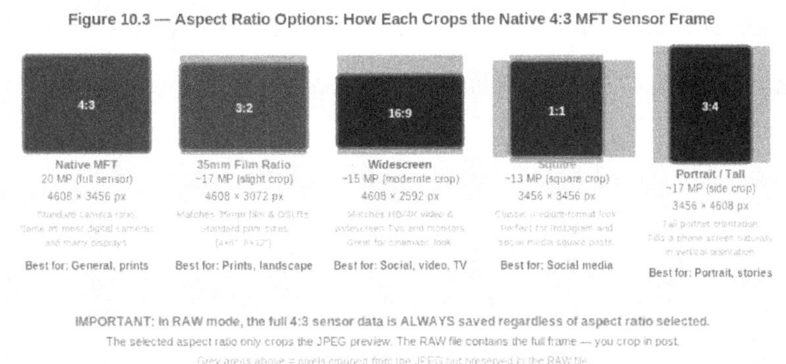

Figure 10.3 — All five aspect ratios shown relative to the native 4:3 sensor. Grey areas are cropped from JPEG but preserved in RAW.

4:3 — The Native MFT Sensor Ratio (Default)

The 4:3 ratio (read as "four-to-three") is the native shape of the Micro Four Thirds sensor in the OM-3. When you shoot at 4:3, the entire sensor is used and no cropping occurs. This is the default and gives you the maximum possible resolution from the camera.

- Pixel dimensions: 4608 × 3456 pixels (approximately 20 megapixels)
- Shape: slightly wider than tall — a compact, square-ish rectangle
- Matches: the native display ratio of most digital cameras, many computer monitors, and square-ish screen formats
- Best for: general photography when you are not sure of the final output medium, scientific/documentary photography where maximum resolution is important, any use where you will crop in post to a specific ratio
- Tip: if you shoot 4:3 and later need a 3:2 or 16:9 crop, you can always crop afterward in software — especially easy with a RAW file

3:2 — The 35mm Film / DSLR Standard

The 3:2 ratio (three-to-two) is the classic 35mm film frame proportion. Almost all full-frame and APS-C DSLRs and mirrorless cameras use 3:2 as their native ratio. Many standard print sizes — 4×6 inches, 6×9 inches, 8×12 inches, A5, A4 — are close to 3:2 proportions. If you regularly print photos at these sizes or are used to composing for 3:2, this is a natural and familiar choice.

- Pixel dimensions: 4608 × 3072 pixels (approximately 17 megapixels — a slight top-and-bottom crop)
- Shape: wider and more rectangular than 4:3
- Matches: standard photo print sizes (4×6", 5×7", A4), most DSLR and full-frame mirrorless cameras, Instagram landscape and portrait posts when printed
- Best for: photographers who regularly print photos, those accustomed to DSLR framing, landscape photography, architectural work

16:9 — Widescreen / Video Format

The 16:9 ratio (sixteen-to-nine) is the standard format for HD and 4K television, most computer monitors, YouTube, and widescreen cinema. It is a wide, panoramic shape — noticeably wider than 4:3 or 3:2.

- Pixel dimensions: 4608 × 2592 pixels (approximately 15 megapixels — a significant top-and-bottom crop)
- Shape: very wide relative to its height — cinematic, panoramic feeling
- Matches: HD and 4K TV screens, widescreen computer monitors, YouTube thumbnails, video frame grabs, Instagram landscape posts on most devices
- Best for: landscape photography with a dramatic wide panoramic feel, architectural and environmental work, social media content creation, photos taken alongside video footage for consistency, photos intended for YouTube thumbnails or widescreen digital display

> **NOTE: 16:9 sacrifices significant resolution**
>
> Selecting 16:9 crops away roughly a quarter of the native sensor — you lose approximately 5 megapixels compared to shooting 4:3. For most screen viewing this is irrelevant, but for large prints it matters. If you want a 16:9 crop AND maximum resolution, shoot 4:3 RAW and crop to 16:9 in post — this gives you the full pixel data with the wide crop shape.

1:1 — Square Format

The 1:1 ratio produces a perfectly square image — equal width and height. Square photography has a long tradition in medium-format film photography (Hasselblad, Rolleiflex), and has been popularised again by Instagram and other social media platforms that favour square posts.

- Pixel dimensions: 3456 × 3456 pixels (approximately 13 megapixels — cropped on both left and right sides)
- Shape: perfect square
- Matches: Instagram square posts, classic medium-format photography aesthetic, certain print sizes (5×5", 8×8")
- Best for: Instagram posts, still life and product photography with symmetrical compositions, portrait photography with a centred, formal quality, street photography in the urban grid tradition

- Composition note: the square frame forces a different way of thinking about composition. Rule-of-thirds placement tends to feel differently in a square — experiment with placing subjects more centrally than you would in a wide frame.

3:4 — Tall Portrait Format

The 3:4 ratio is the 4:3 ratio rotated 90 degrees — the camera's native ratio used in portrait (vertical) orientation. Unlike the other ratios which are all wider-than-tall, 3:4 is taller than it is wide.

- Pixel dimensions: 3456 × 4608 pixels (approximately 17 megapixels — cropped on both sides)
- Shape: vertical rectangle, taller than wide
- Matches: phone screens in portrait orientation (very well), Instagram Stories and Reels (9:16 is even taller, but 3:4 fills most of the screen), portrait prints, social media stories
- Best for: vertical portraits, content creation for Instagram Stories, phone wallpapers, any photo that will be viewed primarily on a phone held vertically
- Note: this ratio is most natural when the camera itself is held in portrait (vertical) orientation — though the aspect ratio setting works regardless of how you hold the camera

The Critical RAW Rule for Aspect Ratios

This is one of the most important things to know about aspect ratios on the OM-3 and most mirrorless cameras:

> **WARNING: RAW files always save the full 4:3 frame regardless of your aspect ratio setting**
>
> When you select 16:9 or 1:1 or any other aspect ratio and shoot in RAW, the .ORF file still contains the COMPLETE 4:3 sensor data. The aspect ratio setting only crops the JPEG preview image and what you see on the LCD. When you open the RAW file in Lightroom or any RAW editor, you will see the full uncropped 4:3 frame. The crop data is stored as metadata — you can apply or remove the crop in software.

This means if you shoot RAW and want a 16:9 final result, you have two options:

- Compose for 16:9 in the camera (using the 16:9 overlay lines as a guide) and then apply the crop manually in your RAW editor
- Or enable the aspect ratio setting — the camera will show you the 16:9 live view crop so you compose correctly, and then apply the crop in post from the full 4:3 RAW file

> **TIP: 4:3 RAW for maximum flexibility**
>
> If you are a RAW shooter who sometimes wants different crops for different purposes, shoot 4:3 RAW for every shot. In post-processing, you can freely crop any photo to 16:9 for a YouTube thumbnail, 1:1 for Instagram, and 3:2 for a print — all from the same RAW

file. This approach is particularly useful for documentary or travel photographers who post the same photos across multiple platforms.

10.4 How to Change Image Quality — Exact Menu Path

The OM-3 offers three ways to access and change the image quality settings. All three change the same setting — choose whichever method is most convenient for your shooting situation.

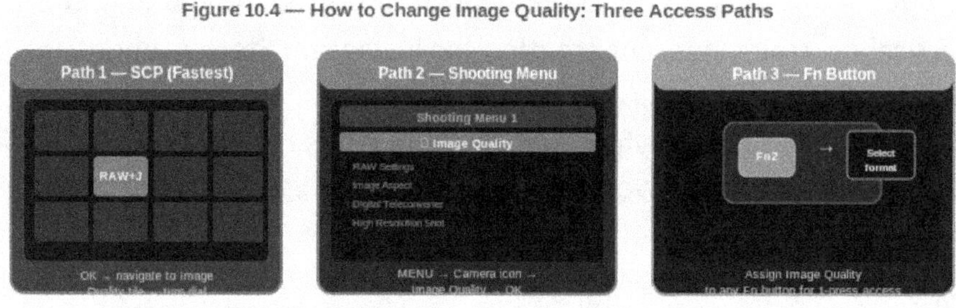

Figure 10.4 — Three access paths: Super Control Panel, Shooting Menu, or assigned Fn button

Method 1 — Via the Super Control Panel (Fastest for Image Quality)

Step 1: Press the OK button to open the Super Control Panel (SCP) from live view.

Step 2: Navigate to the Image Quality tile using the arrow pad. It shows the current quality code (e.g. LF, RAW+LF, RAW) and is usually in the lower-left area of the SCP grid.

Step 3: To quickly cycle through quality options: with the tile highlighted, turn the FRONT DIAL or REAR DIAL. The quality code on the tile changes with each click.

Step 4: Alternatively, press OK on the tile to open a full quality selection screen showing all available options as a scrollable list.

Step 5: Use the UP/DOWN arrows to highlight your preferred quality option.

Step 6: Press OK to confirm. The tile updates to show the new quality code.

Step 7: Half-press the shutter to return to live view. The new quality setting takes effect immediately on the next shot.

Method 2 — Via the Shooting Menu (Most Complete Options)

Step 1: Press the MENU button on the back of the camera.

Step 2: The menu opens. Press LEFT or RIGHT to navigate to the Shooting Menu tab — the camera icon, which is the first tab on the left.

Step 3: Press DOWN to enter the menu list under the Shooting tab.

Step 4: The very first item you will see is Image Quality. If it is not the first item, scroll UP to reach it.

Step 5: Press OK or RIGHT to enter the Image Quality selection screen.

Step 6: A complete list of all quality options appears: RAW, RAW+LF, RAW+LN, RAW+SF, LF, LN, MF, MN, SF, SN. Use the UP/DOWN arrows to scroll through them.

Step 7: Highlight your preferred option. A brief description may appear below the list.

Step 8: Press OK to confirm your selection.

Step 9: Press the MENU button to close, or half-press the shutter to return to live view.

Method 3 — Assign Image Quality to an Fn Button (Best for Frequent Changes)

If you frequently switch between quality modes — for example, toggling between RAW and RAW+JPEG depending on the shoot — assigning Image Quality to a function button gives you instant one-press access:

Step 1: Go to MENU → Custom Menu (gear icon) → Section B (Button/Dial) → Button Function.

Step 2: Highlight the Fn button you want to assign (Fn1, Fn2, Fn3, or another).

Step 3: Press OK to enter the function list for that button.

Step 4: Scroll to find Image Quality in the list and highlight it.

Step 5: Press OK to confirm the assignment.

Step 6: Press MENU to close.

Step 7: Now pressing your assigned Fn button from live view opens the Image Quality selection screen directly. Cycle through options and press OK to confirm — all without opening any menu.

How to Change Aspect Ratio — Exact Steps

The aspect ratio setting is found in the same area as image quality:

Step 1: Press the OK button to open the SCP → navigate to the Aspect Ratio tile (shows 4:3, 3:2, 16:9, etc.) → turn the dial to cycle options OR press OK to enter the selection screen.

Step 2: Or: press MENU → Shooting Menu → Page 1 → Image Aspect → OK → choose your ratio → OK.

Step 3: The live view immediately reframes to show the selected aspect ratio with the uncovered sensor area shown as a grey overlay (in JPEG mode) or transparent frame lines (in RAW mode).

How to Change RAW File Settings

The OM-3 offers three RAW compression options: 12-bit Lossless, 12-bit Lossy, and Uncompressed. For most users, 12-bit Lossless is the correct choice — it preserves maximum quality with moderate file size. Change it here:

Step 1: Press MENU → Shooting Menu → Page 1.

Step 2: Scroll DOWN one item below Image Quality to find RAW Settings (or similar name).

Step 3: Press OK to enter.

Step 4: Options: Uncompressed (largest, ~25MB), 12-bit Lossless (balanced, ~20MB), 12-bit Lossy (smallest RAW, ~15MB, slight quality trade-off).

Step 5: Highlight your preferred option and press OK.

Step 6: Press MENU to close.

Quick Reference — Image Quality Decision Guide

Your Situation	Recommended Setting
You are a beginner who just wants good photos without editing	LF (Large Fine JPEG) — high quality, immediately shareable
You want to occasionally edit some photos but not all	RAW+LN — JPEG for quick use, RAW for when you need it
You are a serious photographer who edits all your shots	RAW — maximum quality and editing freedom
You are shooting an event (wedding, sports) where speed matters	LF or RAW+LN — balance of quality and immediate usability
You are filling a slow or nearly-full card	LN or MF — smaller files, more shots per card
You are shooting for Instagram only (square posts)	LF + set Aspect Ratio to 1:1, OR shoot 4:3 LF and crop in phone
You are shooting for a YouTube widescreen thumbnail	LF + set Aspect Ratio to 16:9, OR shoot 4:3 and crop later
You want the absolute best quality for large prints or archival	RAW (12-bit Lossless) at 4:3

TIP: Change quality settings before you start shooting — not mid-session

Set your image quality and aspect ratio at the start of a shoot session, not in the middle of it. Changing quality mid-session can create confusion when organising files later — half the shots at LF and half at RAW, for example. Set it correctly at the beginning and leave it.

Part 11 — Drive Modes and Burst Shooting

Drive mode determines what happens after you press the shutter — does the camera take one photo, or many? Does it fire immediately, or wait? Does it fire the shutter mechanically, silently, or not at all until it has buffered a burst of pre-captured frames? The OM-3 offers one of the most complete sets of drive modes available on any mirrorless camera at its price level — from the simplest single-shot mode to the astonishing Pro Capture system covered at the end of this part.

Understanding drive modes and choosing the right one for your subject is one of the fastest ways to improve your photography. A bird in flight needs Sequential High. A ceremony where the shutter click would disturb proceedings needs Electronic Silent. A macro subject needs Focus Bracketing. This guide covers every drive mode on the OM-3, explains what it does, when to use it, and how to configure it.

11.1 How to Access and Change Drive Modes — Exact Steps

The OM-3 offers four ways to select your drive mode:

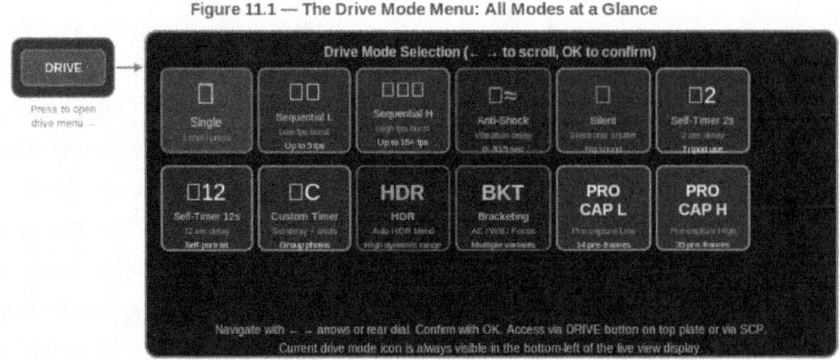

Figure 11.1 — The drive mode selection screen: all eleven modes accessible from the DRIVE button on the top plate

Method 1 — The Drive Button on the Top Plate (Primary Method)

Step 1: On the top plate of the camera, locate the button labeled DRIVE — it sits between the shutter button area and the hot shoe, slightly to the left.

Step 2: Press the DRIVE button once. The drive mode selection screen appears on the LCD (and in the EVF if you are looking through it).

Step 3: All available drive modes are shown as icons in a horizontal row or scrollable list.

Step 4: Press the LEFT or RIGHT arrow button (or turn the rear dial) to move the selection highlight through the modes.

Step 5: When the mode you want is highlighted, its name and a brief description may appear below the icons.

Step 6: Press OK to confirm your selection. The drive mode icon in the lower-left of the live view display updates immediately.

Method 2 — The Super Control Panel

Step 1: Press OK to open the Super Control Panel from live view.

Step 2: Navigate to the Drive Mode tile — it is in the bottom-left area of the SCP grid and shows the current drive mode icon.

Step 3: Press OK on the tile to enter the drive mode selection screen.

Step 4: Use the arrows to select your preferred mode and press OK to confirm.

Step 5: Half-press the shutter to return to live view.

Method 3 — The Shooting Menu

Step 1: Press MENU → Shooting Menu (camera icon) → Page 1.

Step 2: Find Drive / Self-Timer in the list and press OK.

Step 3: The drive mode selection screen appears.

Step 4: Select your mode and press OK. Press MENU to close.

Confirming Your Drive Mode

After selecting a drive mode, look at the bottom-left corner of the live view display. A small icon shows the currently active drive mode at all times — a single square for Single Shot, overlapping squares for burst modes, a clock symbol for self-timers, etc. Check this icon before every important shoot to confirm you are in the right mode.

11.2 Single Shot

Single Shot is the default and simplest drive mode. Each time you fully press the shutter button, the camera takes exactly one photograph. The shutter will not fire again until you release the button and press it again. This applies regardless of how long you keep the shutter button held down.

Aspect	Detail
Symbol	A single square (☐) in the drive menu and live view indicator
Frames per press	1
Shutter type	Mechanical (default)
Best for	Most everyday photography — portraits, landscapes, street, architecture, travel, still life. Any situation where you want deliberate, considered shots rather than a rapid sequence.
Not ideal for	Fast action or unpredictable subjects where a single frame may miss the decisive moment
Buffer	No buffer limitation — single shots can continue until the card is full

TIP: Single Shot for deliberate, thoughtful photography

Many experienced photographers use Single Shot mode even for subjects where burst might seem logical — deliberately choosing one frame instead of hoping a burst contains the right one. This forces you to anticipate the moment and press the shutter at exactly the right time, which sharpens your photographic instincts over time.

11.3 Sequential (Burst) Shooting — Low Speed and High Speed

Sequential shooting modes allow the camera to fire multiple frames continuously as long as the shutter button is held down fully. This is the primary mode for sports, wildlife, children in motion, and any fast-moving subject where timing the perfect single moment is difficult. The OM-3 offers two sequential modes — Low and High speed — each configurable to different frame rates.

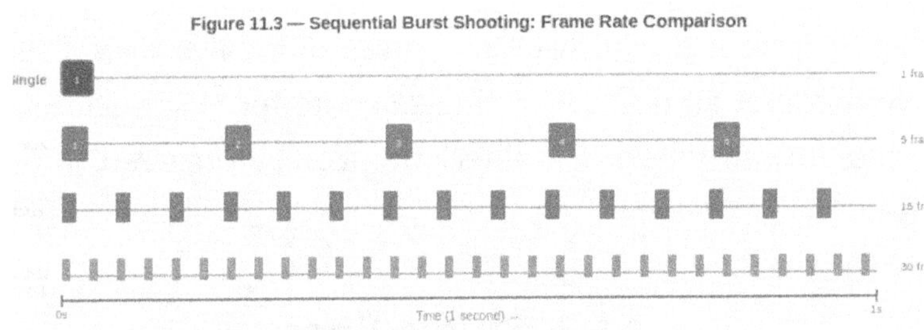

Figure 11.3 — Frame rate comparison: Single (1 frame), Sequential Low (5 fps), Sequential High (15 fps), Pro Capture High (30 fps)

Sequential Low (SL) — Controlled Burst

Sequential Low is the slower burst mode, running at up to 5 frames per second using the mechanical shutter. It gives you multiple frames without overwhelming you with files to sort through afterward.

Aspect	Detail
Symbol	Two overlapping squares in the drive menu
Default frame rate	5 fps (configurable down to 1 fps in Custom Menu C)
Shutter type	Mechanical — standard shutter sound
Flash compatibility	Yes — compatible with flash sync
Best for	Walking or jogging subjects, casual sports, pets moving around, children playing at moderate speed, architecture in light wind. Any subject that moves but not extremely fast.
Buffer capacity	Deep buffer — can sustain many frames before slowing
How to use	Hold the shutter button fully depressed. The camera fires at the set frame rate until you release the button or the buffer fills.

Sequential High (SH) — Fast Action Burst

Sequential High is the high-speed burst mode. It runs at up to approximately 15 frames per second using the mechanical shutter — and higher rates are available with the electronic shutter. This mode is essential for fast-moving subjects where the decisive moment is measured in fractions of a second.

Aspect	Detail
Symbol	Three overlapping squares in the drive menu
Default frame rate	10–15 fps mechanical; up to 30 fps electronic (configured in Custom Menu C)
Shutter type	Mechanical at 15 fps; electronic silent at higher rates
Flash compatibility	At 15 fps mechanical: compatible with some flash. At higher electronic rates: NOT compatible with flash
Best for	Birds in flight, athletes at peak action, motorsport, fast wildlife, children running, any subject with unpredictable fast movement
Buffer capacity	Moderate — at 15 fps the buffer fills more quickly. Fast V60/V90 SD card extends sustainable burst length significantly.
How to use	Half-press to lock focus (use C-AF for moving subjects), then full-press and hold. Review the burst sequence in playback and delete unwanted frames.

Configuring Burst Frame Rates

Step 1: Go to MENU → Custom Menu (gear icon) → Section C (Drive / Release).

Step 2: Find Sequential Low Frame Rate and press OK. Choose from 1 / 2 / 3 / 4 / 5 fps.

Step 3: Find Sequential High Frame Rate and press OK. Choose from 10 / 15 / 20 / 30 fps (availability depends on shutter mode).

Step 4: Press OK to confirm each setting. Press MENU to close.

TIP: Which burst rate to use

For sports and wildlife, Sequential High at 10-15 fps with the mechanical shutter is the most versatile — fast enough to capture peak action while still compatible with flash for indoor sports. For extreme speed (hummingbirds, insects, splashing water) use the higher electronic shutter rates — but be aware of rolling shutter artefacts with very fast lateral motion.

WARNING: High burst rates fill cards very quickly

At 15 fps shooting RAW+LF, a 64GB card fills in approximately 10-12 minutes of sustained shooting. At 30 fps it fills faster still. Use large, fast UHS-II V60 or V90 cards for sustained high-speed burst work, and cull aggressively immediately after the session.

11.4 Self-Timer (2s, 12s, Custom)

The self-timer introduces a deliberate delay between pressing the shutter button and the shutter actually firing. This delay serves several important purposes in photography.

Self-Timer 2 Seconds (Timer 2s)

The 2-second self-timer fires the shutter exactly 2 seconds after you press the button. This is primarily used to eliminate camera shake caused by physically pressing the shutter button — particularly useful for long exposures on a tripod where even the gentle pressure of your finger on the button can cause tiny vibrations that blur the image.

- Symbol: clock icon with a 2
- How to use: set the drive mode to Timer 2s, compose and focus your shot, press the shutter button once. The self-timer lamp on the front of the camera blinks and 2 seconds later the shutter fires. Remove your hands from the camera before the shutter fires.
- Best for: tripod long exposures (landscapes, architecture, astrophotography, waterfalls), macro photography, any shot where you want to fire the shutter without touching the camera
- Alternative: a remote shutter release (wired or Bluetooth via the OM SYSTEM app) achieves the same result without any delay

Self-Timer 12 Seconds (Timer 12s)

The 12-second self-timer gives you time to walk from behind the camera into the frame — enabling you to include yourself in a group photo or self-portrait. The self-timer lamp on the front of the camera blinks slowly for the first 10 seconds, then blinks rapidly in the final 2 seconds to warn you the shutter is about to fire.

- Symbol: clock icon with a 12
- Best for: group photos, self-portraits, family portraits where everyone should be in the shot
- Tip: use in combination with burst drive — after the initial 12-second delay, the camera fires multiple frames automatically, giving you more chances to get a natural expression

Custom Self-Timer (Timer C)

The Custom Self-Timer allows you to set both the delay duration and the number of frames the camera shoots after the delay. This gives maximum flexibility for group photo situations.

Step 1: Select Custom Self-Timer from the drive mode options.

Step 2: Go to MENU → Custom Menu C → Self-Timer Custom.

Step 3: Set the Delay: choose from 1 to 30 seconds. A 5–10 second delay is practical for walking into the frame.

Step 4: Set the Number of Shots: choose from 1 to 10. Setting 3 or 5 shots gives you multiple attempts at a natural expression in a single press.

Step 5: The interval between multiple shots is approximately 1–3 seconds (depending on settings).

Step 6: Press OK to save. Press MENU to close. The custom timer is now active when Timer C is selected.

TIP: Self-timer for group photos

Set the Custom Self-Timer to a 10-second delay with 5 shots. Press the button, walk into the frame, and the camera automatically takes 5 shots — greatly increasing your chances of everyone having their eyes open, looking at the camera, and smiling naturally. Review all five on screen and delete the unwanted ones.

11.5 Anti-Shock and Electronic Silent Shutter

Figure 11.5 — Shutter Types: Mechanical, Anti-Shock, and Electronic Silent

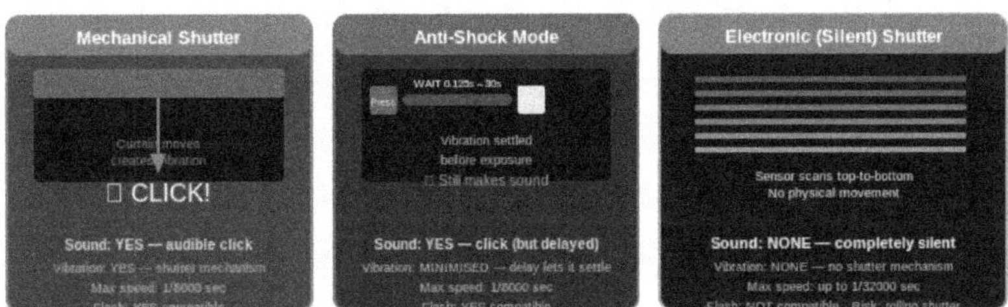

Figure 11.5 — Three shutter types: Mechanical (click, vibration), Anti-Shock (delayed mechanical), Electronic Silent (no sound, no vibration)

Anti-Shock Mode — Eliminating Shutter Vibration

The mechanical shutter in the OM-3 involves physical curtains that move rapidly across the sensor. This movement, while very fast, creates a tiny vibration in the camera body at the exact moment of exposure. In most situations this is imperceptible. But in two specific situations it can cause subtle blur:

- Macro photography at high magnification — where even microscopic camera movement is visible in the photo
- Very long telephoto shots — where at long distances, even tiny vibrations are amplified

Anti-Shock mode addresses this by introducing a configurable delay between when the electronic front curtain opens (silent — no vibration) and when the physical rear curtain closes (which does create a small vibration). By the time the rear curtain fires, the camera has been still long enough for any front-curtain vibration to have fully dissipated.

How to Configure the Anti-Shock Delay

Step 1: Select Anti-Shock from the drive mode options (DRIVE button or SCP).

Step 2: To configure the delay duration: go to MENU → Custom Menu C → Anti-Shock Delay.

Step 3: Available delay times: 0 (immediate, same as regular shutter), 0.125 seconds, 0.25 seconds, 0.5 seconds, 1 second, 2 seconds, 4 seconds, 8 seconds, 16 seconds, 30.5 seconds.

Step 4: For macro photography, 0.25 to 0.5 seconds is usually sufficient. For extreme macro or very long telephoto, try 1 second.

Step 5: Press OK to confirm. Press MENU to close.

TIP: Anti-Shock for macro

Macro photography is where Anti-Shock mode earns its keep. At 1:1 magnification, the camera's IBIS system works hard to keep the subject in frame, but even after stabilization a tiny shutter-induced vibration can cause just enough blur to ruin fine detail. Set Anti-Shock to 0.25 seconds and the difference is immediately apparent in your sharpest macro work.

Electronic Silent Shutter — Completely Soundless Photography

The Electronic Silent (ES) shutter mode completely eliminates the mechanical shutter. Instead of physical curtains moving, the camera's sensor is electronically scanned from top to bottom to read all the pixel data. There is absolutely no moving part, no mechanical sound, and no vibration whatsoever.

Advantages of Electronic Silent Shutter

- Zero sound — completely inaudible. Essential for ceremonies (weddings, funerals, court proceedings), wildlife where the click would startle the subject, performing arts (theatre, classical music concerts), and library or museum environments where silence is required.
- Zero vibration — slightly sharper than mechanical shutter at very high magnifications, and sharper than Anti-Shock at the moment of capture.
- Higher maximum burst rates — electronic shutter enables 20–30 fps or higher, far beyond what mechanical shutter can achieve.

- Higher maximum shutter speed — up to 1/32000 second with the electronic shutter, allowing very large apertures in bright sunlight without a neutral density filter.

Limitations of Electronic Silent Shutter

- Rolling shutter distortion — because the sensor is scanned top-to-bottom rather than exposing all pixels simultaneously, fast-moving subjects can appear skewed or warped. A rapidly rotating propeller may appear bent. A person running fast may lean at an odd angle. This is called rolling shutter and is a fundamental physical limitation of electronic shutter systems.
- Flash incompatibility — electronic shutter cannot synchronize with mechanical flash units. Do not use flash in Electronic Silent mode.
- Fluorescent/LED light banding — some artificial light sources flicker at AC power frequencies (50Hz or 60Hz). Electronic shutter scanning at certain speeds can produce horizontal banding stripes in photos taken under these lights. The OM-3's Anti-Flicker function (Shooting Menu) helps mitigate this.

How to Activate Electronic Silent Shutter

Step 1: Press the DRIVE button or open the SCP → Drive tile.

Step 2: Scroll to the mode labeled Silent (sometimes shown as E-Shutter or S).

Step 3: Press OK to confirm.

Step 4: A small silent/mute icon appears in the live view display confirming the mode is active.

Step 5: Shoot normally. No click will be heard. The camera is completely silent.

WARNING: Electronic shutter and fast action

Do not use Electronic Silent mode for fast-moving horizontal subjects (runners, cars, birds crossing the frame) if distortion-free results are required. The rolling shutter effect on horizontal fast motion can be severe. Use mechanical shutter (SL or SH) for high-speed action. Electronic shutter is best for still subjects that just happen to be in a quiet environment.

11.6 Bracketing Modes

Bracketing is the technique of shooting multiple frames of the same scene with a different variable changed between each frame — exposure, focus distance, white balance, or art filter. This guarantees that at least one frame captures exactly what you intended, or provides multiple versions to choose from or combine in post-processing.

To use any bracketing mode, first select BKT from the drive mode options (DRIVE button or SCP). Then configure the bracketing type and parameters in the Shooting Menu.

AE Bracketing (Automatic Exposure Bracketing)

Figure 11.6a — AE Bracketing: Three Frames at Different Exposures

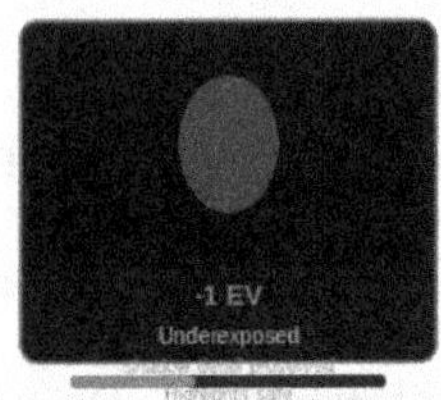

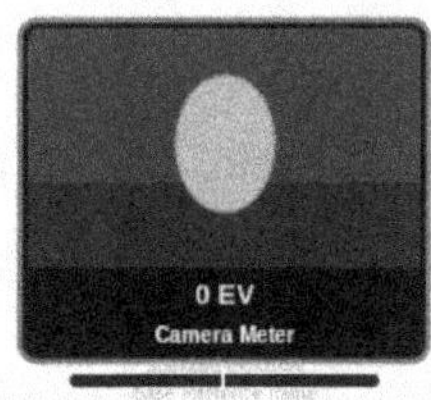

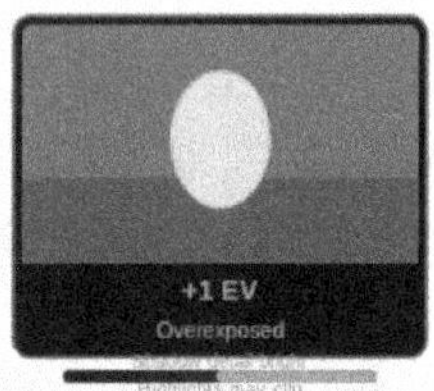

All three frames can be merged in software into a single HDR image with detail in all tonal ranges

Or you select the best-exposed individual frame — the one that preserved the most critical detail

Figure 11.6a — AE Bracketing: three frames at -1 EV, 0 EV, and +1 EV — then combine in software for HDR or choose the best

What AE Bracketing Does

AE Bracketing automatically shoots a sequence of frames at different exposure levels in a single burst. With a 3-frame bracket at 1 EV spacing, you get one underexposed frame (-1 EV), one at the camera's standard meter reading (0 EV), and one overexposed (+1 EV). The camera fires all three frames in rapid succession when you press the shutter once — no need to re-press between frames.

Why Use AE Bracketing?

- HDR compositing — merge the three frames in software (Lightroom, Aurora HDR, Photomatix) to produce a single image with detail in both the brightest highlights and darkest shadows of a high-contrast scene.
- Safety net for difficult lighting — when you are unsure of the correct exposure for a once-in-a-lifetime moment, bracketing guarantees at least one well-exposed frame.
- Exposure selection — review the three frames afterward and select whichever was most successful, discarding the others.

How to Set Up AE Bracketing — Exact Steps

Step 1: Press the DRIVE button and select BKT (Bracketing) from the drive mode options.

Step 2: Press MENU → Shooting Menu → scroll to Page 4 → find AE BKT (or Bracketing Settings).

Step 3: Enter the bracketing settings screen. You will see two parameters: Frame Count and EV Step.

Step 4: Set the Frame Count: 3 frames (most common — under, correct, over) or 5 frames (wider range) or 7 frames (widest range).

Step 5: Set the EV Step: the gap between each frame. 0.3 EV (1/3 stop) is very subtle. 0.7 EV is moderate. 1.0 EV is the standard choice for HDR work. 2.0 EV is for extreme contrast scenes.

Step 6: Press OK to confirm. Press MENU to close.

Step 7: Return to live view. Press the shutter once — the camera fires all selected frames automatically.

TIP: AE Bracket for challenging interior shots

When photographing a room interior where the windows are very bright and the room interior is dark, a 3-frame bracket at 1.0 EV gives you one frame that exposes correctly for the bright window view, one for the room interior, and one in between. Merge them in Lightroom or Photoshop for a natural-looking result with detail both inside and outside.

Focus Bracketing — Stacking for Maximum Depth of Field

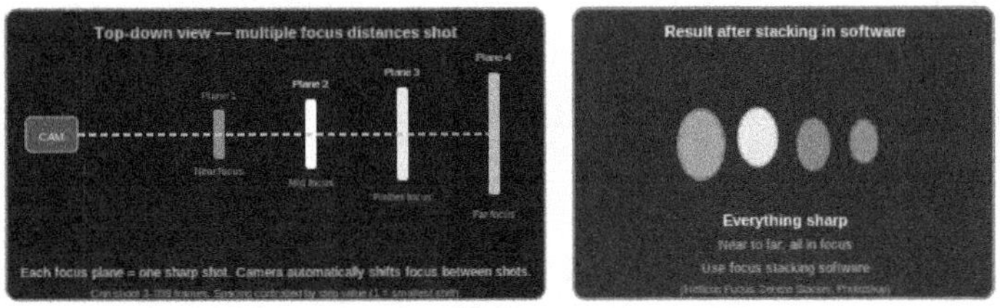

Figure 11.6b — Focus Bracketing: camera automatically shifts focus between frames, creating a series for focus stacking

What Focus Bracketing Does

Focus Bracketing automatically shoots a series of frames, shifting the focus distance slightly between each frame. The camera starts at the closest focus distance you have set and progressively moves focus further away with each shot, continuing until the set number of frames has been captured. Each individual frame has a different shallow plane in focus. In software, you align these frames and blend only the sharp areas from each — a technique called focus stacking — to produce a final image with extraordinary depth of field that would be physically impossible with a single photo.

Why Use Focus Bracketing?

- Macro photography — at 1:1 magnification the depth of field may be only a fraction of a millimetre. A bug's eye may be sharp while its antennae are blurry. Focus stacking solves this by combining multiple frames into a single image where the entire insect is sharp.
- Product photography — photographing a small object (watch, jewellery, electronic component) where the entire product must be sharp but the lens cannot achieve sufficient depth of field at any single aperture.
- Landscape close-up photography — extremely close wildflowers with a focused background.

How to Set Up Focus Bracketing — Exact Steps

Step 1: Compose your shot with the camera on a tripod. Focus bracketing requires complete camera stillness between frames — handheld use is generally not practical.

Step 2: Focus manually (MF mode) or use S-AF to focus on the nearest element you want sharp.

Step 3: Select BKT from the drive mode options.

Step 4: Press MENU → Shooting Menu → Page 4 → find Focus BKT (Focus Bracketing).

Step 5: Set the Number of Frames: start with 10–15 frames and adjust based on results. More frames cover a wider depth range.

Step 6: Set the Focus Differential (step size): a smaller number (1–3) shifts focus in tiny increments — use for extreme macro. A larger number (5–10) gives bigger steps — use for moderate close-up work.

Step 7: Set whether to shoot from Near to Far (most common) or Far to Near.

Step 8: Press OK and close the menu.

Step 9: Press the shutter once. The camera automatically fires all frames in sequence, shifting focus between each.

Step 10: In software (Helicon Focus, Zerene Stacker, Photoshop's Auto-Blend Layers), load all frames and blend to produce the final deeply sharp image.

NOTE: Focus stacking requires post-processing software

Focus Bracketing on the OM-3 saves individual JPEG or RAW files — it does not automatically combine them in-camera. You need focus stacking software on your computer to blend them into a final image. Helicon Focus and Zerene Stacker are the dedicated tools; Photoshop's Auto-Blend Layers is a simpler alternative included with Adobe Creative Cloud. The OM-3 can do some in-camera stacking (covered in menu settings) but the software results are generally superior.

HDR Bracketing — In-Camera HDR Merge

What HDR Bracketing Does

HDR (High Dynamic Range) Bracketing works similarly to AE Bracketing but with an additional step: the camera automatically combines (merges) the bracketed frames into a single HDR image in-camera, without requiring software. It shoots 3 to 5 frames at different exposures and blends them immediately, saving only the final merged image.

- Advantage: completely automatic. Press once, get a finished HDR JPEG with no computer required.
- Limitation: in-camera HDR processing is less sophisticated than dedicated HDR software. Results can look artificial (excessive haloing, unrealistic tone mapping) if the bracket range or scene is not appropriate. For professional-quality HDR, use AE Bracketing and process in software.
- Best for: real estate photography, interior photography for web use, dramatic landscapes where you want HDR but do not have time to process in software.

How to Set Up HDR Bracketing

Step 1: Select HDR or BKT from the drive mode options. (Note: the OM-3 may list HDR as a separate mode from BKT, or as a sub-option within BKT.)

Step 2: Press MENU → Shooting Menu → HDR or Bracketing Settings.

Step 3: Set the Auto HDR options: number of frames (3–5), exposure range (+/-2 EV or +/-3 EV), and tone mapping strength (Low / Standard / Strong).

Step 4: Press OK and close the menu.

Step 5: Use a tripod — the camera must stay absolutely still between the bracketed shots for the merge to work cleanly.

Step 6: Press the shutter once. The camera fires all frames and then processes them into a single HDR JPEG. A brief pause occurs while the merge is computed.

White Balance Bracketing

What WB Bracketing Does

White Balance Bracketing shoots a single frame but automatically saves multiple JPEG copies of that one shot, each with a slightly different white balance correction applied. The sensor data is captured only once — what changes is the in-camera processing applied to produce each JPEG. This lets you compare different WB renderings of the same moment without re-shooting.

- How many copies: 2 or 3 JPEGs (one at your set WB, plus shifted versions)
- Shift direction: Amber-Blue axis (warm to cool), or Green-Magenta axis, or both
- Step size: configurable in Custom Menu G → WB Bracketing

How to Set Up WB Bracketing

Step 1: Go to MENU → Custom Menu G → WB Bracketing.

Step 2: Set the number of frames (2 or 3) and the shift direction (A-B axis / G-M axis).

Step 3: Set the step size — how far apart each WB variation is.

Step 4: Press OK. Press MENU to close.

Step 5: Select BKT from the drive mode options. (On some firmware, WB Bracket is selected in the shooting menu rather than through the drive mode — look for it in the WB settings).

Step 6: Shoot normally. Each press of the shutter saves 2 or 3 JPEG files with different WB renderings.

TIP: WB Bracketing saves only JPEGs, not multiple RAWs

The RAW file (if you are shooting RAW+JPEG) is saved only once — the single sensor exposure. The WB bracketed copies are additional JPEGs only. If you process the RAW file later you can apply any WB you want, making WB bracketing most useful for JPEG-only shooters who want WB options without re-shooting.

11.7 Pro Capture Mode — How to Activate and Use

Pro Capture is one of the most extraordinary features on the OM-3. It solves the fundamental problem of reaction time in action photography: by the time your brain registers the decisive moment and your finger fully presses the shutter, 200-300 milliseconds have passed. At 15 fps, that delay means 3-4 frames have already been missed. Pro Capture eliminates this delay entirely by continuously buffering frames BEFORE you fully press the shutter, then saving those pre-captured frames as part of your burst.

Pro Capture was covered in detail in Part 7.6 of this guide (Focus System) as part of the focus discussion. This section provides the activation steps and practical guide specific to the drive mode context.

Pro Capture L vs Pro Capture H

	Pro Capture L	Pro Capture H
Frame rate (pre-capture)	Up to 15 fps (mechanical shutter)	Up to 30–50 fps (electronic shutter)
Pre-capture frames stored	Up to 14 frames before your press	Up to 35 frames before your press
Shutter type	Mechanical — audible click, no rolling shutter	Electronic — fully silent, possible rolling shutter
Flash compatibility	Compatible with flash	NOT compatible with flash

Best for	Most action photography: birds on branch about to fly, athletes, sporting events, children at play	Extreme speed: insects in flight, hummingbirds, water droplets, peak-of-action moments needing maximum fps
SD card requirement	UHS-I U3 minimum for sustained use	UHS-II V60 or V90 recommended

How to Activate Pro Capture — Exact Steps

Step 1: Press the DRIVE button on the top of the camera.

Step 2: Scroll through the drive mode options until you reach Pro Cap L or Pro Cap H.

Step 3: Press OK to confirm. The display shows a Pro Capture icon.

Step 4: Optionally, configure the number of pre-capture frames: MENU → Custom Menu C → Pro Capture → Pre-Capture Frames → choose your number.

How to Use Pro Capture in the Field

Step 1: Select Pro Capture L or H and your AF mode (C-AF for moving subjects, S-AF for static subjects about to move).

Step 2: Point the camera at the scene where action will occur — the bird on a branch, the starting line, the diver on the board.

Step 3: HALF-PRESS the shutter button and hold it there. This starts the invisible pre-capture buffer. Frames are being recorded continuously but NOT yet saved to the card. Your half-press also activates autofocus.

Step 4: Wait for the decisive moment. The buffer keeps rolling, constantly discarding the oldest frames and replacing them with the newest.

Step 5: When you see (or anticipate) the peak action — the bird lifts its wings, the diver bends their knees — press the shutter button FULLY down.

Step 6: The camera saves all pre-buffered frames (going back as far as your configured frame count before your press) PLUS continues shooting post-press frames in normal burst mode.

Step 7: Release the shutter button when the action sequence ends.

Step 8: Review the burst in playback. You will find frames from before you fully pressed — the moment the wings started lifting, the initial lean of the diver — that you could not have captured with a conventional shutter.

Best Subject for Pro Capture	Why Pro Capture Helps	Recommended Mode
Bird in flight (taking off from perch)	The take-off happens faster than reaction time — pre-frames capture the wing spread	Pro Cap L + C-AF + Sequential H after press
Athlete's peak jump or throw	The peak position lasts less than 50ms — pre-frames guarantee capture	Pro Cap H (max fps) + C-AF
Cat or dog in mid-pounce	The launch from rest is instantaneous — pre-frames catch the crouch-to-launch moment	Pro Cap L + C-AF+TR tracking
Splashing water / liquid drop	The splash peak is unpredictable — pre-frames ensure capture regardless of timing	Pro Cap H + S-AF (pre-focused on drop zone)
Goalkeeper's dive	The dive is a reflex — pre-frames capture the initial body lean before the dive	Pro Cap L or H + C-AF
Child's laughter expression	Peak expression lasts 100ms — pre-frames capture the genuine spontaneous moment	Pro Cap L + Face+Eye detection

TIP: Half-press duration

You can hold the half-press for as long as you need — minutes if necessary. The pre-capture buffer continuously refreshes, dropping the oldest frames as new ones are captured. There is no penalty for waiting a long time before the full press. The buffer always contains your most recent frames up to the configured maximum count.

> **NOTE: Battery consumption during Pro Capture**
>
> Holding the shutter half-pressed continuously runs the sensor, processor, and AF system at full power. Battery drain during an extended Pro Capture wait is significantly higher than in normal shooting. For long sessions — wildlife photography where you may wait 30-60 minutes for a bird to take flight — carry spare batteries and use the battery saver screen setting to reduce LCD brightness.

Part 12 — Flash

Flash photography transforms what is possible in low light, fills harsh outdoor shadows, and adds depth and drama to any scene where a controlled burst of light can make the difference between a mediocre photo and a great one. The OM-3 has a capable built-in pop-up flash and a fully featured hot shoe that accepts external flash units — including wireless multi-flash setups controlled directly from the camera.

This part of the guide covers everything from the basics of popping up the built-in flash all the way through to configuring a professional multi-group wireless flash system. Every flash mode is explained with a real-world use case, and every setting is accompanied by exact steps for applying it on the OM-3.

12.1 Built-In Pop-Up Flash — How to Use It

The OM-3 has a small but capable built-in pop-up flash housed in a compartment on the front of the camera, above the lens mount. When not in use, it sits flat against the camera body and is protected by a hinged cover. When activated, the flash head springs upward and is ready to fire.

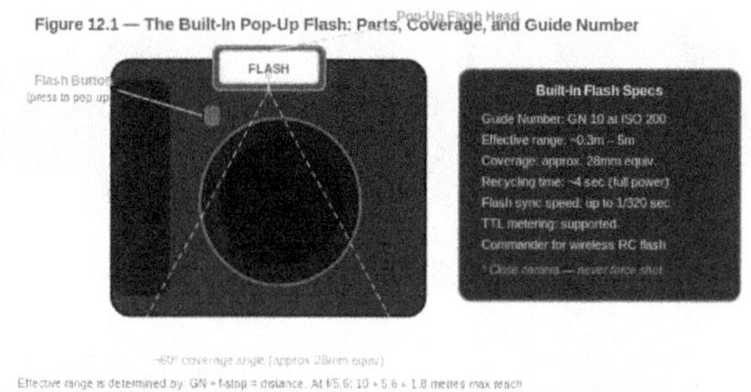

Figure 12.1 — The OM-3 built-in pop-up flash: parts, effective range, and guide number specifications

Understanding the Built-In Flash Specifications

Specification	Value	What It Means for You
Guide Number (GN)	GN 10 at ISO 200	The Guide Number determines the flash's power. GN 10 means: at f/5.6 the maximum effective range is about 1.8 metres (10 ÷ 5.6). At f/2.8 it reaches about 3.5 metres.
Effective Range	Approx. 0.3m to 5m	Do not expect the built-in flash to properly illuminate subjects more than about 4-5 metres away at wide apertures. For subjects further than this, use a more powerful external flash.
Flash Coverage Angle	Approx. 28mm equivalent	The flash illuminates roughly the same area as a 28mm lens on a full-frame camera. With wider lenses, corners may receive less light (vignetting).
Maximum Flash Sync Speed	1/320 second	With the Electronic Front Curtain Shutter enabled, the sync speed can be as high as 1/320 sec. With standard mechanical shutter, it may be limited to 1/250 sec or lower. Do not exceed the

		sync speed — you will see a dark band across the bottom of the frame.
TTL Flash Control	Supported	TTL (Through-The-Lens) metering automatically calculates the correct flash power based on what the camera measures through the lens. You do not need to manually set a power level.
Recycling Time	Approx. 4 seconds at full power	After a full-power flash, the capacitor needs about 4 seconds to recharge before it can fire again. The camera will not allow you to fire a second shot during this recycling period. Using lower power settings dramatically reduces recycling time.
Wireless Commander	Yes (RC optical system)	The built-in flash can act as a commander (controller) for OM SYSTEM RC-compatible external flash units placed off-camera. See Section 12.5 for full wireless flash details.

How to Open the Pop-Up Flash

Step 1: Locate the Flash button on the top plate of the camera. It is the small button in the area to the left of the EVF hump, labeled with a lightning bolt symbol (⚡) or the word FLASH.

Step 2: Press the Flash button firmly once. The flash head springs upward automatically with a soft click.

Step 3: A lightning bolt icon appears on the LCD and EVF, confirming the flash is raised and active.

Step 4: The flash will now fire when you take a photo, according to whichever flash mode is selected (see Section 12.2).

How to Close the Pop-Up Flash

Step 1: When you have finished using the flash, gently push the flash head back down with your finger.

Step 2: Apply smooth, even pressure until the flash clicks flat against the camera body.

Step 3: Do not force it — if it feels stuck, press the flash button once more to electrically release the latch, then push down again.

Step 4: The lightning bolt icon disappears from the display, confirming the flash is closed and inactive.

WARNING: Never force the flash head closed

The pop-up flash is held open by a small spring and locked by a latch. Forcing it closed when it has not been released electrically can break the hinge mechanism. Always push it gently — it should close with minimal pressure. If it seems to resist, press the Flash button briefly to release any electronic lock, then try again.

The Guide Number Explained

The Guide Number (GN) is the mathematical basis for calculating flash exposure manually. The formula is:

Distance (metres) = Guide Number ÷ f-stop

With the OM-3's built-in flash at ISO 200 (GN 10), the maximum useful distance at common apertures is:

Aperture (f-stop)	Max Flash Distance at ISO 200	Max Flash Distance at ISO 800
f/2.8	3.6 metres (about 12 feet)	7.1 metres (about 23 feet)
f/4.0	2.5 metres (about 8 feet)	5.0 metres (about 16 feet)
f/5.6	1.8 metres (about 6 feet)	3.6 metres (about 12 feet)
f/8.0	1.25 metres (about 4 feet)	2.5 metres (about 8 feet)

TIP: Raise ISO to extend flash range

The built-in flash has limited power. If your subject is 4 metres away and you are shooting at f/5.6, the flash barely reaches them. Instead of widening the aperture (which may lose depth of field you need), raise the ISO to 800 or 1600 — the doubled sensor sensitivity effectively doubles the flash's reach.

12.2 Flash Modes — Each Explained with a Use Case

Flash mode determines when and how the flash fires relative to the exposure. Choosing the right flash mode is just as important as choosing the right exposure settings. The wrong flash mode can ruin otherwise technically correct photos — flat, unnatural lighting from a flash at the wrong moment or at the wrong power relative to the ambient light.

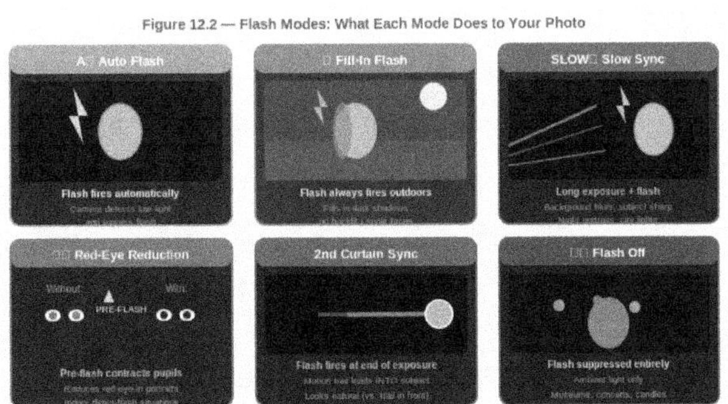

Figure 12.2 — All six flash modes: Auto, Fill-In, Slow Sync, Red-Eye Reduction, 2nd Curtain, and Flash Off

How to Change Flash Mode

Flash mode can be changed in three places:

- Super Control Panel (SCP): Press OK → navigate to the Flash tile (lightning bolt icon) → press OK → select mode → press OK.
- Shooting Menu: Press MENU → Shooting Menu → Page 4 → Flash Mode → select mode → OK.
- Arrow pad shortcut: The RIGHT arrow on the 4-way pad may be pre-assigned as a Flash Mode shortcut — press it from live view for instant flash mode access.

Auto Flash (A⚡)

In Auto Flash mode, the camera decides whether the flash is needed based on the available light. If the camera's metering system determines that the ambient light is insufficient for a correctly exposed photo at the current settings, it fires the flash automatically. If there is enough light, the flash does not fire even though it is raised.

Aspect	Detail
When flash fires	Automatically when the camera judges light is too low
When flash does not fire	When ambient light is sufficient for correct exposure
Shutter speed	Camera selects a shutter speed that balances ambient and flash exposure (may use 1/60 as the minimum)

Best for	General indoor photography, parties, events — the camera handles the flash decision for you
Limitation	Can fire unexpectedly in dim conditions when you would prefer ambient-only light; does not fire when you want fill flash in bright conditions

Real-world scenario: You are photographing a family gathering indoors in a room with mixed lighting — some overhead lights, a window, and some darker corners. The camera uses Auto Flash to fire in the darker areas and hold back in the better-lit areas. Mostly hands-off and generally produces acceptable results.

Fill-In Flash (⚡)

Fill-In Flash (also called Forced Flash or Always-On Flash) fires the flash on every single shot regardless of the ambient light level. Even in bright outdoor sunshine, the flash fires every time you press the shutter. The purpose is to add light to shadows on your subject — particularly the shadows cast on faces by overhead sunlight, or the underside of a hat brim.

Aspect	Detail
When flash fires	Every shot, regardless of ambient light
Shutter speed	Camera selects appropriate sync speed (usually the flash sync speed of 1/250 or 1/320)
Best for	Outdoor portraits in direct sunlight (fills the dark shadows under eyes, nose, and chin); backlit subjects where the subject would otherwise be silhouetted; overcast day portraits where the flat light needs a small boost for catchlights in the eyes
Technique	Often combined with -0.7 to -1.0 FEC (Flash Exposure Compensation) so the fill light looks natural and not overtly flash-lit

Real-world scenario: Photographing a friend on a sunny beach. The sun is bright and directly overhead — their face has deep shadows under their brow and nose. Switch to Fill-In Flash, set FEC to -1.0, and press the shutter. The gentle flash lifts the shadows without making the photo look flash-lit.

Slow Sync Flash (SLOW⚡)

Slow Sync flash combines a long (slow) shutter speed with the flash firing. The long shutter speed records the ambient background and any motion in the scene — producing blur and light trails. The flash fires (usually at the beginning of the exposure, or at the end in 2nd Curtain mode — see below) and freezes the main subject sharply against the blurred background.

Aspect	Detail
When flash fires	Once, at the beginning of the exposure (or end in 2nd Curtain mode)
Shutter speed	Long — typically 1/4 second to several seconds, as needed for the ambient background to register
Best for	Night portraits where you want the background city lights or neon signs to be visible; creative motion blur; concerts with stage lighting
Tripod required?	For sharpness in the background, yes — though the subject can be relatively sharp from the flash even without a tripod
Limitation	If the camera moves during the long exposure, the flash-frozen subject may also show ghosting from the ambient light

TIP: Night portrait with slow sync — the setup

Set Mode Dial to S, shutter speed 1/4 to 1 second, Flash Mode to Slow Sync, ISO 800. Have your subject stand still. The long exposure records the background lights. When the shutter opens, the flash fires instantly and freezes your subject sharp. The background glows with ambient light and motion trails. This technique produces the classic "night portrait" look that makes the subject look naturally integrated into the scene.

Red-Eye Reduction (⚡👁)

Red-eye occurs when flash light enters the eye through a wide-open pupil (which opens in dark rooms), reflects off the blood-rich retina at the back of the eye, and bounces directly back into the lens. The result is the familiar "red-eye" effect in portrait photos.

Red-Eye Reduction mode fires a series of brief pre-flashes before the main exposure. These pre-flashes cause the subject's pupils to contract — reducing the amount of light that can bounce back into the lens when the main flash fires. This significantly reduces (but rarely eliminates completely) the red-eye effect.

Aspect	Detail
How it works	One or several pre-flashes fire briefly, causing pupils to contract, then the shutter opens and the main flash fires for the actual exposure

Delay	A slight delay occurs between pressing the shutter and the actual photo being taken due to the pre-flash sequence — typically 0.5 to 1 second
Best for	Indoor portraits in dark rooms where subjects are looking directly at the camera
Limitation	The pre-flash delay can cause subjects to blink or look away before the actual shot; some subjects find the pre-flash annoying; does not work if subject is not looking at the camera
Alternative	Shoot at a slight angle so the flash-to-subject-to-lens angle is not perfectly reflective; or correct red-eye in post-processing in Lightroom, which takes seconds

2nd Curtain (Rear) Sync Flash

Standard flash fires at the beginning of the exposure (when the first shutter curtain opens). In 2nd Curtain Sync mode, the flash fires at the very end of the exposure (just before the second curtain closes). This changes the relationship between the motion blur and the flash-frozen subject:

- With 1st Curtain (standard): the flash fires first, freezing the subject at the START. Then the long exposure continues and any subsequent motion creates a blur AHEAD of the frozen subject — looking as if the subject is moving backward.
- With 2nd Curtain: the long exposure records the motion trail throughout the exposure, then the flash fires at the END, freezing the subject at the FINISH of the motion. The blur trail FOLLOWS the subject — a much more natural, cinematic look.

Step 1: Go to MENU → Custom Menu F → Sync Order (or 2nd Curtain Sync) → select 2nd Curtain.

Step 2: Set Flash Mode to Slow Sync.

Step 3: Shoot as normal with a slow shutter speed. Motion trails lead naturally behind the subject.

Real-world scenario: Photographing a cyclist at night on a slow 1/4 second shutter. With 1st Curtain, the blur is in front of the cyclist (wrong direction). With 2nd Curtain, the blur trails behind the cyclist — the photo reads as forward motion, which is dramatically more effective.

Flash Off (⚡✕)

Flash Off suppresses the flash entirely, even when it is physically raised. The camera will not fire the flash regardless of how dark the scene is. This allows you to use the built-in flash as a commander for wireless remote flashes without the built-in flash contributing any visible light to the exposure.

Aspect	Detail
When flash fires	Never — even if flash is raised and even if scene is very dark
Best for	Environments where flash is prohibited or unwanted (museums, concerts, ceremonies); situations where ambient light gives you the look you want and you do not want flash interference; wireless flash work where the built-in flash should command but not illuminate
Alternative name	Sometimes labeled as Flash Off, No Flash, or shown as a crossed-out lightning bolt

12.3 Flash Exposure Compensation

Flash Exposure Compensation (FEC) allows you to make the flash fire more or less brightly than the camera's automatic TTL calculation suggests. It works like regular Exposure Compensation — but instead of brightening or darkening the entire photo, it only affects the flash output. The ambient exposure is unchanged.

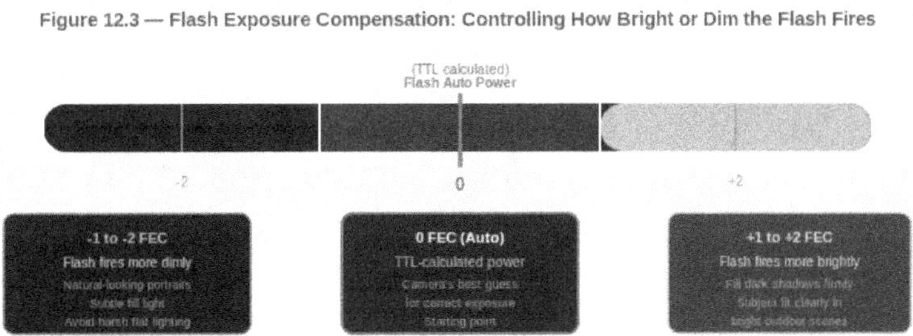

Figure 12.3 — Flash Exposure Compensation scale: negative values dim the flash, positive values brighten it

Why You Need Flash Exposure Compensation

The camera's TTL flash metering is designed to illuminate the subject to the same average exposure as the ambient light — producing a balanced, natural-looking result. But this automatic calculation is not always what you want:

- -0.7 to -1.0 FEC (dimmer flash): the most useful adjustment. Reduces the flash output so it subtly fills in shadows without making the photo obviously look flash-lit. A little fill light is almost always more flattering than full-power TTL flash.
- -2.0 to -3.0 FEC (much dimmer): for extremely subtle catchlight-only flash — just a tiny glint in the eyes in an otherwise ambient-lit portrait.

- +0.7 to +1.0 FEC (brighter flash): when the subject is far away or the background is very bright and the TTL-calculated flash is not powerful enough to properly illuminate the subject.
- +2.0 to +3.0 FEC (very bright): for forceful, dramatic flash-forward lighting where you intentionally want the flash to dominate the exposure.

How to Apply Flash Exposure Compensation — Exact Steps

Method 1 — Via the Super Control Panel (Fastest)

Step 1: Press OK to open the Super Control Panel.

Step 2: Navigate to the Flash Compensation tile — it shows a lightning bolt with a plus/minus symbol. It is typically in the bottom-right area of the SCP.

Step 3: Turn the front or rear dial to move the FEC value in 1/3 EV increments.

Step 4: Or press OK on the tile to open a full scale display and use the arrows to set the value.

Step 5: Press OK to confirm. Half-press the shutter to return to live view.

Method 2 — Via the Shooting Menu

Step 1: Press MENU → Shooting Menu → Page 4.

Step 2: Find Flash Compensation and press OK.

Step 3: Use the arrows to set your preferred FEC value from -3.0 to +3.0 EV.

Step 4: Press OK to confirm. Press MENU to close.

NOTE: FEC is separate from regular EC

Flash Exposure Compensation and Exposure Compensation are independent settings. If you apply both +0.7 EC (to brighten the ambient exposure) and -1.0 FEC (to dim the flash), the ambient background will be brighter while the flash output is reduced. This combination is very useful for outdoor portrait work — brightening the overall scene while keeping the fill flash subtle.

Flash Exposure Compensation Quick Reference

Situation	Recommended FEC	Result

Portrait with on-camera flash — you want natural-looking fill	-0.7 to -1.0 EV	Subtle fill: shadows lifted but photo does not look flash-lit
Outdoor portrait — just want catchlights in the eyes	-1.5 to -2.0 EV	Barely visible fill — just a glint of light in the pupils
Subject 5+ metres away — TTL calculation underexposing them	+0.7 to +1.0 EV	Flash fires harder, reaches further
Group shot — people at different distances	+0.3 to +0.7 EV	Slightly more power ensures people at the back are adequately lit
Dark-skin tones — TTL often underexposes darker subjects	+0.3 to +1.0 EV	Camera's metering can underexpose dark skin; + FEC compensates
Backlit subject with strong background light	+1.0 to +2.0 EV	Flash fights the bright background to properly illuminate the subject
Object photography on white background	-1.0 to -2.0 EV	Prevents the white background from fooling TTL into underexposure

TIP: Start at -0.7 FEC for portraits

In almost all portrait situations, a starting point of -0.7 FEC produces more natural and flattering results than the camera's default TTL calculation. TTL flash tends to produce flat, even lighting that looks obviously flash-lit. Pulling it back by 2/3 stop creates a much more natural balance with the ambient light. This single adjustment will immediately improve most flash portrait results.

12.4 External Flash via Hot Shoe — How to Attach and Sync

The OM-3's hot shoe accepts external flash units (also called speedlights or speedflashes) that are far more powerful than the built-in flash. An external flash can be pointed at a ceiling or wall to bounce diffused light onto your subject, tilted and swivelled for creative directional lighting, and fitted with diffusers or modifiers for softer light quality.

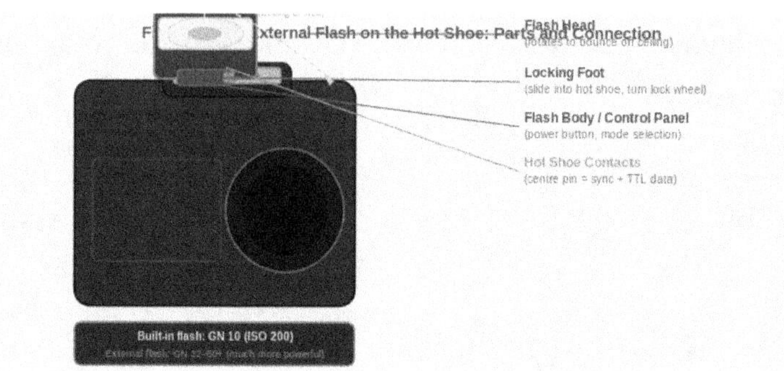

Figure 12.4 — External flash attached to the hot shoe: flash head that rotates for bounce, locking foot, TTL contacts

Compatible External Flash Units

The OM-3's hot shoe uses the OM SYSTEM standard multi-contact interface. Flash units designed for this system offer full TTL integration with the camera:

Flash Unit	Type	Guide Number	TTL Compatible?
OM SYSTEM FL-700WR	Professional wireless speedlight	GN 70 at ISO 200	Yes — full TTL, wireless commander/receiver
OM SYSTEM FL-600R	Mid-level speedlight	GN 60 at ISO 200	Yes — full TTL, wireless RC receiver
OM SYSTEM FL-36R	Compact speedlight	GN 36 at ISO 200	Yes — full TTL, wireless RC receiver
OM SYSTEM STF-8	Macro twin flash	Variable per head	Yes — designed for close-up macro
Godox, Nissin, Yongnuo (with correct adapter or OM mount version)	Third-party speedlights	Varies	Some models offer TTL; check for 'Four Thirds TTL' or 'OM SYSTEM' compatible

Standard PC-sync external flash (via adaptor)	Manual-only studio strobes	Varies	Manual power only — no TTL

How to Attach an External Flash to the Hot Shoe

Step 1: Power OFF the camera and the flash unit before connecting. Attaching a flash while either is powered on can occasionally cause a surge on the contacts — powering off first is good practice.

Step 2: Slide the flash unit's foot into the hot shoe on the top of the camera from the back (most flash units fit into the shoe from the rear, sliding forward into the bracket).

Step 3: Align the flash foot with the shoe channel. Slide it forward until the foot's metal plate is flush with the shoe contacts.

Step 4: Find the locking wheel or lever on the flash foot (usually on the left side as viewed from behind). Turn it clockwise to tighten. Turn until firm but not over-tightened — you should not need force.

Step 5: Power on the camera first, then power on the flash unit.

Step 6: The flash unit should display a ready indicator (often a green light or beep). The camera's display shows a flash icon confirming the external flash is detected.

Step 7: Take a test shot to confirm synchronisation — the flash fires and the photo is correctly exposed.

How to Remove an External Flash

Step 1: Power off both the flash and the camera.

Step 2: Turn the locking wheel counter-clockwise to release.

Step 3: Slide the flash unit backward out of the hot shoe.

Step 4: Store the flash safely. Replace the hot shoe cover on the camera if you have one.

Bounce Flash — The Most Useful External Flash Technique

Direct on-camera flash (pointed straight at the subject) produces flat, harsh lighting with hard shadows directly behind the subject. Bounce flash is the solution: you tilt the flash head to point at the ceiling or a nearby wall, so the light bounces off that large surface and reaches your subject from a much wider, softer angle.

- Ceiling bounce: tilt the flash head straight up (90 degrees). Light bounces off the ceiling and comes down at your subject from above — producing natural, flattering light similar to a large softbox.
- Wall bounce: rotate the flash head to face a white wall to the side of your subject. The light comes from the side — producing more dramatic, directional lighting.
- Important: bounce flash only works well when the ceiling or wall is white or very light coloured. Bouncing off a coloured wall adds a colour cast to your subject.
- FEC for bounce: you often need to apply +0.3 to +0.7 FEC when using bounce flash, because the light travels further (ceiling and back) than direct flash, reducing the effective power.

TIP: A white card on the flash head

Many photographers attach a small white card or commercial bounce card to the back of the flash head when bouncing off the ceiling. This sends a small direct fill beam forward to add catchlights to the eyes while the main light bounces from the ceiling. The result is natural-looking light with lively eyes — one of the best portrait flash techniques available.

Flash Sync Speed — The Maximum Shutter Speed with Flash

Flash sync speed is the fastest shutter speed at which the entire sensor is exposed to flash light simultaneously. At the OM-3's standard maximum sync speed (1/250 sec or 1/320 sec with Electronic First Curtain Shutter), both shutter curtains are fully open when the flash fires. If you try to use a faster shutter speed than the sync limit, the second curtain begins closing before the first has fully opened, and the flash only illuminates part of the frame — creating a dark band across the image.

- Maximum sync speed (standard): approximately 1/250 second
- Maximum sync speed (Electronic Front Curtain): approximately 1/320 second
- If using flash in A, S, or M mode: make sure your shutter speed does not exceed 1/320 sec or you will see a black band at the bottom of the image
- High-Speed Sync (HSS): some OM SYSTEM external flash units (FL-700WR, FL-600R) support High-Speed Sync mode, which lets you use any shutter speed up to 1/8000 sec with flash by pulsing the flash rapidly throughout the exposure. This is useful for outdoor portraits where you want to use wide apertures (shallow depth of field) in bright sunlight while still using flash. Enable HSS on the external flash unit and it activates automatically when you set a shutter speed above the sync limit.

12.5 Wireless Flash Control

Wireless flash (also called off-camera flash) allows you to place one or more flash units away from the camera — to the side, above, below, or behind the subject — and trigger them all simultaneously using an optical infrared signal from the camera's built-in flash. This dramatically expands your lighting possibilities beyond what a single on-camera flash can achieve.

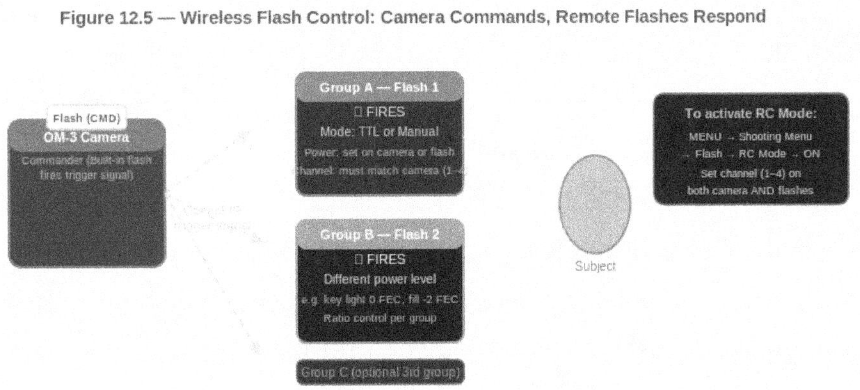

Figure 12.5 — Wireless Flash Control: Camera Commands, Remote Flashes Respond

Figure 12.5 — Wireless RC flash: the OM-3's built-in flash commands remote flash groups A, B, and C independently

How the OM-3 Wireless Flash System Works

The OM-3 uses an optical wireless RC (Radio-Controlled by infrared signal) system. Here is how the system works:

- The camera's built-in flash acts as the Commander (also called Master). It fires a rapid pre-flash sequence of invisible infrared pulses rather than visible light — these pulses contain the command data for the remote flashes.
- Compatible OM SYSTEM RC flash units (FL-36R, FL-600R, FL-700WR) receive these infrared signals through their built-in receivers and fire their main flash in synchronization with the shutter.
- Flash units are organised into Groups: Group A, Group B, and Group C. Each group can be set to a different power level, TTL mode, or manual power level. This lets you use different flash units for different roles — for example, Group A as the key light at -0.3 FEC, Group B as the fill light at -2.0 FEC.
- Communication Channel: a channel number (1 through 4) must be set the same on both the camera and the remote flash units to prevent interference from other photographers using the same system nearby.

Setting Up Wireless Flash — Exact Steps

Step 1: Enable RC Mode on the Camera

Step 1: Press MENU → Custom Menu F → RC Flash (or Shooting Menu → Flash → RC Mode).

Step 2: Set RC Flash to ON.

Step 3: The camera now treats the built-in flash as a commander. The built-in flash fires only the silent trigger signal, not visible light for illumination.

Step 4: Set the Channel: still in the RC menu, find Channel and set it to 1 (or whichever channel you prefer). Note this number — you will need to set the same channel on each remote flash unit.

Step 2: Configure Flash Groups on the Camera

Step 1: Still in the RC Flash settings, you will see Group A, Group B, and Group C settings.

Step 2: For each group you want to use, set the Mode: TTL (camera calculates power automatically), Auto (flash calculates power itself), or Manual (you set power as a fraction of full: 1/1, 1/2, 1/4, 1/8, 1/16, 1/32, 1/64).

Step 3: If using TTL mode, also set the FEC (Flash Exposure Compensation) for that group — e.g. Group A at 0 FEC for key light, Group B at -2.0 FEC for fill.

Step 4: Groups you do not wish to use can be set to OFF.

Step 3: Set Up Each Remote Flash Unit

Step 1: Power on your first remote flash unit (e.g. FL-600R).

Step 2: On the flash unit's control panel, navigate to its wireless settings and set it to RECEIVER (RC) mode.

Step 3: Set the Channel on the flash unit to match the channel you set on the camera (e.g. Channel 1).

Step 4: Set the Group assignment on the flash unit — A, B, or C, depending on which group you want it to respond to.

Step 5: Repeat for each additional remote flash unit, assigning groups as desired.

Step 4: Position and Test

Step 1: Position your remote flash units where you want them. The flash sensor window on the front of each remote unit must have a clear line of sight to the camera — the IR signal cannot pass through solid objects or around corners.

Step 2: Maximum reliable range of the optical wireless system: approximately 5–10 metres indoors, up to 15 metres outdoors in bright daylight (infrared signals can be harder to detect in very bright sunlight).

Step 3: Pop up the built-in flash on the camera.

Step 4: Take a test shot. All remote flash units should fire simultaneously.

Step 5: Review the result and adjust group FEC values or manual power levels as needed.

Multi-Light Portrait Setup Example

Here is a practical three-light wireless flash setup for professional-quality portraits using the OM-3:

Light	Flash Unit	Group	Position	Setting	Role
Key Light	FL-600R or FL-700WR	A	45 degrees to one side, slightly above subject, pointing down	TTL, 0 FEC	Main light — illuminates the face from the flattering 45-degree angle
Fill Light	FL-36R or FL-600R	B	Opposite side of subject, at camera height	TTL, -2.0 FEC	Reduces harsh shadows from the key light to a flattering 3:1 ratio
Hair/Rim Light	FL-36R	C	Behind the subject, pointing toward the back of the head	TTL, -0.7 FEC	Separates the subject from the background with a rim of light
Camera	OM-3 (commander)	—	Camera position, facing subject	RC Mode ON, built-in flash OFF or set to not illuminate	Commands all three groups

TIP: Test each group independently

When setting up a wireless multi-flash system, test each group independently before combining them. Turn Groups B and C off, photograph only with Group A to confirm the key light position and power. Then add Group B and adjust the fill. Then add Group C. This sequential approach saves time compared to adjusting all three at once from a combined result.

Troubleshooting Wireless Flash Problems

Problem	Likely Cause	Solution
Remote flash does not fire at all	Wrong channel, wrong mode on remote flash, or no line of sight	Verify channel matches on camera and flash. Confirm remote flash is set to RECEIVER mode. Move flash so its sensor window faces the camera's built-in flash.
Remote flash fires but exposure is wrong	Group TTL metering issue or incorrect FEC	Start with 0 FEC and adjust. If using manual, set a specific fraction (e.g. 1/4 power) and test.
Remote flash fires sometimes but not consistently	IR signal blocked or range exceeded	Move remote flash closer and remove obstacles between it and the camera. Indoors, IR bounces off walls and ceilings — outdoors, direct line of sight is needed.
Image has two flashes visible (double pop)	Both built-in flash and remote firing visibly	Set the built-in flash to Flash Off mode — it still sends the trigger signal but does not contribute visible light.
Remote flash fires multiple times per shot	RC mode signal bouncing off surfaces	This can happen in reflective environments. Try moving the camera closer to the remote flash or using a different channel.

NOTE: Line-of-sight requirement

The OM-3's optical RC wireless system requires the receiver sensor on each remote flash unit to have a clear view of the camera's built-in flash. Unlike radio-based wireless triggers (such as Godox X-series), the optical system cannot pass through walls, around corners, or across very large distances. For complete freedom of flash positioning, consider adding a dedicated radio trigger (such as Godox X2T) to the hot shoe, which can control compatible Godox flashes via radio signal from any direction and any distance up to 100+ metres.

Part 13 — Video Recording

The OM-3 is a capable video camera — not just a stills camera that happens to shoot video. It records 4K video with full colour, supports LOG profiles for colour grading, offers excellent 5-axis in-body stabilization, has a dedicated 3.5mm microphone input and headphone monitoring port, and provides real-time face and eye tracking autofocus during recording. Understanding how to use these features together makes the difference between mediocre phone-quality video and genuinely cinematic footage.

This part of the guide covers everything from the most basic operation (how to press the record button) through to professional-level concepts like frame rates for slow motion, OM-Log for colour grading, and manual audio control. Work through all sections even if you currently only plan to record casual clips — the knowledge will help you make better decisions even for simple recordings.

13.1 How to Start and Stop Recording

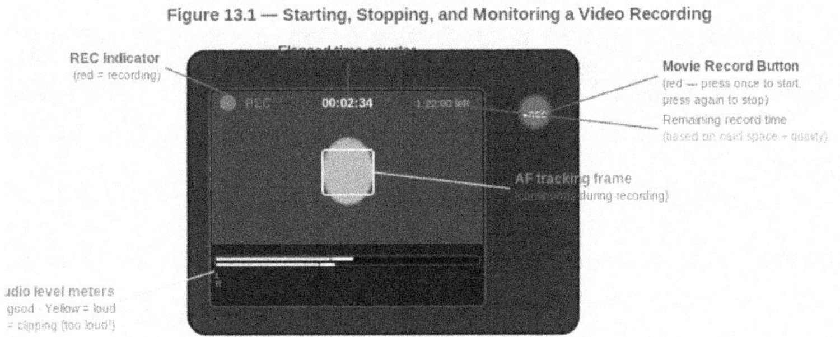

Figure 13.1 — The recording interface: REC indicator, elapsed time counter, audio meters, and AF tracking frame

The Movie Record Button

The OM-3 has a dedicated red Movie Record Button on the top plate, immediately recognisable by its red colour — the only red button on the camera. Press it once to start recording; press it again to stop.

Crucially, you do not need to change the Mode Dial to a video mode before recording. The Movie Record Button works in any shooting mode — P, A, S, M, or even iAuto. When you press the button, recording begins immediately using the video settings in your Video Menu. When you press it again, recording stops and the clip is saved.

Starting and Stopping — Step by Step

> **Step 1:** Point the camera at your subject. If using the LCD as your monitor, tilt it to your preferred angle.
>
> **Step 2:** Press the red Movie Record Button once firmly. The camera begins recording immediately.

Step 3: A red REC indicator appears in the top-left corner of the screen. An elapsed time counter (00:00:00) begins counting in the top center of the screen.

Step 4: Below the scene, audio level meters (L and R) appear at the bottom of the screen — showing the current input level of the microphone. These are important to monitor during recording.

Step 5: Record your scene. The camera continues recording until you stop it.

Step 6: When finished, press the red Movie Record Button once again. Recording stops. The file is processed and saved to the SD card — this may take 1–3 seconds for the card to finish writing. A brief spinning indicator appears.

Step 7: The camera returns to live view mode, ready for another clip or a still photo.

What Appears on Screen During Recording

On-Screen Element	Location	What It Shows
REC (red dot)	Top-left corner	Confirms recording is active. Blinks if there is an issue (card too slow, card almost full).
Elapsed time counter (00:02:34)	Top center	How long the current clip has been recording. Format: Hours:Minutes:Seconds.
Remaining time estimate	Top right	Approximate recording time remaining on the SD card at the current quality setting.
Audio level meters (L / R)	Bottom of frame	Shows the current microphone input level. Green = good level. Yellow = loud but acceptable. Red = clipping (input is too loud — audio will distort).
AF tracking frame	Over the subject	Green box showing where the camera is currently focused. Updates continuously if C-AF is active.
Temperature warning	On screen when hot	If the camera overheats, a temperature icon appears. If it reaches critical level, recording stops automatically.

Recording Using the Shutter Button (Movie Mode)

If you set the Mode Dial to the Video (movie camera) position — if your OM-3 has one — the shutter button may also start and stop recording in that mode. However, the dedicated red Movie Record Button always works regardless of mode. Always use the red button for consistency.

NOTE: Maximum clip length

Individual video clips are limited to 29 minutes 59 seconds per clip due to file system constraints. If your recording exceeds this, the camera automatically stops and starts a new clip seamlessly. For very long recording sessions, check that Unlimited Recording is not capped in the Video Menu settings.

TIP: Use the tilting LCD screen for video

For video work, tilt the LCD screen to a comfortable monitoring angle — particularly if you are vlogging (flip it forward 180 degrees to see yourself), shooting low-angle (tilt up), or shooting from overhead (tilt down). This allows you to monitor focus, framing, and audio levels throughout the recording without holding the camera awkwardly to your face.

13.2 Video Resolution and Frame Rate — What Each Means

Two of the most important video settings are resolution (how many pixels make up each frame) and frame rate (how many frames are recorded per second). Together they determine the quality, cinematic look, slow-motion potential, and file size of your video.

Video Resolutions — 4K, Full HD, and HD

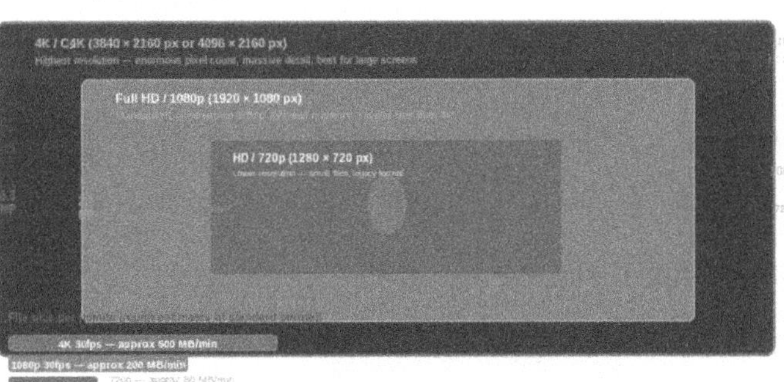

Figure 13.2 — Resolution comparison: 4K contains the most pixels and the finest detail; HD the least

4K (3840 × 2160) — Standard 4K / UHD

Standard 4K records at 3840 × 2160 pixels — exactly four times the pixel count of Full HD. This is the UHD (Ultra High Definition) standard used by 4K televisions and most 4K delivery platforms including YouTube and streaming services.

OM System "Olympus" OM-3

Aspect	Detail
Pixel dimensions	3840 × 2160 (UHD 4K)
Megapixels per frame	Approximately 8.3 MP
File size (approx)	300–600 MB per minute depending on bitrate setting
Best for	Final delivery on 4K TVs and monitors, YouTube and streaming at maximum quality, any project where you want future-proof resolution, documentary work, commercial production
SD card required	UHS-II V60 or V90 for reliable 4K recording at high bitrate
Crop factor note	The OM-3 may apply a slight sensor crop when recording 4K — check the Video Menu for exact crop behaviour at your selected 4K mode

C4K (4096 × 2160) — Cinema 4K

C4K is a cinema-standard 4K resolution that is slightly wider than standard 4K — 4096 pixels wide instead of 3840. This cinema ratio (approximately 1.9:1) is used in digital cinema projection and DCP (Digital Cinema Package) delivery. For most users, standard 4K (3840 × 2160) is more practical, but C4K is the correct choice for cinema or digital film production.

Full HD / FHD / 1080p (1920 × 1080) — The Versatile Standard

Full HD is the most widely supported video resolution in the world. It is the broadcast standard for most television, the minimum quality for professional video production, and the native resolution of the vast majority of displays and projectors.

Aspect	Detail
Pixel dimensions	1920 × 1080
Megapixels per frame	Approximately 2.1 MP
File size (approx)	100–250 MB per minute
Best for	Professional video production for standard delivery, broadcast television, online video where 4K is not required, long recording sessions where card space matters, interview and documentary work
SD card required	UHS-I U3 minimum — most modern cards handle FHD easily

Advantage over 4K	Smaller files, faster workflow, more widely compatible with editing software and delivery platforms, usable at higher frame rates (60fps, 120fps) for slow motion

HD / 720p (1280 × 720) — Legacy Format

720p is an older HD standard. It is rarely used in modern video production because it looks noticeably less sharp than Full HD, especially on modern screens. Its only advantage is smaller file sizes. Most users should avoid 720p unless recording for a very specific legacy platform.

How to Change Video Resolution

Step 1: Press MENU → Video Menu (movie camera icon).

Step 2: Find Movie Quality at the top of the Video Menu. Press OK to enter.

Step 3: A list of resolution and frame rate combinations appears.

Step 4: Use the UP/DOWN arrows to scroll through and highlight your preferred combination.

Step 5: Press OK to confirm. Press MENU to close.

Frame Rates — What Each Means

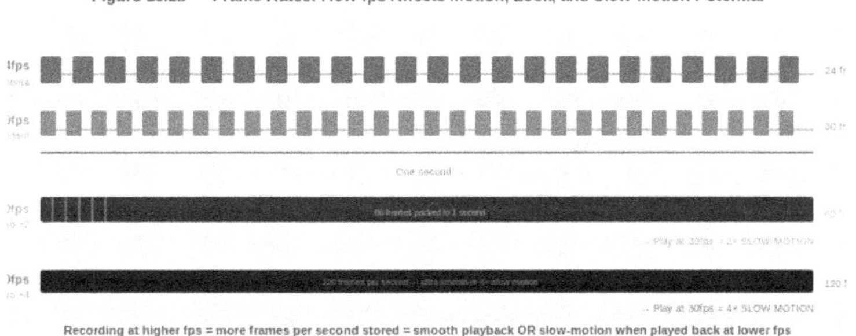

Figure 13.2b — Frame rate comparison: 24fps (cinematic), 30fps (standard), 60fps (2× slow-mo), 120fps (4× slow-mo)

Frame rate — measured in frames per second (fps) — determines how many individual still images are captured each second to create the video. Different frame rates produce very different visual results and serve different creative and practical purposes.

Frame Rate	Where Used	Motion Look	Slow-Motion Potential	Best For

24fps (23.976)	Cinema worldwide	Classic cinematic motion blur — slightly dreamy, film-like quality	Not designed for slow motion	Narrative film, cinematic vlogs, documentary, any project where you want the classic film look
25fps	PAL countries (Europe, Africa, Australia)	Very similar to 24fps — smooth, natural	Not designed for slow motion	European television broadcast, content for PAL markets, YouTube for European audiences
30fps (29.97)	NTSC countries (USA, Japan)	Smooth and natural — the standard for most video content worldwide	Usable at 30fps output for minimal slow-motion	YouTube, social media, television, corporate video, interviews, documentary, general all-purpose video
50fps	PAL slow-motion standard	Extremely smooth motion at normal speed; very slight slow-motion at 25fps output	2× slow motion when played back at 25fps	Sports highlights for PAL broadcast, fast-motion events, wildlife for European delivery
60fps (59.94)	NTSC slow-motion	Ultra-smooth — sports broadcast look, gaming capture look	2× slow motion when played back at 30fps	Sports, wildlife, anything fast-moving where you need smooth or slow-motion playback, YouTube at highest frame rate

120fps	High-speed capture	Motion is too smooth to look natural at 1:1 — designed for slow-motion use	4× slow motion when played back at 30fps	Water splashes, athletics, martial arts, dancing — any fast movement you want to dramatically slow down

Slow Motion — How It Actually Works

Slow motion is achieved by recording at a higher frame rate than you will play back. The concept is simple: if you record 60 frames per second and play them back at 30 frames per second, time appears to move at half speed — every 2 seconds of recorded action becomes 4 seconds of slow-motion playback. Here is the formula:

- Record at 60fps, deliver at 30fps = 2× slow motion (every 1 second of recording becomes 2 seconds of playback)
- Record at 120fps, deliver at 30fps = 4× slow motion (every 1 second of recording becomes 4 seconds of playback)
- Record at 24fps, deliver at 24fps = normal speed

> **NOTE: The camera records at high fps — the slow motion happens in editing**
>
> The OM-3 records 60fps and 120fps video at full speed in real time. The clips appear to play at normal speed when you first review them on the camera. To see the slow-motion effect, you must import the clip into video editing software (Premiere Pro, Final Cut Pro, DaVinci Resolve, CapCut, iMovie) and change the clip's playback speed to 50% (for 60fps) or 25% (for 120fps) relative to a 30fps timeline.

> **TIP: 180-degree shutter rule for cinematic video**
>
> For video that looks cinematic rather than 'news camera' or 'sports broadcast', follow the 180-degree shutter rule: set the shutter speed to approximately double the frame rate. For 24fps video, use 1/50 second. For 30fps, use 1/60 second. For 60fps slow-motion, use 1/120 second. This produces the natural, slight motion blur that the human eye expects in filmed motion. Shutter speeds faster than this make motion look choppy and unnatural; slower makes it look blurry and smeared.

13.3 Video Format Options (MOV / MP4)

The OM-3 can save video files in two container formats: MOV and MP4. A container format is like a box — it holds the video stream and audio stream together in one file. The actual video and audio data inside the box may be compressed using the same codec (H.264 or H.265) regardless of which container you choose. The difference is in compatibility and workflow.

Format	Extension	Compatibility	Recommended For
MOV (QuickTime)	.mov	Excellent compatibility with Apple software (Final Cut Pro, iMovie, QuickTime Player). Good compatibility with Adobe Premiere Pro and DaVinci Resolve on all platforms.	Mac-based editing workflows, Final Cut Pro users, any professional editing environment. MOV supports larger file sizes and some advanced metadata features.
MP4 (MPEG-4)	.mp4	Universal — plays on virtually every device, operating system, and video platform without conversion. Windows Media Player, VLC, YouTube, Instagram, TikTok, smartphones.	Windows users, direct upload to social media platforms, situations where files need to be shared or played without editing software, content for web delivery.

Which Format Should You Choose?

- If you edit on a Mac with Final Cut Pro or iMovie: choose MOV.
- If you edit on Windows with Premiere Pro: either works, but MP4 is slightly more compatible across tools.
- If you want to upload directly to YouTube, Instagram, or share to a phone: MP4.
- If you are a professional using DaVinci Resolve for colour grading: either is fine — Resolve supports both excellently.
- If you shoot OM-Log (covered in Section 13.7): MOV is generally preferred for log footage going into professional colour grading.

How to Change the Video Format

Step 1: Press MENU → Video Menu (movie camera icon).

Step 2: Scroll to find Movie Recording Format or Container Format option.

Step 3: Press OK. Select MOV or MP4.

Step 4: Press OK to confirm. Press MENU to close.

Video Codec and Bitrate

Within each container format, the video is compressed using a codec. The OM-3 uses H.264 (older, more universally compatible) and H.265 (newer, more efficient — same quality at smaller file size). Not all editing software fully supports H.265 without hardware acceleration, so check your editing computer's capabilities before choosing H.265.

Bitrate determines how much data is recorded per second of video — higher bitrate = better quality, larger files. The OM-3 offers three bitrate settings:

Bitrate Setting	Name	Quality	File Size	Recommended For
High	ALL-I (All Intra)	Maximum — each frame compressed independently	Largest (~400-600 MB/min at 4K)	Professional editing workflow, colour grading, any post-production work
Normal	IPB Standard	Very good — groups of frames compressed together	Moderate (~200-350 MB/min at 4K)	General video work, social media content, long recording sessions
Low	IPB Economy	Good but reduced — heavier compression	Smallest (~100-150 MB/min at 4K)	Very long recordings, when card space is limited, casual video

TIP: ALL-I for editing, IPB for sharing

If you plan to edit your video in post-production, use ALL-I (high bitrate). If you are recording footage to share directly without heavy editing, IPB Standard gives you good quality with much smaller files that are easier to handle and upload.

13.4 Microphone Input and Audio Level Settings

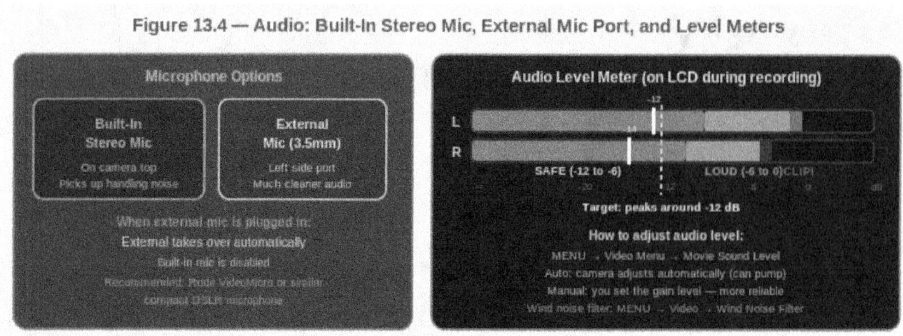

Figure 13.4 — Audio input options (built-in stereo vs. external mic) and audio level meter zones

The Built-In Stereo Microphone

The OM-3 has a built-in stereo microphone located on the top plate of the camera body. It records both left and right audio channels simultaneously, creating a basic stereo field. The microphone is functional for casual video recordings, interviews, and vlogging in quiet environments.

However, the built-in microphone has significant limitations for serious video work:

- It is extremely sensitive to handling noise — any movement of your hands on the camera body, lens adjustments, or button presses are amplified and recorded directly into the audio.
- It picks up the sound of the lens autofocus motor on some lenses, creating audible clicking sounds in the audio track.
- Being mounted on the camera, it is always the same distance from the subject regardless of the shot — for wide shots, the subject is too far away for good audio capture.
- In outdoor conditions, even a slight breeze causes very loud rumbling wind noise.

External Microphone — A Major Improvement

Plugging an external microphone into the 3.5mm microphone input on the left side of the camera immediately deactivates the built-in microphone and uses the external input instead. An external microphone placed close to your subject dramatically improves audio quality:

- A compact shotgun microphone (Rode VideoMicro, DJI Mic Mini, Deity V.Lav) mounted on the hot shoe and plugged into the mic jack points directly at the subject and rejects sounds from the sides.
- A lavalier microphone (small clip-on mic) clipped to the subject's shirt and connected to the camera via a cable gives excellent close-range audio regardless of camera distance.
- A wireless lavalier system (Rode Wireless GO, DJI Mic) transmits audio from a mic on the subject to a receiver in the camera's mic jack — eliminates the cable and allows greater camera-to-subject distance.

TIP: Upgrade audio before upgrading anything else

Viewers will tolerate slightly imperfect video but they will immediately click away from a video with bad audio. The single most impactful upgrade for video quality after your lens is a decent compact microphone. A 20-dollar improvement in audio quality produces a more noticeable result than a 200-dollar lens upgrade.

Setting Audio Recording Levels

The audio recording level controls how much the microphone input is amplified before it is recorded. Getting this right is critical:

- Too low: the audio is quiet and you have to turn it up when editing — amplifying the background noise and making the recording sound hissy.
- Too high: the audio clips (distorts) whenever the sound is loud — creating a harsh, crackling sound that cannot be fixed in editing.
- Correct: the audio level meters should peak at approximately -12 dB during normal speech or music. This leaves headroom for occasional louder moments without clipping.

Auto Audio Level

Auto audio level (Auto Recording Level) lets the camera automatically adjust the input gain to keep the audio at a consistent level. This is convenient and prevents obvious clipping. The drawback is audio pumping — the auto gain system can audibly change the background noise level between quiet passages and louder ones, which sounds unnatural in edited video.

Manual Audio Level

Manual audio level gives you complete, fixed control over the input gain. The level you set stays constant throughout the recording — no pumping, no sudden level changes. This is the correct choice for all professional and semi-professional video work.

Step 1: Press MENU → Video Menu → Movie Sound Level.

Step 2: Change from Auto to Manual.

Step 3: A manual level slider or numeric control appears. The range is typically -40 to 0 dB.

Step 4: Before recording, aim the microphone at your subject and ask them to speak at their normal volume. Watch the audio level meters on the LCD.

Step 5: Adjust the level until peaks reach approximately -12 dB during normal speech. This ensures headroom for louder moments.

Step 6: Press OK and close the menu. Begin recording.

Step 7: Monitor the meters during recording — if a loud sound pushes the meters into the red (clipping), reduce the level for the next take.

Wind Noise Filter

The Wind Noise Filter applies a high-pass audio filter that cuts low-frequency rumbling sounds — primarily wind noise from the built-in microphone. When shooting outdoors in any wind, enable this filter:

Step 1: Press MENU → Video Menu → Wind Noise Filter.

Step 2: Options: Off / Low / Standard / High.

Step 3: Standard removes most wind noise from the built-in mic while retaining good voice quality.

Step 4: High removes the most wind noise but can make voices sound slightly thin or 'telephone-like'.

Step 5: Keep Off when recording indoors — the filter is not needed and may slightly alter the audio quality.

Monitoring Audio with Headphones

The OM-3 has a 3.5mm headphone output on the left side of the camera. Plug standard earphones or headphones into this port during video recording to monitor the audio in real time. This lets you immediately hear if the microphone is picking up unwanted sounds, if the level is too high or too low, and if the autofocus motor is audible in the recording. Audio monitoring is strongly recommended for any serious video work.

To adjust headphone volume: MENU → Video Menu → Headphone Volume → set from 0 to 20.

13.5 Video Stabilization Settings

Shaky, unstable video looks amateur and is difficult to watch. The OM-3's stabilization system for video is one of its strongest features — combining in-body sensor stabilization with additional electronic stabilization for very smooth handheld footage. Understanding the different stabilization modes helps you choose the best balance of smoothness and image quality.

Stabilization Mode	Menu Option	What It Does	Trade-Off	Best For
M-IS 1 (Movie IS 1)	Movie IS → M-IS 1	Combines 5-axis IBIS sensor stabilization with additional electronic (digital crop) stabilization. Maximum smoothness for handheld video.	Slight crop of the frame — field of view narrows slightly (typically 5-10%). Reduces effective resolution marginally.	Handheld walking shots, vlogging, run-and-gun documentary, any situation where you are moving with the camera
M-IS 2 (Movie IS 2)	Movie IS → M-IS 2	Uses 5-axis IBIS sensor stabilization only — no electronic crop. Natural field of view preserved.	Less stabilization than M-IS 1 — some residual shake may be visible in rapid movements.	Mostly stationary handheld shots, slower camera movements, situations where maximum field of view is important
Off	Movie IS → Off	All in-camera stabilization disabled — the lens IS (if any) still functions.	Maximum shake — only usable on a tripod or gimbal.	Tripod recording, motorized gimbal use (some gimbals perform

				better without IBIS), specific creative moving shots

How to Set Movie Stabilization

> **Step 1:** Press MENU → Video Menu → Movie IS (or Movie Stabilizer).
>
> **Step 2:** Select M-IS 1, M-IS 2, or Off.
>
> **Step 3:** Press OK to confirm. Press MENU to close.

Sync IS — Combining IBIS with Lens IS

Some OM SYSTEM lenses have their own optical image stabilization built in — called OIS (Optical Image Stabilizer). When these lenses are attached, the camera and lens work together in what Olympus/OM SYSTEM calls Sync IS — the camera's 5-axis IBIS and the lens's OIS communicate and cooperate to produce better combined stabilization than either could achieve alone. This is especially effective for extreme telephoto video work.

Sync IS is automatic when a compatible lens is attached — there is no separate setting to enable it. The camera detects the compatible lens and enables the combined mode automatically.

> **TIP: Stabilization settings for tripod vs handheld**
>
> When the camera is on a tripod, disable Movie IS (set to Off). IBIS and electronic stabilization can cause subtle 'wobble' artefacts when the camera is mounted on a stable platform because the stabilization system is constantly trying to compensate for movement that does not exist. For tripod shots, always disable stabilization for the cleanest, most stable footage.

13.6 Focusing During Video Recording

Autofocus during video recording on the OM-3 is remarkably capable. The camera can continuously track subjects — including faces and eyes — throughout a recording, producing smooth, cinematic-looking focus transitions rather than the hunting and jumping that plagues many cameras. However, video AF is a nuanced topic and understanding the settings makes a significant difference to the results.

Movie AF Modes

AF Mode for Video	Behaviour	Best For
C-AF (Continuous AF)	Camera continuously adjusts focus to keep the subject sharp throughout the recording. Focus transitions happen smoothly.	Documentary, interview, vlogging, any situation where the subject moves or the camera moves
C-AF + Tracking	Identifies a specific subject at the start of recording and continues tracking it even if it temporarily leaves the frame. Face/Eye detection works within this mode.	Walking subjects, athletes, performers, anyone moving dynamically through the frame
MF (Manual Focus)	You control focus by rotating the lens focus ring during recording. No autofocus motor activity — completely silent for audio.	Narrative filmmaking with planned focus pulls, situations where AF hunts or distracts, lens rostrums, macro video
S-AF (Single AF)	Locks focus when you press the AF button — does not continuously track. Use with care in video as focus is static.	Static interview subjects who do not move, locked-off camera shots on a tripod with a stationary subject

Continuous AF Sensitivity for Video

A key setting for video AF is the C-AF sensitivity (called Movie C-AF Sensitivity in the Video Menu). This controls how quickly the camera re-focuses when it detects a subject has moved.

- Negative values (-1 to -2): the camera re-focuses slowly and smoothly — changes in focus happen gradually, which looks cinematic and intentional. If someone briefly walks in front of the subject, the camera does not immediately jump focus.
- Zero (0): balanced standard tracking — the camera follows subject movement at a moderate speed.
- Positive values (+1 to +2): the camera tracks focus changes very aggressively — immediately snaps to new subjects. Can cause visible focus hunting if the scene has many elements at different distances.

For most video work, -1 or -2 produces the most professional-looking autofocus behaviour. Fast tracking is only useful for very dynamic action-oriented video.

How to Set Movie AF Settings

Step 1: Press MENU → Video Menu.

Step 2: Find Movie AF Mode. Set to C-AF for continuous tracking or MF for manual.

Step 3: Find Movie C-AF Sensitivity. Set to -1 or -2 for smooth, cinematic focus transitions.

Step 4: For face/eye tracking during video: enable Face Priority in the Shooting Menu (this also applies during video recording) and set AF Mode to C-AF.

Step 5: Press OK and close the menu.

TIP: Manual focus pulls for cinematic video

Professional cinematography uses planned, deliberate focus shifts — called focus pulls — from one subject to another. These are done manually by slowly turning the focus ring during recording. Practice focus pulls between two subjects at different distances: start with focus on the near subject, then slowly rotate the focus ring until the far subject becomes sharp. This technique looks intentional and cinematic, where autofocus jumps may look uncontrolled.

13.7 OM-Log and Flat Picture Profiles

Figure 13.7 — OM-Log vs Standard Profile: More Dynamic Range, Needs Colour Grading

Standard / Natural Profile

Punchy, contrasty result — ready to view

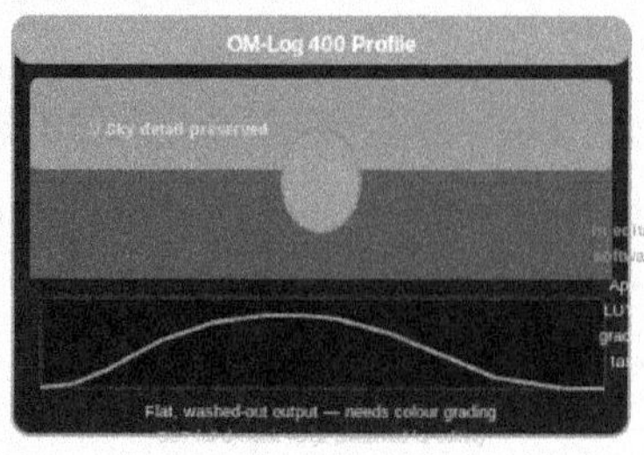

Figure 13.7 — OM-Log (right) preserves full dynamic range but looks washed out until colour graded; Standard profile (left) looks punchy immediately but loses highlight/shadow detail

What Is a Log Profile? (Plain English)

A LOG (logarithmic) picture profile is a special way of recording video that sacrifices immediate visual appeal in exchange for maximum dynamic range and editing flexibility. When you record with OM-Log, the footage coming out of the camera looks flat, washed-out, and low-contrast — like an old faded photograph. This is intentional. The flat look means that both the darkest shadows and the brightest highlights have been squeezed into the recordable range, preserving detail that a standard profile would clip.

In post-production (editing software), you apply a colour grade or LUT (Look-Up Table) to restore the footage to a beautiful, punchy, correctly exposed look — but now with far more detail in the highlights and shadows than standard footage would have. The result can be extraordinary — a dynamic range of 12 or more stops compared to approximately 8 stops for a standard JPEG-style picture profile.

OM-Log 400 — The OM SYSTEM Log Profile

OM SYSTEM's log profile is called OM-Log 400. The 400 refers to the base ISO sensitivity at which the log profile is calibrated — you should set your camera to ISO 400 as your base ISO when using OM-Log for the most predictable results.

Aspect	OM-Log 400
Dynamic range	Approximately 12+ stops — compared to 7-8 stops for standard profiles
ISO recommendation	Start at ISO 400 (the rated base). Adjust exposure from there as needed.
Base exposure	Expose to the right — the histogram should be slightly brighter than you might expect for a standard profile. The flat gamma compresses highlights, meaning the right side of the histogram contains recoverable data that looks bright but is not clipped.
Editing requirement	Must be colour graded in post to look correct. Raw OM-Log footage is not suitable for direct delivery — it must be processed.
LUT support	OM SYSTEM provides official LUTs for OM-Log in OM Workspace software. Third-party LUTs from the Log community are also compatible.

Bit depth recommendation	Record in the highest available bit depth — 10-bit output if available, or highest quality JPEG compression setting. The more bits, the more editing latitude in the grade.

How to Enable OM-Log 400

Step 1: Press MENU → Video Menu → Picture Mode (Movie).

Step 2: Scroll to OM-Log 400 in the picture mode list.

Step 3: Press OK to select.

Step 4: Set your ISO to 400 (or configure Auto ISO with 400 as the minimum).

Step 5: Set Movie Bit Rate to High (ALL-I) for maximum quality log footage.

Step 6: Record your scene. The footage will look flat and washed-out on the LCD screen — this is correct and expected.

Step 7: Import the footage into your editing software and apply a colour grade or OM-Log LUT to restore the look.

WARNING: OM-Log requires colour grading software

Do not enable OM-Log unless you have editing software and some experience with colour grading. Footage shot in OM-Log looks completely wrong without grading — it is not a stylistic choice but a technical workflow requirement. If you need footage that looks good straight out of the camera, use a standard or Natural picture profile instead.

Flat / Muted Picture Profiles — The Alternative to Full Log

For users who want more dynamic range than a standard profile but without the complexity of full log grading, the Muted picture mode is a middle ground. It reduces the contrast and saturation of the footage while staying within a range that looks acceptable without heavy post-processing.

Profile	Contrast	Saturation	Dynamic Range	Post-Processing Needed	Best For
Natural	Normal	Normal	Standard (~8 stops)	None — ready to use	Casual video, social media, interviews where you just

					need a clean, accurate look
Muted (Flat)	Low	Low	Moderate (~9-10 stops)	Colour correction recommended but not mandatory	Semi-professional video where you want editing latitude without full log workflow
OM-Log 400	Very low / log curve	Very low	Maximum (~12 stops)	Mandatory — must be colour graded	Professional production, colour grading workflows, cinematography

> **TIP: Start with Natural, graduate to OM-Log**
>
> If you are new to video, use the Natural picture profile. It looks great straight out of the camera and requires no post-processing. As you develop your editing skills and start colour grading your footage, switch to Muted for a little more latitude. When you are confident with colour grading workflows, move to OM-Log 400 for the maximum creative control. This progression is how most videographers develop.

Recommended Starter Video Settings for the OM-3

For someone starting out with video on the OM-3, these settings provide excellent results with minimal complexity:

Setting	Recommended Starter Value	Why
Resolution	FHD 1920×1080 (Full HD)	Large enough for any screen, smaller files, widely compatible, available at all frame rates
Frame Rate	30fps (or 25fps in Europe/Africa/Australia)	Standard for YouTube, social media, and general delivery

Bitrate	IPB Standard (Normal)	Good quality, manageable file sizes
Format	MP4	Maximum compatibility for sharing and upload
Picture Profile	Natural	Looks great with no editing required
Movie IS	M-IS 1	Best handheld stabilization
AF Mode	C-AF with Face Priority On	Keeps subjects sharp automatically
C-AF Sensitivity	-1	Smooth, natural focus transitions
Audio	External mic if possible; Auto level as a starter	Better audio immediately when ext. mic is connected
White Balance	Set manually (e.g. Daylight outdoors, Tungsten indoors)	Prevents colour shifts mid-clip
Shutter Speed	1/60 (for 30fps, following the 180° rule)	Natural motion blur look

Part 14 — Image Stabilization

The OM-3 has one of the most effective in-body image stabilization (IBIS) systems in the mirrorless camera world. It works by physically moving the camera's sensor in five directions to counteract the camera shake produced by human hand tremors. The result is that you can take sharp photographs at shutter speeds several stops slower than would otherwise be possible — without a tripod.

Understanding exactly what IBIS does, how to control it, and when to use each stabilization mode helps you get the sharpest possible results from every shot.

14.1 What Is In-Body Image Stabilization (IBIS)?

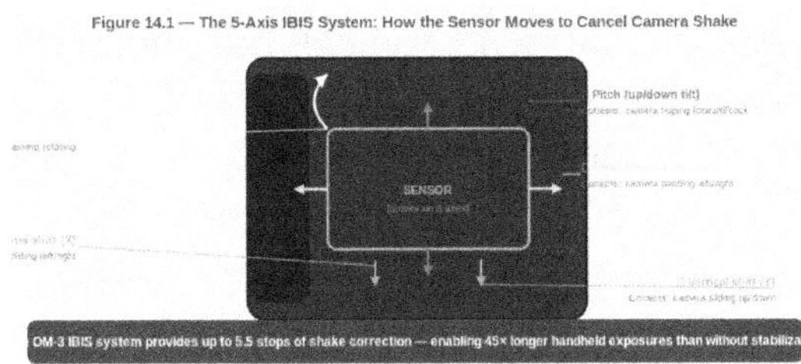

Figure 14.1 — The OM-3's 5-axis IBIS system: the sensor physically moves in five directions to cancel camera shake

How IBIS Works — Plain English

Inside the OM-3, the image sensor is not rigidly fixed to the camera body. Instead, it floats on a precisely controlled electromagnetic suspension system — essentially a tiny, extremely fast gimbal built into the camera. Gyroscopic sensors in the camera detect the direction and speed of camera shake dozens of times per second. A processor calculates the exact opposite movement needed to cancel each shake, and the sensor is moved accordingly.

The result is that while the camera body may be trembling in your hands, the sensor itself stays remarkably still — producing a sharp image even at shutter speeds that would normally result in blur.

The Five Axes Explained

Axis	Type of Movement	Camera Shake It Corrects
① **Pitch**	Sensor tilts forward and backward (up/down rotation)	The camera tipping forward or backward — the most common type of shake, often visible as vertical blur
② **Yaw**	Sensor rotates left and right (horizontal rotation)	The camera panning left or right — the second most common shake, causes horizontal blur
③ **Roll**	Sensor rotates around the lens axis (twist)	The camera rotating as if turning a steering wheel — causes diagonal or circular blur

④ **Horizontal Shift (X)**	Sensor slides left and right	The camera sliding physically sideways — important for macro photography where even tiny shifts matter
⑤ **Vertical Shift (Y)**	Sensor slides up and down	The camera sliding physically up or down — equally important for macro work

How Many Stops Does OM-3 IBIS Provide?

OM SYSTEM rates the OM-3's IBIS at up to 5.5 stops of stabilization compensation (CIPA standard). In practical terms, this means:

- Without IBIS: a typical beginner can handhold a sharp photo at approximately 1/60 second with a standard lens.
- With OM-3 IBIS at 5.5 stops: that same person can handhold a sharp photo at approximately 1/2 second — a 45× longer exposure.
- With Sync IS (IBIS + lens OIS combined): up to 6.5 stops, enabling incredibly slow handheld exposures.

TIP: IBIS does not help with subject motion

IBIS is extraordinarily effective at correcting camera shake — the blur caused by your hands trembling. But it does nothing for subject motion — the blur caused by your subject moving during the exposure. If your subject is moving, you still need a fast shutter speed regardless of IBIS. IBIS helps you handhold the camera steadily; it cannot freeze a moving subject.

14.2 How to Turn IBIS On and Off — Exact Steps

The OM-3's IBIS system is activated and controlled through the Image Stabilization setting in the Shooting Menu or via the Super Control Panel. The setting is labeled IS (Image Stabilization) and offers four options: IS1, IS2, IS3, and Off.

Method 1 — Via the Super Control Panel (Fastest)

Step 1: Press OK to open the Super Control Panel from live view.

Step 2: Navigate to the Image Stabilization tile — it shows a ((•)) icon representing the IBIS sensor.

Step 3: Press OK to open the IS mode selection screen.

Step 4: Use the arrow buttons to navigate between IS1, IS2, IS3, and Off.

Step 5: Highlight your choice and press OK to confirm.

Step 6: Half-press the shutter to return to live view. The IS icon in the display updates.

Method 2 — Via the Shooting Menu

Step 1: Press MENU → Shooting Menu (camera icon) → Page 1.

Step 2: Find Image Stabilization (IS) and press OK.

Step 3: Select IS1, IS2, IS3, or Off.

Step 4: Press OK to confirm. Press MENU to close.

> **NOTE: IS stays on between power cycles**
>
> The IBIS setting is saved when you turn the camera off. When you power on again, IBIS is in whatever mode you last selected. If you turn IBIS off for tripod work, remember to turn it back on when you pick the camera up for handheld shooting.

14.3 Stabilization Modes — What Each Does

Figure 14.3 — Stabilization Modes: Which Axes Are Active in Each Mode

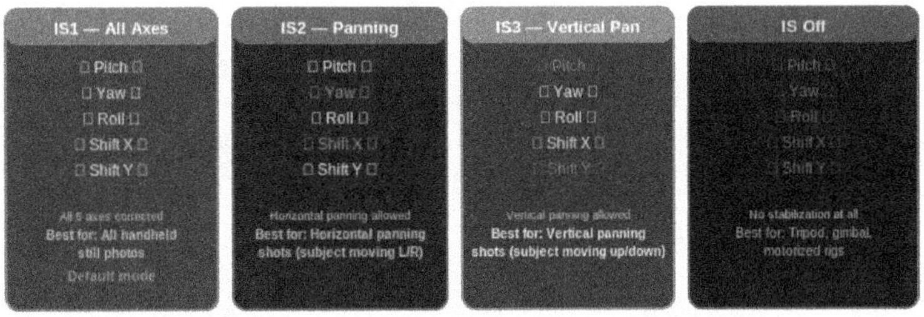

Figure 14.3 — IS mode comparison: which axes are active (green ✓) or intentionally disabled (red X) in each mode

IS1 — All-Direction Stabilization (Default)

IS1 activates all five axes of stabilization simultaneously. This is the correct mode for the vast majority of handheld still photography — portraits, landscapes, travel, street photography, events, and any situation where you simply want the sharpest possible handheld image. The sensor compensates for all types of camera movement in every direction.

e	IS1 Detail
Axes active	All 5 — Pitch, Yaw, Roll, Horizontal Shift, Vertical Shift
Stabilization strength	Maximum — up to 5.5 stops
Best for	All handheld still photography. This is the default and correct mode for 95% of situations.
Also good for	Handheld video where M-IS 1 or M-IS 2 handles video-specific stabilization separately
Potential issue	If the camera is stationary on a tripod, IS1 can cause subtle micro-movements as the system hunts for shake that is not there. Turn Off when using a tripod.

IS2 — Horizontal Panning Mode

IS2 disables stabilization on the horizontal (Yaw/X-shift) axes but keeps it active on all vertical and roll axes. This allows the camera to pan smoothly left and right without the stabilization system fighting the intentional horizontal movement, while still correcting vertical shake and roll that would appear as unwanted jitter during the pan.

Panning is a technique used in sports and action photography where you follow a moving subject with the camera — the subject appears sharp against a motion-blurred background that conveys speed and movement. IS2 makes this technique more reliable by stabilizing the vertical component of the panning motion while permitting the intentional horizontal pan.

Aspect	IS2 Detail
Axes active	Pitch (vertical tilt), Roll (twist), Vertical Shift (Y) — 3 of 5 axes
Axes disabled	Yaw (horizontal rotation), Horizontal Shift (X) — intentionally to allow horizontal panning
Best for	Horizontal panning shots of cars, runners, cyclists, birds flying horizontally
How to pan	Set IS2, use a moderate shutter speed (1/30 to 1/125 for creative blur), track the subject horizontally, and fire a burst as you pan smoothly.

IS3 — Vertical Panning Mode

IS3 is the vertical equivalent of IS2 — it disables stabilization on the vertical (Pitch/Y-shift) axes while keeping horizontal and roll correction active. This allows smooth vertical panning — for example, following a diver dropping from a board, a basketball player jumping, or a bird taking off vertically.

IS3 is used less frequently than IS2 because most action photography involves horizontal movement, but it is invaluable for specifically vertical action sequences.

IS Off — No Stabilization

IS Off completely deactivates the IBIS system. The sensor is locked in a fixed position, identical to a camera without any stabilization.

- When to use IS Off: whenever the camera is on a tripod, a stable surface, or a motorized camera rig. Keeping IBIS on with a stationary camera can introduce subtle instability as the sensor gently drifts trying to detect and cancel vibrations.
- Also use IS Off when using a gimbal stabilizer: some gimbals work better without IBIS because they may conflict with each other. Check your gimbal's recommendations.
- IS Off for video on a tripod: for the cleanest, most stable video from a fixed position, always disable IS.

14.4 Sync IS with Compatible Lenses

Sync IS is an advanced stabilization mode that combines the OM-3's in-body IBIS with the optical image stabilization system (OIS) built into certain OM SYSTEM and older Olympus lenses. When both systems work together in coordination, the combined stabilization is more effective than either system alone — providing up to 6.5 stops of combined correction.

How Sync IS Works

Normally, when a lens with OIS is attached to a camera with IBIS, the two systems can sometimes work against each other or at best work in parallel without communication. OM SYSTEM's Sync IS solves this by having the camera and lens share gyroscope data and coordinate their movements. The lens OIS handles the corrections it is best at (typically pitch and yaw), while the camera's IBIS handles the corrections it is best at (shift, roll, and fine-tuning), and the two systems cooperate without duplication or conflict.

Which Lenses Support Sync IS

Sync IS works with OM SYSTEM and Olympus lenses that have the OIS (Optical Image Stabilization) designation — these are lenses with the IS symbol in their name. Notable compatible lenses include:

- M.Zuiko Digital ED 100-400mm f/5.0-6.3 IS — long telephoto zoom, particularly benefits from combined stabilization
- M.Zuiko Digital ED 300mm f/4.0 IS PRO — super-telephoto prime
- M.Zuiko Digital ED 75-300mm f/4.8-6.7 II — budget telephoto zoom with IS
- Various other OM SYSTEM and Olympus zoom lenses marked with IS

How to Enable Sync IS

Sync IS is automatic — you do not need to select it. When a compatible lens is attached, the camera detects the lens's OIS capability and automatically enables Sync IS whenever the camera's IBIS is set to IS1. The camera communicates with the lens and coordinates the stabilization. A small indicator may appear in the live view or shooting info confirming that Sync IS is active.

TIP: Sync IS for telephoto handheld photography

Long telephoto lenses amplify camera shake dramatically. At 400mm, even tiny vibrations produce significant blur. With Sync IS providing up to 6.5 stops of combined correction, the OM-3 with a compatible IS telephoto lens can produce sharp handheld photos at surprisingly slow shutter speeds — enabling wildlife photography in difficult lighting conditions that would otherwise require a tripod.

Part 15 — Picture Profiles and Color

The OM-3 applies a colour and tone processing profile to every JPEG image it produces. This profile — selected from a range of built-in options — determines how colours look, how much contrast and sharpness is applied, and whether the image is converted to black and white. There are two categories of colour control on the OM-3: Art Filters (dramatic, creative transformations) and Picture Modes (subtle, adjustable colour profiles for realistic results). Both apply only to JPEG files — RAW files store all colour data and are processed entirely by your editing software.

15.1 Art Filters — Every Filter Explained with Its Effect

Art Filters are creative image processing effects that dramatically transform the look of a photo — converting it to a stylised artistic rendering. They go far beyond simple colour adjustments, applying complex tone curves, grain, distortions, colour remapping, and other effects that change the character of the image entirely. Art Filters apply only to JPEG files. When shooting RAW, the Art Filter preview is shown on screen but only the standard RAW data is saved.

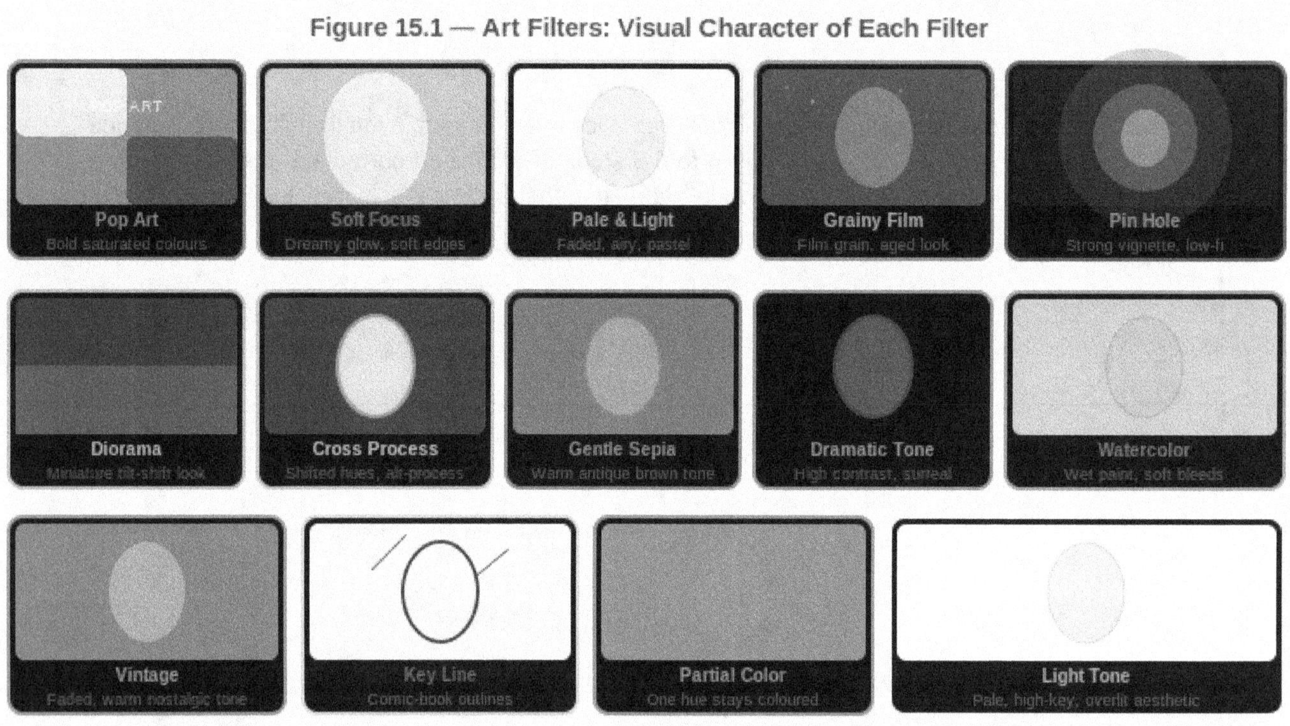

Figure 15.1 — Visual character of each Art Filter: from bold Pop Art to subtle Vintage and delicate Watercolor

How to Access and Apply Art Filters

Step 1: Press MENU → Shooting Menu → Page 3 → find Picture Mode.

Step 2: Press OK to open the Picture Mode selection screen.

Step 3: Scroll DOWN through the list past the standard picture modes (Natural, Vivid, Muted, etc.) until you reach the Art Filter section. The first Art Filter option is usually labeled Art Filter or shows the filter name.

Step 4: Alternatively, use the SCP: press OK → navigate to the Picture Mode tile → press OK → scroll to the Art Filter section.

Step 5: Highlight the Art Filter you want and press OK (or RIGHT arrow) to select it.

Step 6: Some Art Filters offer intensity settings or effect variations — if a small arrow or indicator appears, press RIGHT to access these sub-options.

Step 7: Press OK to confirm. The live view immediately shows a preview of the filter effect.

Step 8: Shoot. Art Filter JPEGs are saved alongside the normal RAW file (if shooting RAW+JPEG). The RAW file is always unaffected.

Every Art Filter Explained

Art Filter	Visual Effect	Technical Description	Best Subjects
Pop Art	Bold, saturated, almost neon colours. High contrast between colour zones.	Dramatically increases saturation to near-maximum. Applies strong colour isolation and contrast. Inspired by Andy Warhol and Roy Lichtenstein's pop art style.	Colourful street scenes, flowers, bold architecture, graphic subjects with strong primary colours
Soft Focus	Dreamy, glowing highlights and soft edges. Gentle overall blur.	Applies a diffusion glow by blending a softened version of the image with the original. Brightens highlights and softens contrast. The effect is strongest in bright areas.	Portraits, flowers, romantic scenes, anything where a soft-edged, ethereal quality is desired
Pale & Light Color	Washed out, pastel, faded appearance. Very light tones throughout.	Reduces saturation significantly and raises the overall exposure point, compressing shadow tones toward a pale grey. The result looks like an old, sun-bleached photograph.	Fashion, portraits with a light airy aesthetic, spring flowers, minimalist architectural subjects
Light Tone	Very high-key, pale, overexposed feel. Bright and delicate.	Similar to Pale & Light but pushes even further toward white. Shadows become pale grey. Highlights approach pure white. Creates an extremely light, almost overexposed look intentionally.	High-key portraits, wedding photography with a dreamy white aesthetic, still life with light subjects
Grainy Film	Black and white or muted tones with visible grain	Converts to desaturated or low-saturation tones and adds a realistic film grain texture. The grain size and	Documentary-style photography, street photography, portraits with a journalistic feel, any subject

	and texture. Aged look.	character change based on the sub-effect setting. Can simulate different film stocks.	that benefits from a timeless, nostalgic quality
Pin Hole	Strong dark vignette around the edges, faded tones, very low-fi look.	Creates a heavy circular vignette (darkening of corners and edges) simulating a pinhole camera's limited lens design. Also reduces saturation and applies a slight colour shift.	Urban scenes, portraits with an artistic edge, anything where you want the sense of looking through a tiny aperture
Diorama	Tilt-shift miniature effect. The center strip appears sharp; top and bottom are blurred.	Applies a vertical blur gradient that imitates the shallow depth of field produced by a tilt-shift lens. Makes scenes look like miniature scale models when photographed from above.	Overhead shots of streets, cities, vehicles, and landscapes. Particularly striking from elevated positions such as bridges, buildings, or hills.
Cross Process	Unusual, shifted colour hues. Greens become more yellow or cyan; skin tones go orange or yellow.	Simulates the look of E-6 slide film developed in C-41 chemistry (or vice versa) — a darkroom technique that dramatically shifts all colour channels. The specific shift depends on the sub-effect variant.	Fashion, music, creative portraits, urban photography. The unusual colour palette creates immediately distinctive images.
Gentle Sepia	Warm brown tones throughout. Classic antique photograph appearance.	Converts to black and white and then tints the entire image with a warm amber-brown hue. A subtle, elegant effect compared to a pure B&W or strong colour effect.	Portraits, historical architecture, vintage-inspired still life, any scene that evokes nostalgia or history
Dramatic Tone	High contrast, dark shadows, surreal tonal rendering. Blue-tinged highlights.	Applies an extreme S-curve tone mapping with very compressed highlights and deeply darkened shadows. Also shifts the colour palette toward blue and cyan, especially in mid-tones. The effect is dramatic and slightly otherworldly.	Landscapes with interesting skies, atmospheric scenes with fog or rain, urban environments, any subject where dramatic mood is desired
Key Line	White or colour background with black outlines emphasising edges — comic book or graphic novel look.	Detects edges in the image and renders them as dark lines over a simplified background. Creates an effect similar to hand-drawn illustration or graphic novel panels.	Architecture, vehicles, portraits, any subject with clear edges and distinct shapes. Works best with subjects that have strong geometric forms.

Watercolor	Soft, painterly washes of colour. Colours bleed into each other. Paper-like texture.	Simulates the look of watercolour paint by desaturating edges, softening transitions between colours, and adding a slight texture. Colour areas are isolated and appear as washes.	Flowers, natural subjects, cityscapes from a distance, portraits. Particularly beautiful with subjects that have soft shapes and pastel-friendly colour palettes.
Vintage	Warm, amber-tinged tones with slight desaturation and vignetting. Nostalgic feel.	Adds a warm tint, reduces saturation slightly, applies a gentle vignette, and may add subtle texture. Simulates the look of photographs from earlier decades.	Travel photography, everyday life scenes, portraits where a timeless warm quality is wanted, social media content with a lifestyle aesthetic
Partial Color	Most of the image is desaturated (black and white) but one specific colour remains fully saturated.	Converts most of the image to black and white, then selectively restores the saturation of one chosen hue. For example: a red rose against a greyscale background, or a blue sky above a monochrome cityscape. You choose which colour to isolate.	Any subject with one dominant colour you want to emphasise. Red subjects (flowers, vehicles, clothing) are the most popular choice. Also effective with yellow, orange, or blue.
Custom (Art Filter variants)	Any of the above, with additional intensity and effect variations	Each Art Filter has up to 4 sub-effect variants accessible by pressing RIGHT when the filter is highlighted. These variations adjust the intensity of the effect, add grain, change the colour tint, or apply additional effects on top of the base filter.	Experiment with variants to find the strength of effect that suits your subject

TIP: RAW protects you from Art Filter experiments

If you shoot RAW+JPEG, you can freely experiment with Art Filters — the JPEG gets the artistic treatment while the RAW file preserves the unprocessed sensor data. If you later decide you prefer a different Art Filter, a standard processing, or no effect at all, you can re-develop the RAW file in software. Shooting RAW+JPEG lets you take creative risks with Art Filters with no downside.

NOTE: Art Filters and video

Art Filters can also be applied to video recording. When an Art Filter is selected as the Picture Mode and you press the Movie Record Button, the video footage is recorded with the filter applied. This is a non-reversible in-camera application — the footage is recorded with the effect baked in.

> If you plan to colour grade the video in post-production, use a standard picture profile (Natural or Muted) or OM-Log instead, and apply creative looks in your editing software where you have full control.

15.2 Picture Mode / Profile Settings

Picture Modes are the standard colour and tone processing profiles applied to JPEG images. Unlike Art Filters which dramatically transform the image, Picture Modes aim to enhance or modify the realistic look of the photo in ways that are useful for photography rather than artistic. Each mode adjusts the combination of contrast, saturation, sharpness, and tonal curve to serve a different photographic purpose.

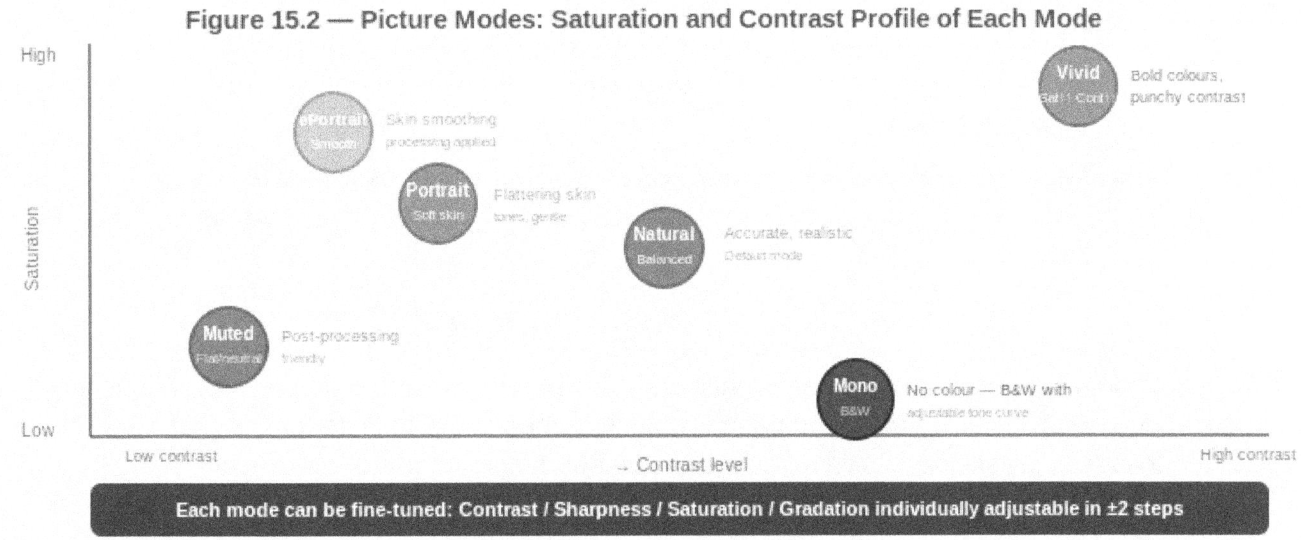

Figure 15.2 — Picture modes plotted by saturation and contrast level. Each can be further fine-tuned individually.

How to Select a Picture Mode

Step 1: Press OK to open the Super Control Panel → navigate to the Picture Mode tile → press OK to enter mode selection.

Step 2: Or: press MENU → Shooting Menu → Page 3 → Picture Mode → OK.

Step 3: The list shows all available picture modes. Use UP/DOWN to scroll. The standard modes are listed before the Art Filters.

Step 4: Highlight your preferred mode and press OK to confirm.

Step 5: The live view immediately updates to show a preview of the mode's effect.

Natural — Accurate, Realistic Colour

Natural is the default picture mode on the OM-3. It applies moderate contrast, moderate saturation, and balanced sharpening — producing colours that look realistic and close to what the scene actually looked like. Nothing is dramatically boosted or suppressed.

Aspect	Natural Mode Detail
Contrast	Normal — balanced between highlights and shadows without crushing either
Saturation	Normal — colours are accurate and lifelike without being enhanced
Sharpening	Standard — crisp enough for most subjects without over-processing texture
Gradation	Normal — standard tone curve
Best for	Everyday photography where you want accurate results. Documentary, travel, landscapes, architecture, product photography. Any situation where faithfulness to the actual colours is more important than visual impact.
When NOT to use	Situations where you want deliberately vivid, muted, or stylised results

Vivid — Enhanced, Punchy Colour

Vivid boosts both saturation and contrast significantly above Natural, producing images with richer colours and more pronounced tonal separation. Colours appear more intense than in real life — skies are bluer, foliage is greener, and skin tones are warmer and more saturated.

- Best for: travel photography where you want impactful, eye-catching results, landscape photography with vibrant colours (autumn foliage, tropical destinations), social media content where images need to stand out on a busy feed.
- Not ideal for: portraits where over-saturated skin tones can look unnatural, or for images intended for post-processing where boosted saturation limits editing flexibility.
- Vivid JPEG output: requires no further enhancement — colours are already at their most vibrant straight from the camera.

Muted — Low Contrast, Desaturated

Muted reduces both saturation and contrast below Natural, producing a flatter, more neutral-looking image that may appear underwhelming on screen but is excellent for photographs that will be edited in post-processing. The reduced saturation and contrast preserve more tonal information in both highlights and shadows, giving the editing software more room to work with.

- Best for: photographers who process their JPEGs in editing software (Lightroom, Photoshop) and want maximum editing latitude. Wedding photographers who need clean skin tones that can be colour graded. Video shooters who want a flat JPEG companion to their RAW file.
- Not ideal for: direct sharing without editing, situations where the image needs to look good straight from the camera.
- Think of Muted as: a LOG profile for JPEG — not beautiful out of camera, but excellent raw material for post-processing.

Portrait — Optimised for Skin Tones

Portrait mode is tuned specifically for photographing people. It applies subtle enhancements that make skin tones look healthy, even, and flattering — typically slightly reducing red-orange saturation to prevent skin from looking ruddy, gently softening contrast to reduce the appearance of skin texture and imperfections, and preserving the overall warmth of skin tones.

- Best for: portrait photography of individuals and groups, candid people photography, event photography where flattering natural-looking skin tones are important.
- Contrast: slightly lower than Natural — softer, less dramatic tonal separation
- Saturation: slightly warm-shifted to complement skin tones
- Sharpening: reduced compared to Natural — prevents excessive texture rendering on skin

Monotone — Black and White

Monotone mode converts the image to black and white (greyscale) in-camera, applying the conversion at the time of capture rather than in post-processing. The RAW file (if saved) retains full colour data — only the JPEG is black and white.

Within Monotone mode, you can apply a simulated colour filter effect that changes how different colours in the original scene translate to grey tones:

Filter (within Monotone)	Effect on Tones
None (no filter)	Standard linear conversion — colours translate to grey according to their brightness. The most neutral conversion.
Yellow filter	Slightly darkens blue skies while brightening yellow subjects. A gentle, natural-looking effect.
Orange filter	More pronounced sky darkening, lighter skin tones. A classic portrait filter effect — dramatic sky with smooth skin.
Red filter	Strongly darkens blue skies to near-black. Dramatically brightens red subjects. The most dramatic filter — landscapes with sky look intense and graphic.
Green filter	Brightens foliage and some skin tones. Good for portraits with green backgrounds or outdoor landscape work. Gives a film-like tone to outdoor subjects.

TIP: Monotone with a red filter for landscape drama

Setting Monotone + Red Filter in bright outdoor conditions produces breathtaking black and white images — clouds appear white against an almost-black sky, creating dramatic tonal contrast that is very difficult to achieve in post-processing without heavy localized adjustments. Excellent for architectural photography and dramatic outdoor scenes.

ePortrait — Portrait with Skin Smoothing

ePortrait applies Portrait mode settings plus an additional in-camera processing step that smooths and evens skin texture. This reduces the visibility of pores, fine lines, and blemishes in the JPEG output without requiring retouching in editing software.

- Best for: casual portrait photography where you want naturally flattering skin without additional editing, wedding and event photography for JPEG-only delivery.
- Limitation: the skin smoothing can look artificial if overdone — it may create a slightly plastic or airbrushed quality in close-up portraits. Use selectively.
- Not for: documentary or journalistic photography where authentic texture is required, or commercial beauty photography where professional retouching is expected.

Custom Picture Modes (Custom 1–4)

The OM-3 allows you to create up to four fully customised picture modes (Custom 1 through Custom 4). Each custom mode starts as a copy of an existing mode and can then be modified with any combination of fine-tuning values. Once saved, your custom modes appear in the Picture Mode list alongside the built-in options.

Step 1: Go to MENU → Custom Menu G → Picture Mode Settings (or directly in the Shooting Menu → Picture Mode).

Step 2: Select one of the Custom 1–4 slots.

Step 3: Choose a starting base mode (Natural, Portrait, Vivid, etc.).

Step 4: Apply your desired fine-tuning (see below).

Step 5: The custom mode is saved and available for selection at any time.

Fine-Tuning Picture Modes — Contrast, Sharpness, Saturation, Gradation

Every picture mode (built-in or custom) can be individually fine-tuned along four parameters. These adjustments stack on top of the mode's base settings, allowing you to perfectly dial in your preferred rendering.

How to Access Fine-Tuning

Step 1: In the Picture Mode selection screen (SCP or Shooting Menu), highlight the mode you want to fine-tune.

Step 2: Press the RIGHT arrow or INFO button — a fine-tuning panel slides in showing the four adjustable parameters.

Step 3: Use UP/DOWN to select a parameter and LEFT/RIGHT to adjust its value.
Step 4: Changes are shown in real time in the live view preview.
Step 5: Press OK to confirm all fine-tuning changes.

Parameter	Range	What It Does	Practical Effect
Contrast	-2 to +2	Adjusts the separation between highlights and shadows — the steepness of the tone curve	-2: very flat, low contrast, pastel shadows. +2: very punchy, bold separation between tones. 0 is the mode's default.
Sharpness	-2 to +2	Adjusts the amount of edge enhancement (sharpening) applied to fine detail	-2: very soft, gentle edges — good for portraits where skin texture softness is desired. +2: crisp, highly defined edges — good for landscapes, architecture, product photography.
Saturation	-2 to +2	Adjusts the intensity and richness of all colours	-2: nearly monochrome appearance, very muted colours. +2: very saturated, almost Art Filter level of colour intensity. For portraits, -1 often produces the most natural skin tones.
Gradation (Tone Curve)	Normal / Low Key / High Key / Auto	Changes the overall tone mapping — how shadows, mid-tones, and highlights are distributed	Normal: standard balanced curve. Low Key: darkens mid-tones and shadows — creates moody, dramatic images. High Key: brightens mid-tones and highlights — creates light, airy images. Auto: adapts dynamically to the scene.

Additional Fine-Tuning for Monotone Mode

In Monotone mode only, there are two additional parameters beyond the standard four:

Parameter (Monotone only)	Options	Effect
Color Filter	None / Yellow / Orange / Red / Green	Simulates a coloured filter placed in front of the lens during film photography. Changes how different colours translate to grey tones. See the Monotone section above for details on each filter.
Toning	None / Sepia / Blue / Purple / Green	Applies a single-colour tint to the greyscale image. None produces pure black and white. Sepia produces the warm antique brown tone. Blue produces a cool, clinical cyanotype look. Other options provide various stylised tints.

TIP: Build a personal custom mode

Spend a session testing each picture mode and fine-tuning adjustment on your typical subjects — your portraits, landscapes, or street photography. When you find a combination that perfectly suits your aesthetic (for example, Natural with Contrast -1, Sharpness +1, Saturation -1 for a slightly muted but crisp portrait look), save it to Custom 1. Then you always have your personal optimal profile one press away.

Part 16 — Playback

Playback is not just about looking at photos you have taken — it is a powerful tool for reviewing your work in the field, catching technical problems early, managing files, and even developing RAW images into finished JPEGs without a computer. The OM-3's playback system offers detailed image analysis, zoom inspection, histogram review, in-camera RAW development, and flexible file management.

Mastering playback lets you be more efficient on a shoot and catch problems while you still have time to re-shoot.

16.1 How to Enter Playback Mode

The OM-3 has a dedicated Playback button — a small button with a triangular play symbol (▶) located on the back of the camera, to the left of the EVF or near the top of the button cluster on the right of the LCD.

Entering Playback from Live View

Step 1: Make sure the camera is powered on and in live view (shooting mode).

Step 2: Press the Playback button (▶) once.

Step 3: The camera instantly switches from the live view to playback mode. The last photo you took appears on the LCD (or EVF if you are looking through it).

Step 4: Navigate through your photos using the methods described in Section 16.2.

Exiting Playback

There are two ways to exit playback mode and return to shooting:

- Press the Playback button again — the camera returns to live view.
- Half-press the shutter button — the camera instantly returns to live view, ready to shoot. This is the fastest way to exit and is useful when a moment appears while you are reviewing photos.

Quick Review After Each Shot

A related feature is automatic quick review. If enabled in Custom Menu D, the camera briefly displays the photo you just took for 1–5 seconds on the LCD before returning to live view. This is different from playback mode — it is a momentary display. You can enable it or disable it in Custom Menu D → Review Time.

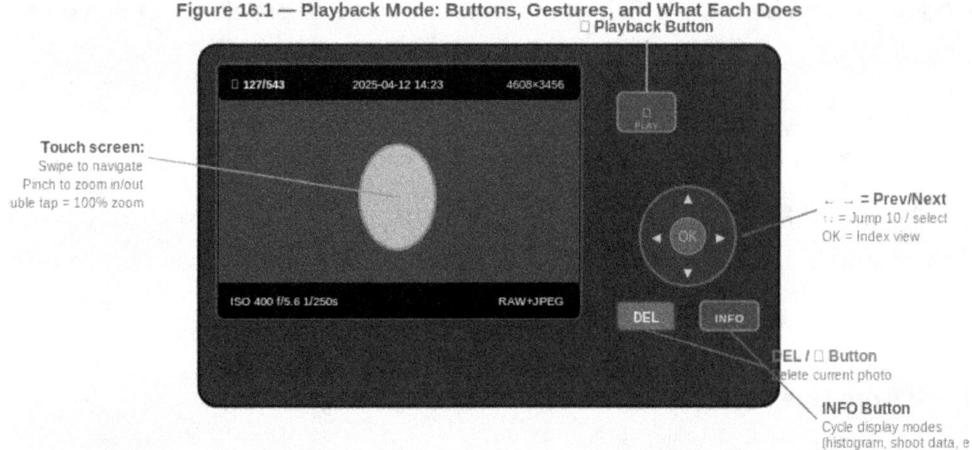

Figure 16.1 — Playback mode: image display, info overlays, arrow pad navigation, delete and INFO buttons, and touchscreen gestures

16.2 Scrolling Through Images

Single-Image View — Arrow Keys

When a single photo is displayed, use the arrow pad to navigate:

Button / Gesture	Action
LEFT arrow (◀)	Previous photo — moves to the photo before the current one
RIGHT arrow (▶)	Next photo — moves to the photo after the current one
UP arrow (▲)	Jump backward 10 photos at a time — useful for moving quickly through a long burst sequence
DOWN arrow (▼)	Jump forward 10 photos at a time — fast navigation
Hold LEFT or RIGHT	Fast scroll — the camera skips through images rapidly
Swipe left on touchscreen	Same as LEFT arrow — previous photo
Swipe right on touchscreen	Same as RIGHT arrow — next photo

Index / Thumbnail View

To see multiple photos at once as thumbnails, which is useful when reviewing a large number of shots to find a specific one:

Step 1: In single-image playback view, rotate the rear dial LEFT (counter-clockwise as viewed from above).

Step 2: The view zooms out, showing 4 thumbnails on screen at once.

Step 3: Rotate the rear dial further left to see 9, 25, or 100 thumbnails per screen.

Step 4: Navigate the thumbnail grid with the arrow pad — highlighting the thumbnail you want.

Step 5: Rotate the rear dial RIGHT (clockwise) or press OK to zoom back into single-image view on the selected photo.

Calendar View

For organizing photos by date, the calendar view shows a monthly calendar with a tiny thumbnail on each date that contains photos:

Step 1: From single-image view, rotate the rear dial LEFT repeatedly past the largest thumbnail index view.

Step 2: Eventually a calendar view appears, showing the current month with small thumbnails on each date that has photos.

Step 3: Use arrow keys to move between dates.

Step 4: Press OK on a date to see all photos from that day.

Step 5: Exit by rotating the rear dial RIGHT to return to thumbnail view, then single-image view.

TIP: Calendar view for travel photography

When you are travelling and have photos from many days on one SD card, calendar view is the fastest way to jump to photos from a specific day. Much faster than scrolling through hundreds of images chronologically.

16.3 Zooming In on a Photo During Playback

Zooming into a photo during playback is essential for checking critical focus, verifying fine detail, and confirming that your photo is truly sharp at the pixel level. The OM-3 supports up to 14× magnification during playback review.

How to Zoom In

Step 1: Display the photo you want to inspect in single-image view.

Step 2: Rotate the rear dial RIGHT (clockwise) to zoom in. Each click increases the zoom level: 2× → 4× → 7× → 10× → 14×.

Step 3: Once zoomed in, use the arrow pad to pan around the image — LEFT/RIGHT/UP/DOWN move the view within the photo.

Step 4: A small navigation map may appear in a corner of the screen showing which part of the full image you are currently viewing.

Step 5: Rotate the rear dial LEFT to zoom back out, one level at a time.

Step 6: To return to single-image view from any zoom level, press OK or half-press the shutter.

Alternative: Touch Gestures

Touch Gesture	Action
Double tap on the LCD	Instantly zooms to approximately 100% view at the tapped location — quick focus check
Pinch out (spread two fingers)	Zoom in — smooth continuous zoom control, as on a smartphone
Pinch in (pinch two fingers together)	Zoom out
Drag with one finger when zoomed in	Pan around the zoomed image
Double tap again when zoomed in	Returns to full-image view

TIP: Use 7× or 10× for focus check

7× or 10× zoom is the practical level for checking focus accuracy. At these zoom levels, you can see whether the eye of a portrait subject is truly sharp, or whether the focus landed on the eyebrow or eyelash instead. Zooming to 14× shows individual pixels — useful for extreme detail check but less useful for general focus verification.

16.4 Viewing Image Info, Histogram, and Highlight Warning

The INFO button during playback cycles through different overlay display modes, each showing different information about the current photo. Pressing INFO repeatedly cycles through these modes.

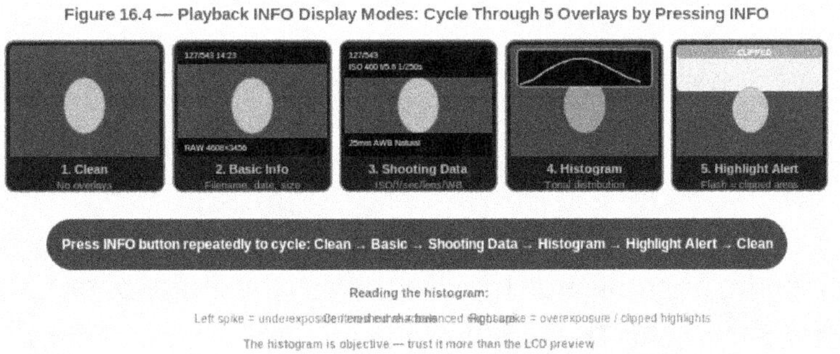

Figure 16.4 — The five INFO display modes in playback: Clean, Basic Info, Shooting Data, Histogram, and Highlight Alert

The Five Playback INFO Modes

Mode	What It Shows	When to Use
1. Clean (No Info)	The photo with no overlay. Fills the whole screen.	Pure review — judging composition, colour, and impact without distraction. Ideal for reviewing images with a friend or client.
2. Basic Info	Top bar: filename, index (e.g. 127/543), date/time. Bottom bar: image size, RAW/JPEG indicator.	Quickly finding a specific photo, tracking which card slot or folder a photo is in.
3. Shooting Data	Detailed EXIF overlay: ISO, aperture, shutter speed, focal length, metering mode, white balance, exposure compensation, picture mode, flash status.	Learning from your photos — understanding which settings worked and which did not. Essential for photographers trying to improve.
4. Histogram	Full RGB histogram overlaid on the photo showing tonal distribution. Shows separate red, green, blue channels plus overall luminance.	Objective exposure analysis — seeing whether a photo's brightness is balanced, underexposed, or overexposed.

		More reliable than judging the LCD preview by eye.
5. Highlight & Shadow Alert	Any area that is clipped to pure white (overexposed) blinks or flashes. Some firmware also shows clipped shadows in blue.	Quality control — immediately spotting parts of the photo where you have lost detail. If important areas are flashing, consider reshooting at a darker exposure.

Reading the Histogram

The histogram is a graph of the brightness distribution across the entire photo, with the darkest tones on the left and the brightest on the right. The height of the graph at any point shows how many pixels in the image are at that specific brightness level.

- A histogram spike pressed against the LEFT edge indicates underexposure — large areas of the photo are at pure black with no detail.
- A histogram spike pressed against the RIGHT edge indicates overexposure — large areas are at pure white with no detail (clipped highlights). This is generally worse than left-edge clipping because clipped highlights are very difficult to recover even in RAW.
- A histogram that spreads smoothly across the middle without touching either edge indicates good exposure with detail preserved in both highlights and shadows.
- Remember: the ideal shape depends on the scene. A photograph of a dark night sky should have most of its histogram on the left — that is correct. A photograph of a bright snow scene should have most on the right. The histogram tells you the distribution; you judge whether that distribution is correct for your intended image.

WARNING: Clipped highlights usually cannot be recovered

When the histogram shows a spike at the right edge and the Highlight Alert display shows large flashing areas, the brightest parts of your image have been recorded as pure white with no recoverable detail. This is often impossible to fix in post-processing, even in RAW. If you see significant highlight clipping during playback review, consider reshooting with -0.7 to -1.0 EV exposure compensation to protect the highlights.

16.5 Deleting Images — Single and Multiple

Deleting a Single Image

Step 1: In playback mode, display the photo you want to delete.

Step 2: Press the Delete button (the button with a trash can or ⌫ symbol, located near the arrow pad).

Step 3: A confirmation dialog appears: "Erase this image?" with Yes/No options.

Step 4: Use the UP arrow to highlight Yes (the default is usually No for safety).

Step 5: Press OK to confirm. The image is permanently erased from the SD card.

Step 6: The camera automatically advances to the next (or previous) photo.

WARNING: Deleted photos are NOT recoverable on the SD card

Once a photo is deleted on the OM-3 and the card is used again, the file is permanently lost. The camera does not have a trash or recycle bin. Unlike a computer, there is no way to restore deleted photos directly on the camera. Specialist data recovery software can sometimes recover recently deleted files from an SD card if nothing has been written over them — but success is not guaranteed. Always use Delete carefully.

Deleting Multiple Images (Batch Delete)

To delete several photos at once without having to navigate to each one and press Delete individually:

Step 1: Enter playback mode.

Step 2: Press MENU → Playback Menu → Erase.

Step 3: Options appear: Selected Images / All Images / Date Range (varies by firmware).

Step 4: Select Selected Images to choose specific photos to delete.

Step 5: A thumbnail grid appears. Use the arrow pad to navigate between photos.

Step 6: Press OK to tick each photo you want to delete. A checkmark or delete icon appears on ticked photos.

Step 7: When you have selected all photos to delete, press MENU or a dedicated Delete button to confirm.

Step 8: Confirm the deletion of all selected photos. The camera deletes them in sequence.

Deleting All Photos

To delete all photos on the card without re-formatting it:

Step 1: Press MENU → Playback Menu → Erase → All Images.

Step 2: A strong warning appears asking you to confirm.

Step 3: Select Yes to delete every non-protected photo on the card.

Step 4: Alternatively, for a faster and more thorough erase that also resets the card's filesystem, use Card Format in the Setup Menu (see Part 2.3). Format erases everything on the card and prepares it fresh.

16.6 Protecting Images from Deletion

Protection is a small flag applied to a photo that prevents it from being accidentally deleted with the Delete button. A protected photo shows a lock icon in playback and refuses deletion attempts. However, protection does NOT prevent a card format from erasing the photo — formatting erases everything on the card regardless of protection status.

How to Protect an Image

Step 1: Display the photo you want to protect in single-image playback view.

Step 2: Press MENU → Playback Menu → Protect.

Step 3: Alternatively, if the camera has a dedicated protection shortcut or OK → Protect option, use that.

Step 4: The photo is marked as protected. A small lock or key icon appears in the playback display.

To remove protection: repeat the same procedure on the protected photo. Protection is a toggle — applying it to an already-protected photo removes the protection.

When to Use Protection

- Your best shots from a shoot — protect them immediately after taking them so you do not accidentally delete them during culling.
- Photos you have carefully retouched in-camera using RAW Development (Section 16.9) — protect them to preserve your work.
- Client-facing or time-sensitive photos that must survive until you can transfer them to a computer.
- Before passing the camera to someone else to review (e.g. a client at a shoot) — protect the important shots so they cannot be accidentally deleted.

NOTE: Protection does NOT survive a card format

Card Format (in the Setup Menu) erases everything on the card regardless of whether photos are protected or not. Protection only prevents deletion via the Delete button. If you need to permanently preserve important photos, transfer them to a computer or cloud storage — do not rely on in-camera protection.

16.7 Rotating Images

The OM-3 automatically detects the camera's orientation at the moment of capture and saves this information as metadata in the file. Most modern playback software (and the OM-3 itself) uses this metadata to automatically rotate photos shot in portrait orientation so they display correctly.

However, occasionally you may want to manually rotate a photo — for example, if you held the camera at an unusual angle and the auto-rotation is wrong, or if you want to change the displayed orientation for a specific creative reason.

How to Rotate an Image

Step 1: Display the photo you want to rotate in single-image playback view.

Step 2: Press MENU → Playback Menu → Rotate.

Step 3: Use the arrow pad to select the rotation direction: 90° clockwise, 90° counter-clockwise, or 180°.

Step 4: Press OK to apply the rotation. The photo now displays in the chosen orientation.

NOTE: Rotation is metadata only

When you rotate a photo in-camera, the pixel data is not actually rotated — only the orientation metadata is updated. Most modern software honours this metadata and displays the photo rotated correctly. Some older software may not read the metadata and show the photo in its original orientation. If this matters, export a rotated copy using editing software rather than relying on in-camera rotation.

16.8 Slideshow

The slideshow function plays through photos on the SD card automatically, displaying each one for a set interval. It is useful for showing your work to others without having to manually press the arrow keys, or for reviewing a shoot in a way that feels continuous and flowing.

How to Start a Slideshow

Step 1: Enter playback mode.

Step 2: Press MENU → Playback Menu → Slideshow.

Step 3: Configure the slideshow settings before starting:

Step 4: — Interval: choose 2 seconds, 3 seconds, 5 seconds, or 10 seconds per photo.

Step 5: — Background Music (BGM): select On or Off. Music files may be included with some firmware.

Step 6: — Repeat: choose whether the slideshow repeats when it reaches the last photo, or stops.

Step 7: — File Type: some firmware lets you choose Still Photos Only / Movies Only / Both.

Step 8: Select Start to begin the slideshow.

Controlling a Slideshow

Action	Effect
Press OK during slideshow	Pauses the slideshow on the current photo
Press OK again	Resumes the slideshow
Press LEFT/RIGHT	Manually skip to previous/next photo without pausing
Press UP/DOWN	Adjust the display interval on the fly
Press MENU or the Playback button	Stop the slideshow and return to manual playback

TIP: Slideshow on an HDMI-connected TV

If you connect the OM-3 to a television or monitor via HDMI, slideshow playback appears on the external screen. This is a great way to review a day's photos with a group, or to present your work at an event. Use a proper HDMI cable — the OM-3 has a Micro-HDMI port.

16.9 RAW Development In-Camera — Step by Step

RAW Development is a powerful feature that lets you develop a RAW file into a finished JPEG directly in the camera, with no computer required. You can adjust white balance, exposure, noise reduction, sharpness, picture mode, and other settings — then save the result as a new JPEG file while leaving the original RAW file unchanged. This is extraordinarily useful for photographers who want to share high-quality photos in the field, or who want to experiment with different edits before committing to a computer-based workflow.

What You Can Adjust in RAW Development

Setting	Range / Options	What It Does
Picture Mode	Natural / Vivid / Muted / Portrait / Monotone / Art Filters	Change the entire look of the image — apply a different colour profile or Art Filter than was originally set
Exposure Compensation	-5.0 to +5.0 EV	Brighten or darken the image in post — significant latitude because RAW data is still intact
White Balance	AWB / all presets / custom / K value	Change the white balance completely — as if you had shot with that WB setting originally
WB Compensation	2-axis fine-tune (A-B, G-M)	Fine-tune the colour temperature on both axes
Noise Reduction	Auto / Low / Standard / High / Off	Apply different noise reduction intensity
Contrast	-2 to +2	Adjust the tonal contrast
Sharpness	-2 to +2	Adjust edge definition
Saturation	-2 to +2	Adjust colour intensity
Gradation	Normal / Low Key / High Key / Auto	Adjust the overall tone curve shape
Aspect Ratio	4:3 / 3:2 / 16:9 / 1:1 / 3:4	Crop to a different aspect ratio

How to Develop a RAW File In-Camera — Step by Step

Step 1: Enter playback mode and navigate to the RAW file you want to develop. A RAW file shows a small RAW indicator in the corner of the display.

Step 2: Press MENU → Playback Menu → Edit (sometimes labeled RAW Data Edit or RAW Development).

Step 3: If you have multiple photos open, select the specific RAW file to develop.

Step 4: The RAW development screen appears, showing the image with a panel of adjustable parameters beside it.

Step 5: Navigate through the parameters using the arrow pad. Adjust each setting to taste — the preview updates in real time so you can see the effect of each change.

Step 6: Start with the most impactful adjustments: Exposure Compensation, then White Balance, then Picture Mode.

Step 7: Fine-tune with Contrast, Sharpness, Saturation, and Noise Reduction.

Step 8: When you are satisfied with the result, press OK (or the dedicated Save button — varies by firmware).

Step 9: The camera creates a new JPEG file on the SD card with your developed version. The original RAW file is unchanged.

Step 10: Review the new JPEG in playback to confirm.

TIP: Use RAW Development for quick client previews

At an event, you can develop a few key RAW photos right in the camera with optimised white balance and exposure, then share them immediately via the OM SYSTEM app (covered in Part 17) to social media or to your client — all while the event is still in progress. The original RAW files are preserved for your full post-production workflow later.

Batch RAW Development

Some firmware versions offer batch RAW development, where you can apply the same set of adjustments to multiple RAW files simultaneously. Look for Batch Edit or similar in the Playback Menu. This is powerful for applying the same colour grade or exposure fix to a series of similar shots.

Part 17 — Connectivity and Transferring Photos

Getting photos off the OM-3 and onto your phone, computer, or the internet is a fundamental part of photography workflow. The OM-3 offers multiple connection methods: Bluetooth and Wi-Fi to your smartphone, USB-C to a computer, and full tethered shooting for studio work. Each method has its strengths and appropriate uses.

Figure 17.1 — Connecting the OM-3 to Your Smartphone via the OM SYSTEM App

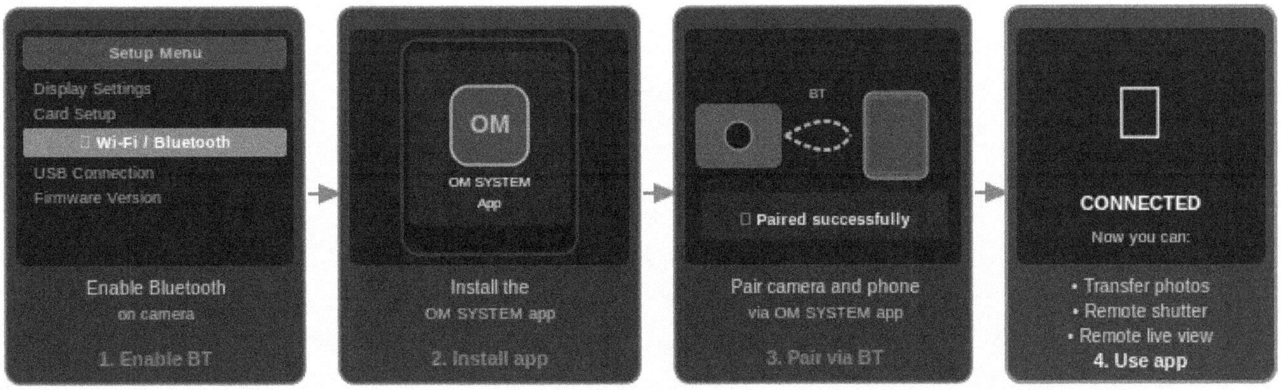

Figure 17.1 — Four-step smartphone app connection: enable Bluetooth → install app → pair devices → use app features

17.1 Connecting to the OM SYSTEM App — Step by Step

The OM SYSTEM App (formerly Olympus Image Share, or OI.Share) is the official smartphone application for remote control and photo transfer. It is available free for both iOS (iPhone and iPad) and Android phones and tablets. Once connected, the app gives you remote live view, shutter control, photo transfer, and camera setting adjustments.

Installing the OM SYSTEM App

Step 1: On your smartphone, open the app store: Apple App Store for iPhone/iPad, or Google Play Store for Android.

Step 2: Search for OM SYSTEM or OM Image Share.

Step 3: Install the official OM SYSTEM Corporation app — verify the publisher to avoid unofficial apps with similar names.

Step 4: Open the app after installation. Grant the app the permissions it requests (Bluetooth, Wi-Fi, camera, location, photos) — all are required for proper operation.

Enabling Bluetooth on the OM-3

Step 1: Press MENU on the camera → Setup Menu (wrench icon) → Wi-Fi / Bluetooth.

Step 2: Select Bluetooth On/Off and set it to On.

Step 3: A Bluetooth icon appears in the camera's live view display, indicating Bluetooth is active.

Step 4: Leave the camera powered on with Bluetooth active while you continue with the app.

Pairing the Camera with Your Phone

Step 1: Launch the OM SYSTEM app on your smartphone.

Step 2: Tap Add Camera or Pair New Camera — the exact label varies by app version.

Step 3: Select OM-3 (or Olympus/OM SYSTEM Camera) from the list of camera models.

Step 4: The app instructs you to put the camera into pairing mode. On the OM-3: MENU → Setup Menu → Wi-Fi / Bluetooth → Pair New Device.

Step 5: Confirm pairing on the camera when prompted — press OK to confirm.

Step 6: The phone and camera establish a Bluetooth connection. The app confirms pairing was successful.

Step 7: The phone is now paired. Future connections will be automatic — you do not need to pair again for subsequent sessions.

NOTE: Bluetooth is always on — Wi-Fi activates on demand

Bluetooth is a low-power always-on connection that lets the camera and app communicate for things like remote shutter and photo transfer triggering. When you actually transfer photo files (which are large), the app switches over to a Wi-Fi direct connection for speed — then switches back to Bluetooth when done. This is automatic; you do not need to manage it.

What the App Lets You Do

- Remote live view — see what the camera sees on your phone screen in real time
- Remote shutter control — fire the shutter from your phone at any distance within Bluetooth range (typically 10 metres)
- Photo transfer — select individual photos or groups and download them to your phone over Wi-Fi
- Adjust camera settings remotely — shutter speed, aperture, ISO, white balance, drive mode, and more
- Video recording — start and stop recording remotely
- Add location data to photos — the phone's GPS can be added to the EXIF data of photos taken on the camera.

17.2 Transferring Photos via Wi-Fi to Your Smartphone

Transferring photos from the OM-3 to your smartphone via Wi-Fi is the fastest way to share images online, preview them on a large phone screen, or back them up without a computer. Transfer speeds are typically 5–15 MB/second — fast enough to move several dozen JPEGs in a minute, or a handful of large RAW files.

How to Transfer Photos — From the App

Step 1: Ensure the camera is powered on and paired with your phone via the OM SYSTEM app (see Section 17.1).

Step 2: Open the OM SYSTEM app on your phone. The app should connect to the camera automatically — a connection indicator appears.

Step 3: Tap Import Photos (or Photo Browse / View Images — terminology varies).

Step 4: The app may briefly initiate a Wi-Fi connection with the camera. A progress indicator shows the connection forming.

Step 5: A thumbnail view of photos on the camera appears in the app.

Step 6: Tap each photo you want to transfer, or use Select All for the current folder.

Step 7: Tap Download (or Save / Import).

Step 8: The photos are transferred over the Wi-Fi connection. Transfer time depends on file size and count.

Step 9: When complete, the photos appear in your phone's normal photo library for sharing via any app.

How to Transfer Photos — From the Camera

You can also initiate transfer directly from the camera during playback:

Step 1: In camera playback, display the photo you want to transfer.

Step 2: Press MENU → Playback Menu → Send to Smartphone (or Share / Connect to Phone).

Step 3: Select which photos to send — current photo only, or select multiple.

Step 4: The camera connects to the app on your phone (which must be running in the background or foreground).

Step 5: The transfer begins. Progress is shown on both the camera and phone.

Transfer Quality Options

Transfer Size	Description	When to Use

Original size	Full resolution JPEG as saved on the card — full megapixel count	Archiving important photos, sharing to social media at maximum quality, printing
Resized (2MP)	Automatically resized to 2-megapixel (small) for faster transfer	Quick social media sharing, sending preview images to a client, when data speed is limited
Video transfer	Videos are typically transferred at original resolution	Sharing short video clips recorded on the OM-3

TIP: Transfer only JPEG, not RAW, for speed

RAW files on the OM-3 are 20-25 MB each — transferring 10 RAW files takes several minutes. JPEG Large Fine files are 5-8 MB and transfer 3-4× faster. For quick sharing or review, shoot RAW+JPEG and transfer only the JPEGs. Leave the RAW files on the card for later computer processing. This is the fastest workflow for travel and event photography.

17.3 Bluetooth Remote Shutter Control

Using the OM SYSTEM app as a remote shutter control is one of the most practically useful Bluetooth features. It lets you trigger the camera from your phone at a distance of up to approximately 10 metres, making it perfect for self-portraits, group photos (without running from behind the camera in a self-timer countdown), long exposure photography where even a light touch of the shutter button causes vibration, and unattended wildlife photography.

How to Use the Remote Shutter — Step by Step

Step 1: Mount the OM-3 on a tripod, stand, or stable surface. Frame your shot using the LCD or EVF.

Step 2: Ensure the camera is paired with your phone via the OM SYSTEM app.

Step 3: Open the OM SYSTEM app. The home screen should show connection status and main controls.

Step 4: Tap Remote Control (or Remote Shooting).

Step 5: A live view stream from the camera appears on your phone screen, with a shutter button icon below it.

Step 6: You can also adjust camera settings from the app: aperture, shutter speed, ISO, white balance, and drive mode.

Step 7: Tap the shutter button on your phone screen to fire the camera.

Step 8: The shutter fires on the camera, the photo is saved to the SD card, and a preview appears in the app.

Step 9: Continue shooting as needed. The connection remains active until you close the app or go out of Bluetooth range.

Remote Shutter Use Cases

Scenario	How Remote Shutter Helps
Self-portrait / selfie with proper camera	Frame yourself from outside the shot, trigger via phone — far better than self-timer with unlimited retakes
Group photo where you want to be in it	Press shutter from your phone instead of running from behind a camera. Everyone looks natural because there is no countdown anxiety.
Long exposure photography	Zero vibration — the shutter fires without any physical contact with the camera. Critical for exposures longer than 1 second.
Wildlife at a feeder or nest	Set up the camera near the subject area, step back several metres, trigger when the animal appears. The animal is not disturbed by your presence at the camera.
Astrophotography	Fire the shutter without accidentally bumping the tripod. Essential for multi-minute exposures where any vibration destroys the shot.
Macro photography of timid subjects	Approach the subject, step back to a normal distance, trigger remotely without the subject detecting you moving.

17.4 Connecting to a Computer via USB-C

The OM-3 has a USB-C port on the left side of the camera, behind the rubber door covering the connection ports. Connecting the camera to a computer via USB-C enables four different operating modes, selectable on the camera: Storage (simple file copying), MTP (media protocol for Windows), Tethered Shooting (remote camera control), and Charging (power only).

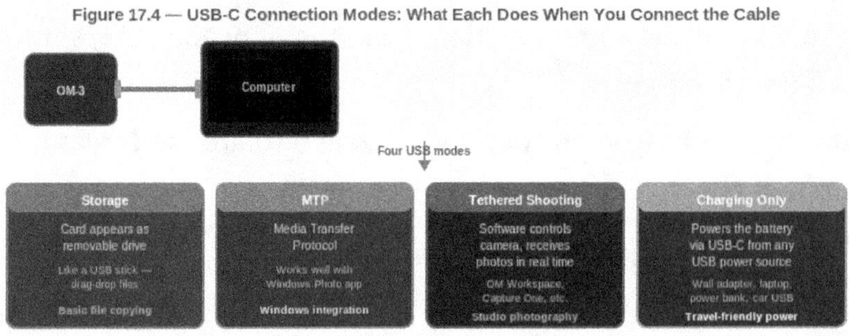

Figure 17.4 — Four USB-C connection modes: Storage, MTP, Tethering, and Charging — each with different functions

How to Connect USB-C

Step 1: Power the camera OFF before connecting — this protects the USB connection from any electrical spike.

Step 2: Locate the USB-C port on the left side of the OM-3, under the rubber connection port door.

Step 3: Open the rubber cover and plug in a USB-C cable. The other end goes to your computer's USB port (USB-C or USB-A with adapter cable).

Step 4: Power the camera ON.

Step 5: The camera displays the USB Connection Mode selection screen (if the USB mode is set to Auto — the default).

Step 6: Use the arrow keys to highlight your chosen mode: Storage / MTP / Tethered / Charging.

Step 7: Press OK to confirm.

The Four USB Connection Modes

Storage Mode

The camera's SD card appears on your computer as a removable drive — similar to plugging in a USB stick or external hard drive. You can drag and drop files between the card and your computer using any file browser. This is the simplest mode and works on Windows, macOS, and Linux without any additional software.

- Best for: basic file copying to a computer; users who just want to get photos off the card; one-time transfers or archive operations
- Limitation: does not use any specialized photo software — you manually navigate folders (DCIM/100OLYMP/) to find your photos

MTP Mode (Media Transfer Protocol)

MTP is a standardised media protocol used primarily on Windows. When the camera connects in MTP mode, Windows treats it as a Media Device (similar to a smartphone), allowing Windows Photos app and other media applications to see the camera and import photos with proper metadata preservation.

- Best for: Windows users who want seamless integration with Windows Photos app, Adobe Lightroom's Import from Camera feature, or similar photo management software
- Also works on macOS but less commonly used there (macOS treats both modes similarly)

Tethered Shooting Mode

In Tethered mode, the camera is controlled remotely by software running on the computer. The computer can change camera settings, trigger the shutter, and receive each photo as it is taken — displaying the photo on the computer screen within seconds of capture. See Section 17.5 for details.

Charging Only Mode

The USB-C connection powers the battery in the camera without triggering any data communication. This is useful when you simply want to charge the camera from a laptop, USB wall adapter, or USB power bank without the computer attempting to mount the card or detect the camera.

- Best for: charging while travelling; charging from any USB power source including laptops, power banks, car USB ports, and airline seat USB outlets
- A fully depleted OM-3 battery typically charges to 100% in approximately 4 hours via standard USB charging. A 45W+ USB-C PD (Power Delivery) charger can charge faster.

Setting the Default USB Mode

If you always want the camera to default to a specific USB mode without asking each time:

Step 1: MENU → Setup Menu → USB Connection Mode.

Step 2: Select: Auto (asks each time) / Storage / MTP / Tethered / Charging.

Step 3: The camera will now use this mode automatically whenever USB-C is connected.

17.5 Tethered Shooting

Tethered shooting is a professional workflow where the camera is connected to a computer by cable and controlled by software on the computer. As you take photos, each image is transferred to the computer within seconds and displayed on the large monitor for immediate review — enabling precise control over composition, focus, and lighting in studio or controlled settings.

Benefits of Tethered Shooting

- Instant large-screen review — every photo appears on your monitor within 2-3 seconds of capture. You can check focus, composition, and exposure at full size on a calibrated monitor far more accurately than on the camera LCD.
- Direct-to-computer file storage — photos save directly to a computer folder, bypassing the SD card entirely. This eliminates the risk of card failure mid-shoot and removes the step of later copying files from card to computer.
- Client collaboration — in a commercial portrait or product shoot, the client can watch photos appear on the monitor in real time, giving immediate feedback on what is and is not working.
- Live histogram and focus analysis — tethering software typically provides more detailed analysis tools than the camera itself, including full-resolution histogram inspection and precise focus point verification.
- Remote camera control — change settings, trigger the shutter, and focus from the computer without touching the camera. Useful for setups where the camera is in an awkward or dangerous position.

Software Options for Tethering

Software	Platform	Cost	Notes
OM Workspace	Windows, Mac	Free	OM SYSTEM's own tethering software. Full camera control, RAW processing, basic editing. Best starting point for OM-3 tethering.
Adobe Lightroom Classic	Windows, Mac	Subscription	Integrates tethering directly into your main editing workflow. Tethered shots appear in your Lightroom catalog immediately.
Capture One Pro	Windows, Mac	Subscription or one-time purchase	Professional tethering with fine control. Industry standard in commercial

			studios. Compatible with OM SYSTEM cameras.
Smart Shooter 5	Windows, Mac	One-time purchase	Dedicated tethering software with extensive automation features. Supports OM SYSTEM cameras.

How to Set Up Tethered Shooting with OM Workspace

Step 1: Download and install OM Workspace on your computer from omsystem.com (free).

Step 2: Connect the OM-3 to the computer via USB-C cable.

Step 3: Power on the camera. When the USB mode selection appears, choose Tethered.

Step 4: Open OM Workspace on the computer.

Step 5: In OM Workspace, go to the Camera Control or Tethered Shooting section.

Step 6: The software detects the connected camera. A camera view and control panel appears.

Step 7: Configure where tethered photos should be saved — a specific folder on your computer.

Step 8: Begin shooting. Each photo appears on your computer monitor within seconds of capture.

Step 9: Use the software to adjust camera settings as needed — the camera responds in real time.

Step 10: When finished, disconnect by first closing the software, then powering off the camera, then unplugging the cable (in that order to prevent any data corruption).

TIP: Keep an SD card in the camera during tethering

Even during tethered shooting, keep an SD card in the OM-3. Most tethering software allows you to save photos simultaneously to both the computer and the card — giving you a built-in backup in case the USB cable gets accidentally unplugged or the computer crashes mid-shoot. This redundancy has saved many commercial shoots from disaster.

NOTE: Wireless tethering alternative

For photographers who want tethering without cables, some software and OM SYSTEM firmware support wireless tethering over Wi-Fi. This is typically slower than USB-C tethered shooting but eliminates cable constraints. The setup procedure involves configuring the camera's built-in Wi-Fi as an access point and connecting the computer to it directly. Consult OM Workspace documentation or your chosen software's manual for specifics.

Part 18 — Customising the Camera

The OM-3 is designed to be configured to the way you personally like to shoot. Out of the box, the camera uses factory-default button assignments, control panel layouts, and menu structures that work well for most new users. But as you develop your own shooting style — your favourite settings, the controls you reach for most often — you can reconfigure the camera to match. A camera that fits your hand, your workflow, and your eye is one you will reach for more often and enjoy using more.

This part covers four levels of customisation: reassigning function buttons, rearranging the Super Control Panel, saving complete camera setups to custom positions on the mode dial, and creating your personal My Menu for one-press access to your most-used settings.

18.1 Assigning Functions to Fn Buttons — Step by Step

Function buttons (Fn buttons) are buttons on the camera body that can be assigned to any of 60+ camera functions. When you press an Fn button in live view, the assigned function is activated instantly — no menu navigation required. This is by far the fastest way to access settings you change frequently, and it transforms the camera from a general-purpose tool into one perfectly tuned to your workflow.

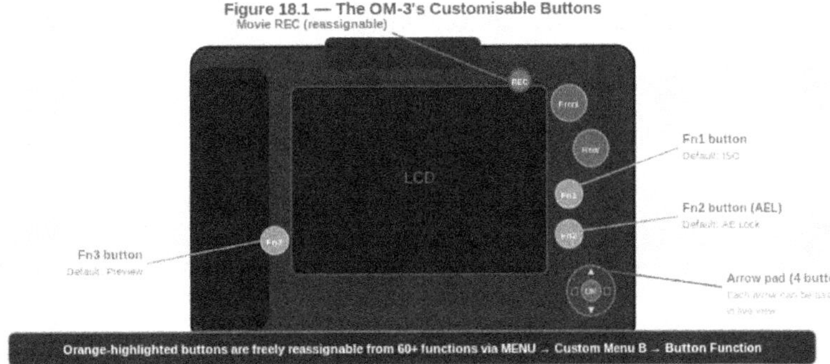

Figure 18.1 — The OM-3's reassignable buttons: Fn1, Fn2 (AEL), Fn3, plus the Movie Record button and arrow pad

Which Buttons Can Be Reassigned

The OM-3 offers a surprising number of buttons that accept custom function assignments:

- Fn1 — the primary function button, usually located on the top-right of the back of the camera
- Fn2 — the AEL button (default: AE Lock); can be fully reassigned
- Fn3 — the Preview button on the front of the camera (default: depth-of-field preview); can be fully reassigned
- Movie Record button — the red button on the top plate; can be reassigned when you don't use it for video

- Arrow pad buttons — UP, DOWN, LEFT, and RIGHT arrows can each be assigned to a function when pressed in live view

What You Can Assign

When you open the Button Function menu to reassign a button, you are presented with a long list of available functions. Some of the most useful include:

Category	Useful Functions
Exposure	ISO, Exposure Compensation, Flash Compensation, Metering Mode, AE Lock
Focus	AF Mode, AF Area Mode, AF-ON (back-button focus), Focus Peaking, Magnify, Face+Eye toggle
Image quality	Image Quality / RAW, Aspect Ratio, Picture Mode, White Balance, Gradation
Drive / burst	Drive Mode, Bracketing, Pro Capture, Anti-Shock, Live Composite, Live Bulb/Time
Stabilization / video	Image Stabilization mode, Movie IS, OM-Log toggle, Movie REC start/stop
Display / review	Peaking on/off, Histogram on/off, INFO cycle, Level gauge, Playback direct
My Menu	Open My Menu (bypasses the main menu system for instant access to your saved settings)

How to Reassign an Fn Button

Step 1: Press MENU → Custom Menu (gear icon, fourth tab) → section B (Button/Dial).

Step 2: Select Button Function and press OK. A screen appears showing all customisable buttons and their current assignments.

Step 3: Use the arrow pad to highlight the button you want to reassign. The current assignment is shown next to the button name.

Step 4: Press OK to enter the function selection list. A long list of assignable functions appears, organised by category.

Step 5: Scroll through the list (UP/DOWN arrows or rear dial) to find the function you want.

Step 6: Press OK to select the function. The button is now assigned.

> **Step 7:** Press MENU repeatedly to close. Test by pressing the reassigned button in live view.

Recommended Starter Fn Button Assignments

If you are unsure how to use the button customisation, here are practical starter assignments that work well for most photographers:

Button	Recommended Function	Why
Fn1	ISO	ISO is the setting most frequently changed as light varies. One-press access.
Fn2 (AEL)	AF-ON (back-button focus)	Separates focus from shutter. Professional workflow.
Fn3 (Preview)	Peaking on/off	Quick toggle when checking focus; off when not needed.
Arrow UP	Exposure Compensation	Quick EC access without reaching for the SCP.
Arrow LEFT	White Balance	Changing WB between scenes (outdoor/indoor) is common.
Movie button (if rarely used for video)	My Menu	Open your custom shortcut menu with one press.

> **TIP: Don't assign functions you already have dials for**
>
> The front and rear dials already give you immediate access to aperture, shutter speed, and ISO in your chosen shooting mode. Save your Fn buttons for things not already on a dial.

18.2 Customising the Super Control Panel

The Super Control Panel (SCP) — the grid of tiles that appears when you press OK from live view — is already a very efficient way to access many camera settings in one screen. But you can customise which tiles appear and in what order, tailoring the SCP to show only the settings you actually use.

What Can Be Customised

- Which functions appear as tiles on the SCP grid
- The position of each tile on the grid
- Whether certain tiles are hidden entirely (to simplify the display)
- The overall SCP style (compact vs expanded, tile appearance)

Enabling SCP Customisation

Step 1: Press MENU → Custom Menu (gear icon) → section D (Display/Sound).

Step 2: Find Live View Settings or SCP Settings (exact name may vary by firmware).

Step 3: Locate Super Control Panel customization or Info Settings.

Step 4: Inside, you will see a list of all functions that can appear on the SCP with checkboxes or toggles.

Step 5: Check the functions you want visible. Uncheck the ones you don't need.

Step 6: Use a reorder option if available to rearrange tile positions.

Step 7: Press OK or MENU to save. Return to live view, press OK to bring up the SCP, and verify your changes.

Recommended SCP Tile Priorities

Most important tiles to keep (settings you change often but are not on a dedicated button or dial):

- ISO, Exposure Compensation, Flash Compensation — core exposure
- Metering Mode, White Balance, Picture Mode — look and exposure calculation
- AF Mode, AF Area Mode — focus control
- Drive Mode, Image Quality, Aspect Ratio — shooting modes
- Image Stabilization mode — toggle IBIS on/off from live view

Less critical tiles you might hide to simplify:

- Flash Mode (if you rarely use flash)
- Color Space (set once, rarely changed)
- Noise Filter (set once based on preference)

18.3 Saving Settings to Custom Modes (C1, C2, C3)

The OM-3's Mode Dial has three Custom Mode positions labeled C1, C2, and C3. Each of these positions can store a complete camera configuration. By turning the Mode Dial to C1, C2, or C3, you instantly recall that complete configuration — the fastest way to switch between completely different shooting setups.

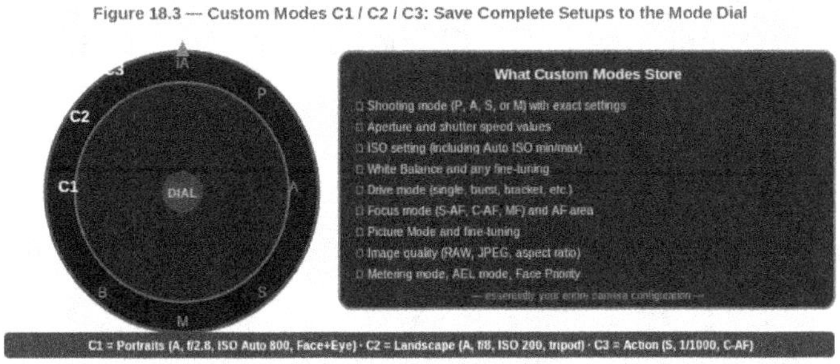

Figure 18.3 — The three Custom Mode positions on the Mode Dial can each store an entire camera setup

What Gets Saved in a Custom Mode

- Shooting mode (P, A, S, or M) and the specific aperture/shutter values
- ISO setting, including Auto ISO configuration
- White Balance selection and any fine-tuning values
- Drive mode — single, burst speeds, self-timer, HDR, bracketing, Pro Capture
- Focus mode (S-AF, C-AF, C-AF+TR, MF), AF area mode, Face/Eye priority
- Picture Mode and fine-tuning (Contrast, Saturation, Sharpness, Gradation)
- Image quality (RAW, JPEG size, compression), aspect ratio
- Metering mode, AEL behaviour, Flash Compensation, Exposure Compensation
- Image Stabilization setting (IS1/IS2/IS3/Off)

NOTE: What is NOT saved in Custom Modes

Custom Modes do not save the state of physical controls (lens aperture ring, flash head position). They also do NOT save your Fn button assignments or SCP layout — these are global settings that apply to all modes.

How to Save a Custom Mode

Step 1: Set up the camera exactly how you want it for a specific scenario: choose shooting mode, aperture, ISO, Auto ISO limits, WB, drive mode, focus mode, and any other settings appropriate.

Step 2: Take a test shot to verify the settings work as intended.

Step 3: Press MENU → Shooting Menu → look for Reset/Custom Mode (or Save to Custom Mode).

Step 4: Select Custom Mode Settings (or similar).

Step 5: Choose the slot you want to save to: C1, C2, or C3.

Step 6: Select Set (or Save / Assign / Register). Confirm. The configuration is stored in that slot.

Step 7: Test: turn the Mode Dial to C1, C2, or C3. The camera instantly reconfigures to match the saved settings.

Recommended Custom Mode Setups

Custom Mode	Portrait Photographer	Landscape Photographer	Wildlife Photographer
C1 (primary)	A mode, f/2.8, Auto ISO 200-1600, WB Auto, S-AF + Face/Eye, Single shot, Portrait picture mode	A mode, f/8, ISO 200, WB Daylight, S-AF, Single shot, Natural picture mode, 2-second timer	S mode, 1/1000, Auto ISO 400-6400, WB Auto, C-AF+TR, Sequential High, Natural
C2 (secondary)	A mode, f/4, Auto ISO 400-3200, WB Auto, S-AF + Face/Eye, ePortrait mode	A mode, f/11, ISO 200, WB Daylight, MF, Single shot + bracketing 3-frames 1EV	S mode, 1/2000, Auto ISO 800-12800, WB Auto, C-AF+TR, Pro Capture H
C3 (specialty)	M mode, 1/125 f/4 ISO 400, Flash Fill (indoor flash portraits)	M mode, 30s f/11 ISO 200, MF (astrophotography)	M mode, 1/4000 f/4 ISO 1600, S-AF, Silent electronic shutter

TIP: Custom modes save seconds, which saves shots

In the middle of a shoot, the difference between a good shot and a missed shot is often a few seconds. Turning a dial to C1 instantly reconfigures every setting, rather than manually changing each one separately.

18.4 My Menu — How to Create and Use a Personal Shortcut Menu

My Menu is a special user-configurable menu tab that holds only the settings you choose to put in it. Unlike the main menu system which contains hundreds of items, My Menu holds only your personal selection — perhaps 5 to 10 settings you use most often. When you need to change one of these, My Menu gives you direct access without navigating through the full menu tree.

The Power of My Menu + Fn Button

The real magic of My Menu comes from assigning it to an Fn button. Once you do this, pressing that Fn button opens My Menu directly — skipping every other menu tab entirely. Your most-used settings are now one button-press away.

How to Build Your My Menu

Step 1: Navigate through the main menu to any setting you want to add to My Menu.

Step 2: Highlight the setting name (do not enter it — just select it).

Step 3: Press the INFO button. A popup appears asking if you want to add this item to My Menu.

Step 4: Confirm with OK. The setting is added to your My Menu list.

Step 5: Repeat for each setting. You can add up to 5 (sometimes more depending on firmware) items.

Step 6: To access My Menu: press MENU, then navigate to the My Menu tab (usually far left or far right of the tabs row).

Step 7: For fastest access: assign an Fn button to My Menu via Custom Menu B → Button Function → [Fn button] → My Menu. One press opens My Menu directly.

Managing My Menu Items

Step 1: Press MENU → navigate to the My Menu tab.

Step 2: Highlight the item you want to remove.

Step 3: Press the INFO button while highlighting — this brings up a remove option.

Step 4: Confirm removal. The item disappears from My Menu (remains in the main menu elsewhere).

Step 5: To rearrange: use the Reorder function if your firmware supports it, or remove and re-add in desired order.

Recommended My Menu Items

- Format Card — frequently accessed and usually buried in the Setup Menu
- Image Quality — switch between RAW and RAW+JPEG quickly
- Noise Filter — adjust for high-ISO scenes
- Aspect Ratio — switch between 4:3 and 1:1 for different platforms
- Image Stabilization Mode — quick toggle between IS1, IS2, IS3, Off
- Firmware Version — quick check without deep menu diving
- Copyright Settings — for updating EXIF copyright per project

TIP: My Menu + Fn button = power user workflow

The combination reduces 10-second menu navigations into single-second interactions. A small investment in customisation time pays back every time you pick up the camera.

Part 19 — Maintenance and Camera Care

A well-maintained camera works better, lasts longer, and delivers more reliable results. The OM-3 is built to be rugged — weather-sealed, freeze-proof, and dust-resistant — but regular care is still important. This part covers the routine maintenance that keeps your camera performing at its best.

19.1 Cleaning the Sensor — Built-In Ultrasonic Cleaner

Every time you change lenses, tiny specks of dust have an opportunity to enter the camera body and settle on the sensor. These show up as dark spots in your photos — usually most visible in plain skies, smooth backgrounds, and when shooting at narrow apertures (f/11 or smaller) where the dust is rendered sharply.

Figure 19.1 — SSWF Ultrasonic Sensor Cleaner: Vibrates Dust Off the Filter

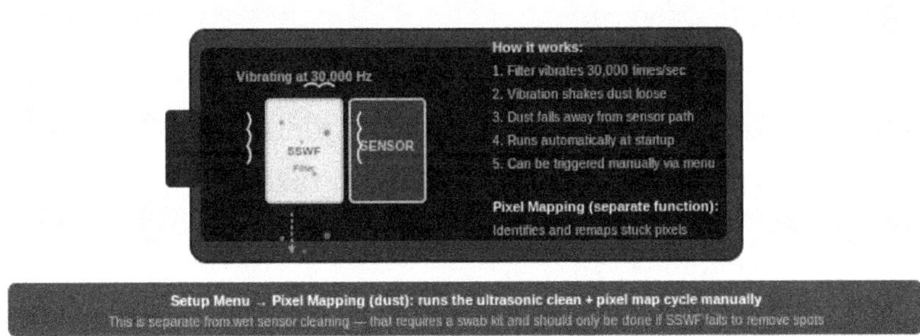

Figure 19.1 — The SSWF (Supersonic Wave Filter) sits in front of the sensor and vibrates at 30,000 Hz to shake dust loose

How the Ultrasonic Cleaner Works

The OM-3 inherits Olympus's industry-leading Supersonic Wave Filter (SSWF) technology. Just in front of the image sensor is a transparent filter that vibrates at approximately 30,000 times per second — so fast that dust particles literally shake off and fall away. This vibration is silent, takes less than a second, and runs automatically every time you turn on the camera. For most users in normal conditions, this built-in cleaning is sufficient without ever needing manual intervention.

When Automatic Cleaning Isn't Enough

- After heavy lens changes in dusty environments (beaches, deserts, dusty roadsides)
- After prolonged exposure to pollen (spring outdoor photography)
- When dark spots appear in your photos, particularly visible in smooth areas or bright skies
- If a spot persists after power-cycling the camera

Manual Triggering

Step 1: Press MENU → Setup Menu (wrench icon).

Step 2: Find Sensor Cleaning (may also be Dust Reduction or Pixel Mapping — the ultrasonic cleaning is usually part of Pixel Mapping).

Step 3: Select Start or Execute and press OK.

Step 4: The camera runs the cleaning cycle — takes about 3 seconds. The LCD shows a brief progress indicator.

Step 5: When complete, the confirmation message appears. Press OK.

Wet Sensor Cleaning (Last Resort)

If the SSWF fails to remove persistent spots, wet sensor cleaning with specialised swabs is the next step. This is an advanced procedure requiring care:

WARNING: Wet sensor cleaning can damage the camera if done wrong

Only use sensor-cleaning swabs and fluid specifically rated for camera sensors. Never use cotton swabs, tissues, or any household cleaning product — they will leave fibres or residue and can scratch the sensor. If not confident, take the camera to a professional camera service centre.

Step 1: Work in a clean, dust-free room. Avoid fabric-fibre-filled rooms.

Step 2: Ensure the battery is fully charged.

Step 3: In the Setup Menu, find Manual Sensor Cleaning Mode. Activate it — the shutter opens and stays open.

Step 4: Apply 2-3 drops of sensor cleaning fluid to a sensor-cleaning swab sized for Micro Four Thirds.

Step 5: In a single gentle continuous motion, wipe across the sensor from one side to the other. Do not press hard.

Step 6: Flip the swab and make one pass in the opposite direction if needed.

Step 7: Exit the cleaning mode. Take a test shot at f/22 of a blank surface. Review for remaining spots.

19.2 Cleaning the Lens and Camera Body

The lens and camera body accumulate dust, fingerprints, rain spots, and sunscreen residue during normal use. Regular cleaning keeps everything working well.

Cleaning the Lens

Step 1: First, use a rocket-style air blower to blow off loose particles. This is important — wiping with a cloth when grit is present can scratch the glass.

Step 2: Use a clean microfibre cloth (specifically for optics — not general household microfibre). Wipe from centre outward in a spiral.

Step 3: For stubborn smudges, apply one drop of professional lens-cleaning fluid to the cloth (never directly to the lens).

Step 4: Never use breath condensation, household glass cleaner, eyeglass wipes, or tissues — these can leave residue or cause scratches.

Step 5: Work in an area free of dust and airborne particles.

Cleaning the Camera Body

- Wipe the body with a slightly damp microfibre cloth to remove dirt, sweat, sunscreen, or water.
- Pay attention to the hot shoe contacts, lens mount contacts, and card/battery door.
- Use a cotton swab to clean between buttons and around dials where dust collects.
- Do NOT use solvents, alcohol, or aggressive cleaners — they can damage the rubber seals and rubber grip surfaces.
- Never submerge the camera. Weather sealing protects against splashes and rain, not submersion.

LCD and EVF Eyepiece

Use the same optics-dedicated microfibre cloth. Avoid abrasive cleaners that can damage anti-reflective coatings. The EVF eyepiece can be removed (pull straight back) for thorough cleaning and then reattached.

19.3 Charging the BLS-50 Battery

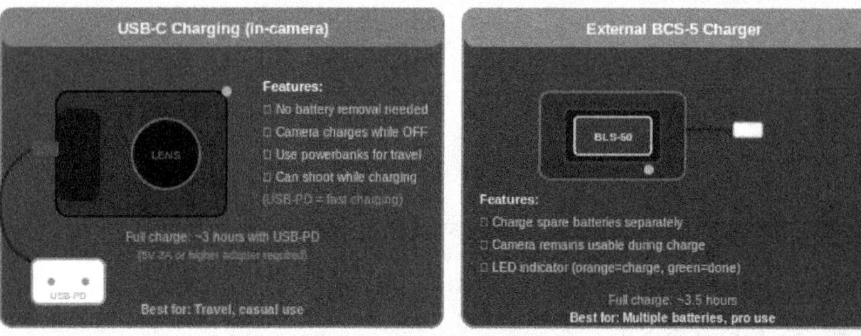

Figure 19.3 — Two ways to charge the BLS-50: in-camera via USB-C or externally with the BCS-5 charger

Method 1 — USB-C Charging (In-Camera)

The OM-3 supports charging the installed battery directly via its USB-C port — convenient for travel because you don't need to remove the battery or carry a separate charger.

Step 1: Turn the camera OFF (recommended).

Step 2: Open the USB-C port door on the left side of the camera.

Step 3: Plug a USB-C cable into the camera's USB-C port.

Step 4: Plug the other end into a USB power source: USB-PD wall adapter (recommended for fastest charging), computer USB port, or USB powerbank.

Step 5: The charging indicator LED lights orange during charging, turns green when fully charged.

Step 6: Full charge: approximately 3 hours with USB-PD adapter at 5V 3A or higher. About 4-5 hours from a standard USB-A computer port.

NOTE: What is USB-PD?

USB Power Delivery (USB-PD) is a high-power USB charging standard. Most modern smartphone and laptop chargers support it. A basic USB-A charger still charges the camera but much more slowly.

Method 2 — External BCS-5 Charger

The optional external charger charges the battery independently of the camera. Essential if you own spare batteries — charge one while shooting with another.

Step 1: Remove the BLS-50 battery from the camera: open the battery door on the bottom, slide the orange battery lock lever, pull the battery out.

Step 2: Insert the battery into the BCS-5 charger: align the contacts (only fits one way).

Step 3: Plug the BCS-5 into a wall outlet using its included power cord.

Step 4: The LED on the charger turns orange during charging. Changes to green when fully charged.

Step 5: Full charge: approximately 3.5 hours.

Step 6: Remove from charger and install back in the camera.

TIP: Charge batteries the night before

The BCS-5 charger handles one battery at a time. For three batteries, budget roughly 10 hours total — best to start the night before a shoot.

19.4 Battery Care and Storage Tips

Lithium-ion batteries like the BLS-50 are the power source for the OM-3. Proper care extends their usable life (typically 3-5 years) and maintains consistent capacity. Poor care can reduce life to 1-2 years or less.

Daily Use Best Practices

- Avoid fully draining the battery. Running to 0% repeatedly shortens lifespan. Charge when the camera shows 20-30% remaining.
- Avoid leaving the battery at 100% for long periods. Batteries held at full charge for weeks develop reduced capacity. For long storage: 40-50% charge.
- Remove the battery from the camera if not used for more than a week. Trickle drain continues even when off.
- Carry spare batteries in a protective case. Avoid loose batteries in pockets or bags where terminals could short-circuit against coins or keys.

Temperature Considerations

Temperature Range	Effect on Battery
Below freezing (0°C / 32°F and colder)	Capacity drops significantly. Keep battery in inside pocket between shots — body heat helps. At -10°C or colder, plan for 50% reduced capacity.
Normal ambient (10-30°C / 50-86°F)	Ideal operating range. Full capacity, normal lifespan.
Hot environments (30-40°C / 86-104°F)	Capacity is normal but lifespan shortens with prolonged heat. Avoid direct sun or a hot car.
Extreme heat (above 40°C / 104°F)	Risk of damage. Battery may refuse to charge until cool. Permanent capacity loss possible.

Long-term storage	Best: 15-25°C, dry, 40-60% charge. Check every 2-3 months and top up if below 30%.

Signs a Battery Is Wearing Out

- Life feels noticeably shorter than it used to be
- Charges quickly but drains rapidly
- Camera reports lower and lower 'full' battery percentage
- The battery feels warm or puffy — replace immediately; swollen batteries can be a safety hazard
- After 500-800 charge cycles, consider replacement — capacity has declined 30-40%

19.5 Updating the Camera Firmware — Step by Step

Firmware is the software that controls every aspect of your camera. OM SYSTEM periodically releases firmware updates to fix bugs, add features, improve AF, and support new lenses. Keeping firmware up to date can significantly improve camera behaviour.

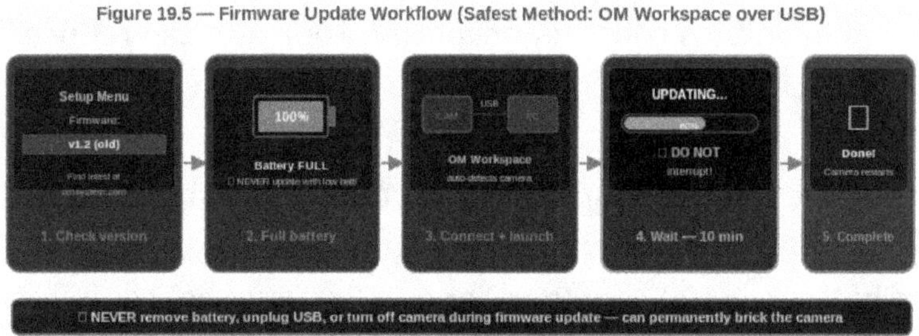

Figure 19.5 — Firmware update flow: check version → full battery → USB + Workspace → wait → complete

Checking Your Current Firmware Version

Step 1: Press MENU → Setup Menu (wrench icon).

Step 2: Find Firmware Version and press OK.

Step 3: The current camera firmware version is displayed (e.g. v1.1, v1.2).

Step 4: If a compatible lens is attached, the lens firmware version is also shown.

Step 5: Note the current version for reference.

Finding the Latest Firmware

Use only the official OM SYSTEM download. Before updating:

- Visit the official OM SYSTEM support site (omsystem.com or regional variant).
- Find the OM-3 page and the Firmware section.

- Check the latest version number. If it matches yours, no update needed.
- Read the release notes first — they describe what has been fixed or added.

Updating via OM Workspace (Recommended)

The safest method is OM SYSTEM's free OM Workspace application:

Step 1: Ensure the camera battery is fully charged. Essential — an interrupted firmware update can permanently damage (brick) the camera.

Step 2: Install OM Workspace on your computer (Windows or Mac) from the OM SYSTEM website.

Step 3: Open OM Workspace and update it to the latest version first.

Step 4: Connect the OM-3 to your computer via USB-C cable.

Step 5: Power on the camera. At the USB connection prompt, select Storage or PC Control.

Step 6: OM Workspace auto-detects the camera. A message appears if a firmware update is available.

Step 7: Click Update Firmware. Read and accept the release notes.

Step 8: The update begins. The camera LCD shows a progress bar. Takes approximately 10 minutes.

Step 9: During the update: DO NOT disconnect USB, remove battery, or turn off camera. Any interruption can brick the camera.

Step 10: When complete, the camera restarts automatically. Verify the new version in the Setup Menu.

Step 11: Disconnect the camera from the computer. Take a test photo to confirm everything works normally.

WARNING: NEVER interrupt a firmware update

If the camera turns off, USB disconnects, or battery dies during a firmware update, the camera may be permanently bricked — requiring service-centre repair (potentially expensive or unrecoverable). This is the single most important rule. Before starting: battery full, USB connection secure, power source stable, no interruptions during 10-minute process.

Alternative Method — SD Card Update

Step 1: Download the firmware file from the OM SYSTEM website.

Step 2: Format an SD card in the camera.

Step 3: Copy the firmware file to the root of the card using your computer.

Step 4: Eject and insert the card into the camera.

Step 5: In the camera: Setup Menu → Firmware Version → Update.

Step 6: The camera detects the firmware file and offers to apply. Confirm and wait — no-interruption rule applies.

19.6 Resetting the Camera to Factory Defaults

A factory reset returns the camera to its original out-of-the-box state. All custom settings, Fn button assignments, Custom Modes (C1/C2/C3), SCP configurations, My Menu items, and wireless pairings are erased. After a factory reset, the first-time setup wizard runs again.

When to Perform a Factory Reset

- Camera behaves erratically after many customisations
- You are selling or giving away the camera
- You cannot locate a troublesome setting to correct it
- After a firmware update that has made strange changes
- Before giving the camera to someone else to use temporarily

WARNING: Factory Reset cannot be undone

Once confirmed, all customisations are erased. Custom button assignments, three Custom Modes, My Menu, Picture Mode fine-tuning, Custom White Balance readings, and wireless pairings are all deleted. This cannot be reversed. Before resetting, take photos of your key settings on your smartphone so you can reconfigure them afterward.

How to Perform a Factory Reset

Step 1: Back up any important shots from the SD card to a computer. Factory reset does NOT erase card contents but best to be safe.

Step 2: Take screenshots or notes of your key settings: Custom Modes, Fn button assignments, My Menu items, Picture Mode fine-tuning.

Step 3: Press MENU → Setup Menu (wrench icon).

Step 4: Find Reset (sometimes Reset Settings or Factory Reset).

Step 5: Press OK. A confirmation prompt asks if you really want to reset.

Step 6: Choose Full (resets everything including language, date, time) or Basic (resets most but keeps language, date, time). Full is the true factory state.

Step 7: Confirm with OK. The camera processes for a few seconds and restarts.

Step 8: After restart, the first-time setup wizard runs: select language, set date and time, time zone.

Step 9: All menus are now at factory defaults. Reconfigure Fn buttons, My Menu, and Custom Modes as needed.

TIP: Export your settings before resetting

If you invested significant time in customising the camera, some firmware versions support exporting settings to an SD card before reset, then importing them back afterward. Check Setup Menu → Save/Load Settings. This also transfers settings between multiple OM-3 bodies.